T0295974

Trade Unions and Society

First published in 1974, *Trade Unions and Society* examines the process by which trade unions sought and achieved recognition in the three decades after 1850. It shows a parallel process: on the one hand, trade unionists struggling to attain the indispensable Victorian virtue, 'respectability', without sacrificing their essentially protective functions; on the other hand, employers recognizing the value of an ordered system of industrial relation in which trade unions could exert discipline and control over their workers. While this was going on, middle-class radicals (often themselves employers) continued their attack on aristocratic domination of political institutions and looked to a 'labour aristocracy' as allies. The book shows the manner in which, thanks to their own efforts and those of their indefatigable publicists, unionists became identified with the respectable elite of the working class. It deals with a crucial period in the trade union development but looks at it not merely from the point of view of the unions, but also that of the employers, politicians, the press, intellectuals, political economists, giving for the first time a rounded picture of trade unionism and industrial relations in the third quarter of the nineteenth century. This book will be of interest to students of economics and history.

Trade Unions and Society

The Struggle for Acceptance, 1850-1880

W. Hamish Fraser

Routledge
Taylor & Francis Group

First published in 1974
by George Allen & Unwin

This edition first published in 2022 by Routledge
2 Park Square, Milton Park, Abingdon, Oxon, OX14 4RN

and by Routledge
605 Third Avenue, New York, NY 10017

Routledge is an imprint of the Taylor & Francis Group, an informa business

© 1974 W. Hamish Fraser

Publisher's Note
The publisher has gone to great lengths to ensure the quality of this reprint but points out that some imperfections in the original copies may be apparent.

Disclaimer
The publisher has made every effort to trace copyright holders and welcomes correspondence from those they have been unable to contact.

A Library of Congress record exists under ISBN: 0874715148

ISBN: 978-1-032-21835-9 (hbk)
ISBN: 978-1-003-27025-6 (ebk)
ISBN: 978-1-032-21838-0 (pbk)

Book DOI 10.4324/9781003270256

Trade Unions and Society

The Struggle for Acceptance
1850–1880

W. Hamish Fraser

London · George Allen & Unwin Ltd
Ruskin House   Museum Street

First published in 1974

ISBN 0 04 331063 X

Printed in Great Britain
in 10 point Times Roman type
by Unwin Brothers Limited
The Gresham Press
Old Woking, Surrey

To my parents

Contents

Introduction

The search for a system that will produce peace in industrial relations is as old as industry itself, but it was not until the middle of the nineteenth century that there was any widespread recognition that trade unions were an essential element in any viable system of industrial relations. How this came about in the three decades after 1850 is the theme of this book. It was a gradual process that involved a change of attitude on the part of both trade unionists and of employers, as well as a fundamental alteration in public opinion.

It is hard not to see the third quarter of the nineteenth century as, in so many ways, a lacuna in British history. The very confidence in itself that permeates society gives the period a uniqueness. The middle classes, above all, had reason to feel confident that at last they were coming into their own, though all levels of society were touched by it. It was a confidence built on stability, the kind of stability symbolised by those mid-century monuments to civic pride and prosperity, the great town halls of the industrial cities of the North. Gone was the trepidation of the 1840s. Yet to come was the self-doubt of the 1880s. For three decades one can see 'victorianism' at its high noon.

The confidence was firmly based on economic prosperity. The abandonment of protection, coinciding with Californian gold discoveries of the late 1840s had allowed a great expansion of trade. After a decade of relative stagnation, annual exports quadrupled in value in less than twenty years. All industries expanded to meet the demand. Industrialising states needed the products of British engineering and machinery exports led the export boom with a tenfold increase in value, but coal, iron, textiles and ships all made their contribution to the growth. Prices and profits held, rising to a peak in the boom years of the early 1870s, and only in the last years of the period are the signs of crisis to be found. Improved trade and profits brought the business class a security there had not been in half a century, and with it came a confidence to negotiate with their workers, to make concessions, and to tolerate some erosion of managerial rights.

The gains of an expanding economy were not evenly shared, but improvements in the standard of living of the working classes are unquestionable. Average money wages rose by nearly 50 per cent, while real wages increased by just under 40 per cent. To take merely one useful indicator of affluence: per capita consumption of sugar, having remained surprisingly steady for half a century before 1850, suddenly pulled away and trebled over the next thirty years.

There was also a new political confidence. The events of 1848 had not brought revolution: 'the good spirit of our middle classes' (as Lady Palmerston saw) had stood revealed in the ranks of the special constables on the tenth of April. The propertied classes felt confident enough to think in terms of political concessions and parliamentary reform began to be considered once again. The very instability of political groupings in the 1850s and 1860s was indicative of widespread agreement on issues of domestic policy. Even parliamentary reform did not provide that catalyst of political change that the corn laws had done in the 1840s or that Ireland was to do in the 1880s. Even the least perceptive began to identify a working man with the necessary 'virtue, prudence, intelligence, and frugality' which entitled him 'to enter into the privileged pale of the constituent body of the country'. Perhaps he had always existed; he was no different from the 'proud mechanic' of earlier decades; he was no different from those artisans who had sought to make chartism an educational crusade. But, only in the secure years after 1850 was he able to be clearly differentiated from the 'dangerous classes'.

It was in this atmosphere that trade unions made the transition from those rather mysterious conspiracies that middle-class observers had seen in the 1830s, with so much in them that was dangerous to society, to the respectable, legalised – indeed privileged – bodies that annually sent their sober delegates to the meetings of the Trades Union Congress. Trade unions built up their membership and their financial strength and achieved a new level of stability. They spread from local societies into powerful bodies with efficient organisation and professional administration. Employers adjusted to their new strength and industrial relations became less a matter of a struggle for mastery and more a negotiable set of working rules in which both sides made concessions.

The confidence and the concord lasted for a quarter of a century before the doubts and questioning began. By the end of the 1870s prices were falling sharply and profits were less secure; unemployment in the staple industries was rising; the political demands of the workers had not ended with reform; the first stirrings of a renewed questioning of capitalism began to appear. Concessions were less easy. Employers now sought increased productivity and cost consciousness came to dominate their thinking on industrial relations. Skilled men, faced with the threat of unemployment, had less confidence in the security of their position and showed less faith in the continuing progress of capitalism. Even their powerful unions were rocked by the altered circumstances: Stonemasons' and Ironfounders' Societies both came near to bankruptcy in 1879 and the great Amalgamated Society of Engineers teetered on the brink of crisis. Changed circumstances brought changed attitudes. Traditional goals and traditional structures began to be critically examined and fundamental adjustments made.

In many ways too, therefore, for trade unionism, and for industrial relations also, the third quarter of the nineteenth century is not so much the start of a new direction as an exceptional product of exceptional circumstances. But, in other ways, the period does mark a decisive breakthrough. Never again were the working classes to be treated with the fear and suspicion of the first half of the nineteenth century. The recognition, the status, the role that trade unions won in these three decades was never again lost. There were many more struggles. By the last decades of the century size and organisation of industry altered and changed the nature of capitalism and trade unions altered in response. But, as Clegg, Fox and Thompson have argued, even Taff Vale, which left the unions utterly vulnerable to an employers' onslaught, was not used as an opportunity for crushing unionism. Most employers accepted their right to exist and governments certainly did. The three decades after 1850 were crucial. The issue of trade unionism and its role was debated in these years in all its aspects and the debate was decided in favour of unionism. After 1875, the existence of unionism and the vital role of unions in an organised and voluntary system of industrial relations was never seriously threatened.

The material for this book was collected over many years and during that time I have received guidance and help from more people than it is possible to mention. Special thanks are, however, due to Professor Asa Briggs, who supervised research on trades councils which I undertook at the University of Sussex and some of the results of which is incorporated in the present work. As he has been to so many students, Professor Briggs was a source of both encouragement and inspiration. Most of my colleagues at the department of economic history at the University of Strathclyde have had their brains picked at some time for information and I should like to thank all of them. Two in particular, Professor S. G. E. Lythe and Dr J. T. Ward gave a great deal of assistance. They read most of the manuscript and helped remove the worst infelicities of style and encouraged reconsiderations of rash judgements. I am very grateful to them. Mr Eric Young, also of the University of Strathclyde, gave me valuable help with the chapter on trade unions and the law and Mr Ian MacDougall, who has done so much towards discovering and preserving Scottish labour records, has been an ever-helpful friend, willingly answering numerous enquiries.

At the many libraries whose collections I used, I received unfailing kindness and courtesy from the librarians and staff and I wish to thank those of the British Museum, the National Library of Scotland, the British Library of Political and Economic Science, the Bishopsgate Institute, the Picton Library, Liverpool, the Mitchell Library, Glasgow, the Library of the TUC, the public libraries of Aberdeen, Birmingham, Bolton, Bradford, Edinburgh, Darlington, Leeds, Manchester, and Newcastle and the libraries of the Universities of Aberdeen, Birmingham, Edinburgh, Glasgow, Leeds, London, Manchester, Nottingham, Sheffield, Strathclyde and Sussex. My thanks also to the archivists of both Newcastle and Glasgow city archives.

Officials of a number of trade unions and trades councils took time to guide me through their archives and to answer queries, and thanks are due to the secretaries and staff of the National Union of Furnishing Trade Operatives, the Amalgamated Society of Woodworkers, the Edinburgh branch of the National Union of Printing, Bookbinding and Paperworkers, and the Edinburgh Trade Council. Mr Julius Jacobs, a former secretary of the London Trades Council gave me full access to the minutes of the Council which are in his possession and he and Mrs Jacobs were liberal hosts on many occasions.

I am obliged to the following people for information and advice at different times: Mr W. H. Marwick, Dr W. H. Chaloner, Professor Sidney Pollard, Mr E. P. Thompson and Mrs Barbara Smith. Much of the material on Scottish unionism was collected while undertaking a project on the development of unionism in nineteenth-century Scotland, which was generously financed by the Social Science Research Council and by the Twenty-Seven Foundation, and I received valuable assistance on that project from Miss Lois Miller and Mr Charles Munn.

Acknowledgement must also be made to the Company of Scottish History for permission to use material formerly printed in the *Scottish Historical Review*, Vol. 1, October 1971.

Lastly, I am indebted to my wife, Helen, who throughout the writing of this book has shown great patience and tolerance as well as having given tangible help with proof-reading. Without her it would not have been possible.

The judgements, the errors of fact that remain and all else in the text remains my own responsibility.

W. HAMISH FRASER
University of Strathclyde

Chapter 1

Trade-union Growth, Structure and Policy

Accurate returns of total trade-union membership in Britain are not available before the 1890s and, therefore, for the mid-Victorian period we are dependent on the reasoned guesses of a few interested contemporaries. It was estimated that there were 600,000 unionists in 1859; Frederic Harrison talked of there being 'not short of half a million' in 1865; George Potter suggested 800,000 in 1867 and George Howell thought there were 1,600,000 in 1876.[1] Whatever the exact value of these figures they support the conclusion that between 1850 and 1880 there was a substantial growth in the number of unions and in the number of unionists. Taking a sample of fifteen important unions, in both England and Scotland, Sidney and Beatrice Webb calculated that their membership rose from 24,737 in 1850 to 125,339 in 1880, an increase of more than 500 per cent.[2]

The growth was not steady, for membership of individual unions could fluctuate quite erratically. Preparations for a major strike usually brought a flow of new members who would disappear just as rapidly if the strike failed. The trade cycle also played its part, for at times of depression and of high unemployment workers were less willing to take the risk of belonging to a union, especially if the union was powerless to prevent wage cuts. In times of boom, with the union in a position to press for advances and the workers feeling secure enough to ignore employers' hostility to unions, membership tended to rise. Broadly, the overall pattern was one of growth from the last years of the 1840s to 1852, when there was a set-back. A revival in 1853 brought steady expansion until the financial crisis of 1857, with a subsequent depression in many of the main industries, slowed down the rate of growth for two or three years. The first half of the 1860s saw sustained growth in most unions, only for it to be halted once again in 1867, 1868 and 1869. From 1870 to 1875 all unions were expanding at an un-precedented rate amid boom conditions, but the onset of depression in the second half of the decade decimated most of them. Many disappeared entirely and others lost most of the gains in member-ship they had made since 1870. And within that broad pattern every union was subject to its own peculiar fluctuations.

We are equally dependent on interested observers for estimates of the strength of unionism in particular crafts and between different parts of the country. At the beginning of the 1850s that painstaking observer of London life, Henry Mayhew, estimated that about 10 per cent of the workers in the average London craft were in a trade society.[3] In 1867, Alfred Mault, secretary of the Midlands-based General Builders' Association, gave his estimates of unionisation in the building trades to the Royal Commission on Trades Unions: 10·3 per cent of carpenters and joiners, 17 per cent of masons, 18·75 per cent of bricklayers, 30 per cent of plasterers, 9·75 per cent of plumbers, glaziers and painters and 6 per cent of brickmakers.[4] In 1879, George Howell, concerned to show the strength of unionism, and despite the losses in the years after 1875, claimed a higher percentage: 50 per cent of carpenters and joiners, 66 per cent of masons, 60 per cent of bricklayers, 33 per cent of plasterers and 16 per cent of painters.[5] Outside the building trades Howell estimated that one in three engineers was in the Amalgamated Society of Engineers, in 1879,[6] while a decade earlier William Allan had thought it somewhere between two-thirds and three-quarters.[7] Ironfounders seem to have maintained a high level of unionism. Daniel Guile told the Royal Commission that in strong districts five out of six ironfounders were members of his society[8] and, in 1879, Howell estimated an overall average of two out of three. Other estimates of union strength given to the Royal Commission were 25 per cent of cabinetmakers, 90 per cent of cotton spinners, 90 per cent of provincial printers and 85 per cent of London bookbinders,[9] while Howell thought 75 per cent of boilermakers were unionised in 1879.

The main geographical areas of union strength followed the distribution of industry. The North West was the strongest with its cotton factories and engineering works, followed by the industrial Midlands, though Birmingham was a black spot because of the small scale of most of its industry. Despite great weakness in the woollen industry, Yorkshire as a whole was quite strong, as was the North East. The West of Scotland was well organised, and

Edinburgh had one or two strong unions, but taken as a whole, Scotland was generally regarded as weak. Some London trades societies were strong, but the high level of casual labour in the metropolis made the overall picture not very bright. In the mining areas the level of unionisation varied quite drastically throughout the period, with the ups and downs of mining unions. Indeed, in all areas and in each industry there were quite marked fluctuations in membership in response to the ebb and flow of the trade cycle or to the internal problems of unions.

I

In the building trades the largest society was the Operative Stone-masons' Friendly Society, formed amid the Owenite enthusiasm of 1833. Its main areas of strength were Manchester, Birmingham and Bristol, but under the able leadership of its secretary from 1847 to 1872, Richard Harnott,[10] it grew from 4,671 members in 1850 to more than 26,000 in 1876, with 373 branches,[11] before the end of the building boom of the seventies began to take its toll and it fell back to under 13,000 in 1880. The society covered England and Wales. In Scotland there was the United Association of Operative Masons, formed in 1852 and with 6,000 members in 1880. The bricklayers were divided between the London and Manchester Orders of the Operative Bricklayers' Society, two quite distinct and mutually hostile bodies. The two Orders had split in 1848 and the expansionist policies of Edwin Coulson, secretary of the London body from 1860 to 1891 created great bitterness. Attempts at an accord between them were usually short-lived. Until the end of the 1870s the Manchester Order was the larger with 7,350 members in 1875. The London Order grew from 200 to 300 at its formation to over 5,500 in 1866. By 1870 this had fallen to 1,441, but a steady recovery in the 1870s took it to 6,749 in 1877 and despite a fall in the depression it had, by the 1880s, surpassed the Manchester Order.[12]

The best-known builders' society of the period was undoubtedly the Amalgamated Society of Carpenters and Joiners, formed by the amalgamation of twenty local – mainly London – societies in 1860. It began with only 600 members, but from 1862, when the efficient and dedicated Hull joiner, Robert Applegarth, took over as general secretary, it grew steadily: 3,320 in 1865, 10,178 in 1870, 14,917 in 1875, and 17,764 in 1880. With headquarters in London, its more than 300 branches by the end of the seventies covered

England, Wales and Ireland and there was a number of branches in the United States. A similar amalgamation, the Associated Carpenters and Joiners, was formed in Scotland in 1861 and had about 7,000 members in the mid-1870s. Outside the amalgamations was the Manchester-based General Union of Carpenters and Joiners whose history went back to 1827. It was steadily passed in membership by the Amalgamated Society, but it still had more than 10,000 members in 1875. However, in the following years the Amalgamated Society began a war of attrition against the General Union, deliberately setting out to 'poach' whole lodges and by the middle of the following decade the membership of the General Union had fallen to under 2,000.[13] Besides these large bodies, many small local societies of carpenters and joiners remained in existence, particularly in London. George Potter's union, the Progressive Joiners' Society, for example, had a mere 130 members.[14]

Local societies of plasterers came together in a National Association of Operative Plasterers in 1860. Its general secretary, based first in Liverpool and later in Birmingham, was Charles Williams and although he was a man of considerable ability and enthusiasm, the Association grew only slowly and was under 4,000 members at the end of the 1870s. It suffered from frequent splits, such as in 1870 when most of the London branches broke away to form a Metropolitan Association.[15] Other building trade unions remained small and of little significance. The United Operative Plumbers' Association covering Birmingham, the North of England and Scotland grew only slightly to just over 2,000 members after its formation in 1865 and it, too, suffered from lodges breaking away, particularly the Scottish ones. The painters, who had been suffering for decades from an influx of unskilled and casual labour, found it the most difficult to organise on a national basis. About sixty North of England societies were loosely linked in the Manchester Alliance from 1855, but not until 1873 was George Shipton able to organise a mainly London Society, the Amalgamated Society of House Decorators and Painters.[16] A Manchester-based Brickmakers' Society achieved considerable notoriety in the 1860s with its policy of sabotage, boycott and machine smashing against machine-made bricks, but, by the 1870s, the battle had been fought and lost. In London attempts to organise the brickmakers in the 1860s were short-lived.

At the forefront of British industry in the mid-century was the iron industry and its related machine-building and shipbuilding industries and it was here that the strongest unions developed.

Above them all stood the Amalgamated Society of Engineers, formed in September 1850 by an amalgamation of the Manchester-based Journeymen Steam Engine and Machine Makers' Friendly Society ('the Old Mechanics'), the Steam Engine Makers' Society and a number of London unions of millwrights and smiths. Right from the start it was larger than any other union, with 12,000 members by the end of its first year. Its rate of growth was spectacular: 21,000 by 1860, 35,000 by 1870, 44,692 in 1880. It covered fitters, turners, smiths, patternmakers and millwrights in locomotive building, in machine-building – particularly textile machines – in steam-engine making and in marine engineering. Lancashire, Cheshire, Yorkshire, Tyneside and London were its strongest areas but by the end of the 1860s it had spread to all parts of the country and beyond. Its 312 branches in 1868 included 35 in Scotland, 13 in Ireland, 9 in Australasia, 4 in Canada, 11 in the United States, 1 in Malta, 1 in Constantinople and 1 in France.[17] Not all eligible workers joined the A.S.E. and a number of small rival societies persisted, such as the Steam Engine Makers' Society, with just over 4,000 members in 1880; the United Patternmakers' Association with 800 members; the United Machine Workers with 300 members, and, in Scotland, the Associated Blacksmiths with 2,000 members, in 1880. In addition there was a proliferation of tiny specialist engineering societies on a local basis.[18] None of these presented a threat to the domination of the A.S.E., but they were a source of frequent irritation and dispute at certain works.

In the foundries the moulders and ironfounders had been organised since the beginning of the century in the Friendly Society of Iron Moulders, changing its name in 1854 to the Friendly Society of Iron Founders. Its outstanding secretary was Daniel Guile, general secretary from 1863 to 1881, under whom membership grew from around 8,000 in 1860 to over 12,000 at the end of his period of office. In Scotland the Scottish Iron Moulders' Union, which became the Associated Iron Moulders of Scotland, grew fairly steadily to around 4,000 members in 1880. Alongside the moulders in the foundries were smaller groups of iron dressers and coremakers usually organised in their own societies. In the brass foundries of the Midlands the workers were, from 1866, organised in the United Journeymen Brassfounders' Association with 1,900 members in 1880, and in 1872 W. J. Davis created the Amalgamated Brassworkers' Society with 5,000 members in 1880.

The actual makers of the iron, the puddlers and millmen of

Staffordshire, Teesside, Yorkshire, Durham and central Scotland were slow to organise on a permanent basis. The Staffordshire men formed a union in 1863, which became the Associated Ironworkers of Great Britain. A split in 1865 caused the North of England to form their own National Amalgamated Association of Iron-workers under the presidency of John Kane. Kane's body, with around 5,000 members in 1866, became the best known. The Staffordshire millmen continued with their own separate body.[19]

The vital fuel of British industry was coal and by 1873 more than half a million workers were employed in the industry. The miners, however, proved notoriously difficult to organise on a permanent national basis. It was not for want of effort, but isolation of miners' villages, differences in work conditions at different collieries and in different coal fields and the hostility of the coal owners proved major barriers to permanency. A National Association under Martin Jude had had a short-lived existence in the 1840s, but by 1850 there were no national links and what organisation there was was on a county or even more localised basis. In 1855, however, under the leadership of Alexander McDonald, a university-educated miners' agent from Lanarkshire, a Scottish Miners' Association was formed, loosely linking what remained of county organisations in Fife, Midlothian, Ayrshire, Renfrewshire, Stirlingshire and West Lothian. Three years later the Yorkshire miners succeeded in forming a permanent associa-tion, the South Yorkshire Miners' Association, which after the appointment of John Normansell as secretary in 1864 became one of the best-organised miners' unions. A much weaker West Yorkshire Association appeared in 1863 but for a time its existence was a very precarious one. Some traces of unionism persisted in Northumberland and Durham in the 1850s, but it usually made an appearance only at times of strike. However, in 1862 an organisa-tion, which proved to be permanent, the Northumberland Miners' Mutual Confident Association, was formed to resist the reintro-duction of the yearly bond, with Thomas Burt as its secretary from 1865. Five years later, the Durham men followed their neighbours' example with the Durham Miners' Association of which William Crawford became general secretary in the 1870s. In Lancashire, Thomas Halliday was the main force behind the revival of mining unionism and in the early 1860s he was able to form a federation of most of the Lancashire unions.[20]

Much of this revival of mining unionism in the 1860s was due to the efforts of Alexander McDonald in the 1850s to renew contacts between miners' unions, mainly for the purpose of pressing for improved conditions in the mines, through parliamentary legislation. The efforts bore fruit in 1863 when the National Association of Coal, Lime and Ironstone Miners was formed, linking unions in all the main mining areas. Unity was not maintained for long, however, and in 1869 a breakaway body was formed by those who favoured a more centralised organisation and one which would create a national organisation for industrial purposes and not confine united action between regions to parliamentary lobbying, as McDonald's body did. The main strength of the Amalgamated Association of Miners, as the new body was called, lay in Lancashire and in Wales, where it was responsible for organising the South Wales miners in a union. It proved a substantial rival to the National Association between 1869 and its demise in 1875. In 1873, at the height of the boom, the Amalgamated Association was claiming 99,145 members compared with the National Association's 123,406.[21] Despite the collapse of the Amalgamated Association in 1875, due to a number of disastrous strike defeats, the National Association was not able to maintain its existence in the face of the depression. Even most of the county organisations broke up and only in Fife and Northumberland and Durham was a really widespread organisation maintained.

In the textile industry the cotton mills of Lancashire housed the major concentrations of labour: and there union organisation among the cotton workers was effective and extensive. It was, however, largely made up of local societies. Frequent attempts were made to link together these local bodies, but any organisations that did emerge were fairly loose federations. John Doherty's General Union of Spinners had collapsed in the early 1830s. An attempt at a new federation was made in 1842 when the Association of Operative Cotton Spinners, Twiners and Self-Acting Minders of the United Kingdom was formed, which sought to unite both hand-mule spinners and the workers on the new self-acting machines. Rivalry between the two groups put a great strain on the Association and it faded away after 1847, when the Bolton and Oldham spinners' societies withdrew. A new amalgamation was constructed in 1853, again consisting of hand-mule spinners and self-actor minders. It survived the big Preston strike of that year but steadily declined in importance, since the two main areas of Bolton and Oldham were not associated with it. A further federation in 1860 remained weak and unco-ordinated and not until 1869 was a permanent Amalgamated Association of

Operative Cotton Spinners, Self-Acting Minders, Twiners and Rovers of Lancashire and Adjoining Counties formed. By 1880 this body, although weakened by a major strike in 1878, had just under 12,000 members.

In weaving, there were some powerloom weavers' associations in the 1840s and probably some informal federation of a few of them in the early 1850s. From 1854 when the Blackburn Weavers' Association was formed a number of district associations of weavers' societies appeared, clustered around the main centres: Padiham had one in 1856, Darwen in 1857, Accrington, Preston and Haslingden in 1858, Clitheroe in 1860, Bolton in 1865, Nelson in 1866. New district associations continued to be formed throughout the period and by 1880 there were at least thirty of these. It was as a result of a breakaway from the Blackburn Association in 1858, and at the prompting of Thomas Birtwistle, an official of the Accrington Association, that the East Lancashire Power Loom Weavers' Association was formed, which survived both the cotton famine of the 1860s and a nine-weeks' strike of great bitterness in 1878. It was reorganised in 1878 as the North-East Lancashire Weavers' Amalgamation, linking fourteen district associations with almost 16,000 members. In 1884 this was widened into the Northern Counties Amalgamated Association of Weavers. In the preparatory sections of the industry, an attempt in 1857–8 to form a federation of Cardroom Operatives came to nothing and not until 1886 was a permanent Cardroom Amalgamation formed. These federations of weavers and spinners never at any time contained all the cotton unions. Very many local societies remained completely independent or were organised in other smaller federations.[22]

The woollen and worsted mills of Yorkshire were in complete contrast to Lancashire, for there was very little organisation among the woollen workers before the 1880s. Influenced by developments in Lancashire, some of the more-skilled workers did organise small unions. In the 1860s, for example, most of the main wool and worsted towns had their local societies of overlookers and, in some, societies of spinners appear from time to time, but the great mass of workers in the industry were untouched by unionism and even when an organisation came into existence during a strike it never succeeded in establishing itself.

Unionism among the hosiery workers of Nottingham and Leicestershire had a long and frequently notorious history, but in the 1850s and 1860s the industry was being transformed by technical developments and the position of the hand framework knitter working outside the factories was being undermined by the new rotary power and circular power machines. The hand workers were organised in many small local unions, but in 1866 these succeeded in federating in a United Framework Knitters' Society, but it split in 1871 between the hand workers in factories and those working outside. In addition, there was a Rotary Framework Knitters' Society and a Circular Framework Knitters' Union. In the main towns these unions were able to build up a strong organisation, but they failed almost completely in organising the large number of workers in the many villages of the area and this encouraged the movement of the industry from the towns to the villages.[23]

Nottingham was also the centre of an expanding lace industry. A Lace Makers' Society was formed in 1850 covering most sections of the industry. A split occurred in 1867 between workers in different processes, but in 1874 they were re-united in the Amalgamated Operative Lace Makers.[24]

Iron, coal, textiles – the fourth pillar of Britain's industrial dominance was shipbuilding. Until the mid-1860s the Thames remained the most important area, but the development of iron-shipbuilding, combined with bad business methods had by the end of the sixties brought a switch to Tyneside, Merseyside and Clyde-side; it also brought a change in the nature of shipbuilding unionism. The wooden shipbuilders, the shipwrights, had been able to develop powerful local unions which, in most areas, fairly effectively controlled entry, rules and remuneration in the trade. With the development of iron-shipbuilding, however, their position was eroded and new workers in iron moved into the industry. The United Society of Boilermakers, formed in 1834, added Ironshipbuilders to its title in 1852 and began to expand steadily in shipbuilding. From under 2,000 members in 1850 it rose to almost 18,000 in 1880. Shipwrights' societies continued and they were successfully united in a national organisation in 1882, but their fate was irrevocable decline: even on the remaining woodwork in shipbuilding they found themselves being squeezed out. In Scotland especially, the Associated Carpenters took over more and more of the finishing jobs.

This period also saw the traditional crafts trying to move from a local to a national basis – tailors, shoemakers, cabinetmakers, printers and bookbinders. All of these had a long history of combination in local societies. An Amalgamated Association of

Operative Tailors was formed in 1866 with headquarters in Manchester, though the London Operative Tailors remained aloof until destroyed by strike and court actions in 1867. There was also a separate Scottish Association formed about the same time. An Amalgamated Cordwainers' Society was formed in 1863, linking some London and provincial societies of boot and shoemakers.[25] It consisted mainly of hand-sewing workers, though thanks to the efforts of George Odger, of the London West-End Ladies' Shoemakers' Society, it was not committed to any opposition to machine-made work. However, discrimination against factory workers undoubtedly took place and in 1873 representatives from the factory-based industry of Northamptonshire and Leicestershire broke away to form the National Union of Boot and Shoe Riveters and Finishers,[26] which grew to over 6,000 members by 1880. Again, the Scottish shoemakers were separately organised in local societies, with a national society surviving for only a few years in the 1860s. In cabinetmaking, the Alliance Cabinetmakers' Association established in 1865 spread from London, but for long faced opposition from independent local societies.

Trade unionism had been well-established in printing and bookbinding since the eighteenth century, but despite numerous attempts to create national organisations there was still divided organisation. Most provincial printers were in the Provincial Typographical Association, which had been formed in 1849 amid the ruins of an earlier National Typographical Association. Its headquarters were in Manchester and by the end of the 1870s had well over 5,000 members in about 80 branches. The London and Scottish printers, however, remained separate. The London Society of Compositors dated from the end of the eighteenth century and the Scottish societies, although they had been affiliated to the National Typographical Association in the forties, formed their own Scottish Typographical Association in 1853.[27] Among the bookbinders there was a Bookbinders' Consolidated Union dating from 1840 covering mainly provincial workers but moving into London in 1857 to compete with the London Consolidated Lodge of Journeymen Bookbinders, which had Thomas Dunning as its secretary. In the 1860s the Consolidated Union moved into the other important bookbinding centre, Edinburgh, which had retained its independent Union Society of Journeymen Bookbinders, and forced amalgamation in 1872. Also in 1872 the Consolidated Union opened its doors to machine rulers and by this steady expansionist policy had achieved a membership of just under 2,000 by the end of the 1870s. There were other tiny but powerful societies, particularly in London, that retained their independence, such as the Vellum Binders' Society, which had been formed in 1823, and the Day-Working Binders, who had broken from the London Consolidated Lodge in 1850.

Some of the most powerful, though numerically small, unions consisted of skilled craftsmen in specialist trades confined to limited areas. For example, with the bulk of its membership around the Birmingham region, the Flint Glass Makers' Society maintained a very effective organisation with about 2,000 members. The best-known such unions were those of the Sheffield light metal trades – file smiths, table-knife grinders, edge-tool grinders, saw makers, saw grinders, saw-handle makers and a host of such highly specialised workers – who were all organised in tiny societies striving to maintain a firm control over their particular craft.

While most of the societies of the period were organisations of skilled workmen, organisation among the unskilled was not unknown. From 1853 there was a Harbour Labourers' Society on Clydeside,[29] and short-lived bodies of general labourers existed in Glasgow at the end of the 1850s.[30] A builders' labourers' society appeared during the London lock-out of 1859 and the Royal Commission on Trades Union heard of a number of organisations of builders' labourers.[31] In general, however, organisation among the unskilled proved difficult to achieve and even more difficult to maintain: low earnings, a low level of education, occupational mobility and the casual nature of their work proved massive barriers for the unskilled to overcome and made them particularly vulnerable to economic fluctuations. However, the exceptional economic conditions of the first few years of the 1870s, with a high demand for labour, gave even the unskilled workers a strong bargaining position and in these years a number of unions of the unskilled appeared.

The most important new area of organisation was among the agricultural labourers, notoriously the most poorly-paid of workers. The first abortive efforts in this direction had taken place in the mid-sixties, when farm servants in many of the main farming areas of Scotland had formed protective societies, and when there was some organised activity in Dorset and in Lincolnshire. But the honour of really inspiring 'the revolt of the field' must go to Warwickshire, where in February 1872, under the secretaryship of the Barford Methodist, Joseph Arch, a Warwickshire Agricultural Labourers' Union was formed. Other areas, Lincolnshire,

Huntingdonshire, Kent and Sussex quickly followed and, in April, delegates from twenty-six counties, meeting at Leamington Spa, formed the National Agricultural Labourers' Union with Arch as its chairman. A year later it had almost 72,000 members in 982 branches. A number of unions continued to exist outside the National and some of these were united in 1873 in a Federal Union of Labourers, with about 50,000 members. Internal disputes and the onset of the agricultural depression in the second half of the 1870s began to take their toll of the agricultural unions and by 1881, membership of Arch's union had slumped to 15,000 and the decline continued throughout that decade.[32]

Another important new area of organisation at the beginning of the 1870s was the railways. Some societies of engine drivers and firemen appear from time to time from the 1840s; in 1866 there was an Enginemen and Firemen's United Society with its own journal. Not until 1871, however, did a permanent organisation appear, largely due to the assistance of M. T. Bass, the brewer. A national union of railwaymen, the Amalgamated Society of Railway Servants was formed and, by the following year, there was a Scottish society of the same name. It was intended to cover all grades, but in 1880 both the engine drivers and the signalmen broke away to form their own separate organisations.[33]

The year 1871 also brought a significant breakthrough among the dock workers of London's east end. Resisting a 25 per cent cut in wages, they formed the Labour Protection League, which in October 1872 claimed a membership of 30,000, including not only stevedores and dockers, but other workers on the waterside.[34] Barge men were in the Amalgamated Lightermen and Watermen's Association and there was some organisation of seamen.

Numerous new organisations of the unskilled, previously unorganised, workers made a brief appearance at the beginning of the 1870s. Dustmen, shop assistants, postal workers, carmen and even policemen developed organisations for a few months in these years. The London gas stokers organised the Amalgamated Gas Stokers' Union during their strike in 1872 which blacked out a large part of London. The builders' labourers formed the General Amalgamated Labourers' Union. At the end of 1872 there was even an attempt to link the new unions of transport workers, when a conference of representatives of the Lightermen's Society, the Carmen's Association, the Amalgamated Society of Railway Servants and the Labour Protection League resulted in the formation of the Amalgamated Labour Union. It was intended to co-ordinate strike activity with a council made up of representatives of the four societies to which all disputes had to be submitted before a strike was embarked upon:[35] there is no evidence that it actually succeeded in regularising procedures.

Few of the unions survived the onset of large-scale unemployment brought by the depression in the second half of the seventies. Many had crumbled earlier in the face of bitter employer opposition. But, contrary to what was once believed, unionism among the unskilled workers did not die out entirely. Little pockets of organisation persisted and, in the London docks, from their organisation within the Labour Protection League the stevedores were able to build and maintain what was virtually a closed shop until the end of the 1880s.

There were literally hundreds of small societies with only a few score members usually confined to one particular locality: basketmakers, cocoa fibre mat makers, composition and ornamental frame makers, glass blowers, gilders, gold beaters, organ builders, tobacco pipe makers, portmanteau makers, french polishers, wire workers and wood carvers, to name only a handful. In Staffordshire, Glasgow, London and in the West Country there were a number of potters' societies, covering the specialist tasks of potting. Most coopers were organised in their own local society, as were sail makers and ship riggers, tinplate workers and rope workers. Even small unions of handloom weavers still existed at the end of the 1870s. Some of these unions were really no more than friendly societies, but, at times of dispute, could be brought into action as trade unions. All were subject to the vicissitudes of the trade cycles and to the energy – or lack of it – of their secretaries.

II

A multitude of trade societies produced a multitude of variations in structure and there is no common pattern. The majority of societies remained small, with limited resources coming either from regular 1d or 2d contributions or from occasional levies. The funds would be used either for a brief strike or to provide small sums for widows, orphans or disabled members of the trade. Usually such donations were made on an *ad hoc* basis, with the approval of a trade meeting, which was the normal manner in which any major decisions were taken. With the growth of national trade organisations such primitive democracy was no longer possible and more formal rules and regulations were necessary, but the variety remained.

The most spectacular of the larger national societies was the Amalgamated Society of Engineers, which the Webbs in their *History* regarded as providing a 'new model' for other craft unions. While it is true that the A.S.E. did point the direction for some future trade-union development, it took a long time before other trades achieved the efficiency of the engineers and, indeed, many did not attempt to emulate its structure. The A.S.E. had the advantage of building on two well-established unions, the Steam Engine Makers' Society and the 'Old Mechanics' and it combined features of both. The Steam Engine Makers' Society had been largely a friendly society, paying sickness allowance among its members, but no out-of-work, i.e. unemployment or strike, benefit. The 'Old Mechanics', on the other hand, paid out-of-work benefit but no sickness allowance. The benefit side of the new society was, therefore, based on an amalgamation of the two bodies and provided a full range of benefits – out-of-work as well as sickness and superannuation. It combined to an extent and with an effectiveness such as had not before existed the advantages of both a trade and a friendly society. For the high weekly due of 1s a member was eligible for up to £19 18s per year unemployment benefit;[36] 10s per week for 26 weeks and 5s per week thereafter sickness benefit; up to 9s per week superannuation benefit; a lump sum of £100 on permanent disablement; £12 funeral allowance; and in certain circumstances of high unemployment up to £6 emigration assistance.

The one society to deliberately model itself on the A.S.E. was the Amalgamated Society of Carpenters and Joiners. There were differences in the level of some benefits, but, to all intents, the pattern was the same. A number of other societies such as the Friendly Society of Ironfounders, the United Society of Boilermakers and the Flintglass Makers' Society offered a similar substantial range of benefits in return for high dues, but the friendly benefit side in these long pre-dated the formation of the A.S.E.

In many other societies, in contrast, trade and sickness funds were quite distinct. In the Operative Stonemasons' Society, for example, for 5½d a week a member could join the trade section, which entitled him only to funeral benefit, superannuation and support in the event of a strike. It was optional to pay a further 3½d for the sickness fund. The London Order of the Operative Bricklayers' Society had no sickness fund until the 1870s and the contribution until then was only 3d per week.[37] The National Association of Plasterers was little more than a loose federation: subscriptions and benefits varied from area to area. In the cotton industry subscriptions in the spinners' societies varied from 4d to 9d per week, while among the weavers subscriptions were 2d or less. It was the local societies that fixed their own rates. The weavers' unions, which always saw their main function as wage bargainers, offered little friendly benefits other than funeral allowance, but some of the spinners' unions did develop an unemployment, accident and superannuation side.

In the Provincial Typographical Association, until the 1870s, benefits were paid by the branches and varied greatly, though few went beyond burial allowance, out-of-work relief and a tramping benefit. In contrast, the powerful London Society of Compositors offered no benefits other than for unemployment. The organisation of tailors, cabinetmakers, bookbinders and shoemakers were generally simply trade societies with only a nominal friendly society side, which began to be developed in the 1870s. Almost all the light-metal trade societies of Sheffield, on the other hand, had extensive benefits, with particularly high unemployment benefit aimed at keeping any surplus labour out of the labour market. As a result, in order to remain solvent, the dues of some of the Sheffield societies could be as high as 5s a week. In all the Scottish societies trade and benefit funds were distinct[38] and many well-organised Scottish unions had no friendly benefits. One reason for this was the refusal of the Scottish Registrar of Friendly Societies to register unions which did not keep their industrial activities quite separate from their friendly society function[39] – a decision that anticipated the Hornby v. Close ruling of 1867; another was the continued existence of a large number of friendly societies and sickness clubs in Scotland, often covering one trade but unconnected with the trade societies. Yet another reason, however, was the persistent refusal of Scottish unionists to pay high dues.

For those societies that did adopt a benefit side one of the great attractions of it was that it brought in members and, perhaps more important, helped to cut down on the turnover of membership, which was the bane of so many societies. But only a few societies adopted extensive friendly benefits. The A.S.E., the Amalgamated Carpenters, the Ironfounders and the Boilermakers with their sickness, unemployment, accident, superannuation, emigration and funeral benefits were the exception rather than the rule. Most societies offered little more than funeral and out-of-work benefits, with perhaps some help to members tramping in search of work. Funeral benefit reflected the deep-seated desire of workmen to avoid, even in death, the stigma of pauperism. Out-of-work benefit was really an extension of trade policy, since its primary purpose was to ensure that unemployment did not drive men to 'take situations on terms injurious to the trade'.[40]

Where societies did provide some measure of sickness benefit it was more commonly done by a special levy than by payment as of right. In other cases, the benefit and trade sides were kept distinct, with membership of the former optional. The success of the large societies did, however, encourage emulators. But the leaders of unions were much keener on introducing friendly benefits than were the rank and file and wherever such an innovation was proposed in a society it was likely to stir up a fair amount of opposition. In 1880 the majority of unions still lacked a significant benefit side.

The introduction of friendly benefits did much to encourage centralisation of power in trade unions, but a variety of administrative structures persisted. An organisation of the size and complexity of the A.S.E. required professional and efficient administration and, here again, it was able to draw upon the past experience of the 'Old Mechanics', which from 1843 had had a full-time general secretary and an elected executive council. The A.S.E., when it opened its doors in January 1851, had a similar administration, with an executive council of thirty-seven elected by the London district and a full-time general secretary appointed by the executive. On paper the supreme body was the delegate meeting of the whole society, but, in practice, this met rarely and all effective power was in the hands of the executive, which was the arbiter on the use of the Society's money. The executive, in turn, was generally amenable to guidance from the general secretary.

Membership of the Society was organised in branches – almost 400 of them by the end of the 1870s – and these in turn were linked regionally by district committees. The branch dealt with the collection of dues, the distribution of benefits and the admission of members. Its powers to use the Society's money were strictly circumscribed, in the constitution, since all money belonged to the whole society and, at the end of each year, the funds held by the different branches were equalised under the guidance of the executive council, a matter that usually caused considerable bitterness and disagreement.[41] Since the branches held most of the money, however, they were in practice left with a substantial amount of discretion on its use. The executive could disallow any disbursement made by a branch, but it was difficult for the executive to take effective action after the money had been spent.

Similar administrative structures were to be found in other big societies. In the Friendly Society of Ironfounders there had been a fairly steady trend towards centralisation since the end of the 1830s. The trend was accelerated with the appointment of a full-time general secretary in 1853 and, by the 1860s, the power of the secretary, backed by the London-based executive, was 'virtually absolute'.[42] In the Amalgamated Society of Carpenters the executive was elected by members within a twelve-mile radius of the head office, which was in London until 1871 and then in Manchester. The general secretary was elected by the whole membership each year and, as was shown in 1871 when Applegarth clashed with the executive committee of the Society, in the last analysis power lay, not with the executive but with the general council representing the whole society. However, on most matters the executive made the final decisions. The executive of the Boilermakers' Society was selected by the twenty lodges of the important Tyne District, each in rotation nominating one of the seven members. This pattern of executive councils chosen by the members in one geographical area was very common and often this involved a moveable headquarters, as each district claimed its rights. With the appointment of full-time officials there was pressure to stabilise the ruling body in one place, but such centralisation of power did not meet with undivided support. As late as 1877 a proposal in the London Order of Bricklayers to restore a moveable executive was blocked only by the chairman's casting vote.[43]

As societies grew in size there was undoubtedly a tendency towards centralisation, but traditional democratic procedures were often clung to. In the Operative Stonemasons, the moveable executive had very little real power, and strike or disciplinary decisions were not at the discretion of the executive, but by a vote of the whole society. The use of referenda to test members' opinion was popular in most societies well into the 1870s, though officials gradually placed a curb on the 'proposition mania' of some branches and began to take steps to ensure that only the executive could initiate major rules' revision. The sheer complexity and cost of getting together a delegate meeting of a large national society encouraged a trend that left more and more decision-making to the central executive. Power at the centre was increased also when it was recognised that all funds belonged to the Society as a whole and that any decision to spend the funds, say on strike action, ought to have the approval of some central authority.

The process of centralisation was usually carried a stage further with the expansion of permanent staff, such as the appointment of full-time district officials. A forceful general secretary, backed by his officials, could dominate a society no matter what limits the constitution laid down. The classic example of this was the United Society of Boilermakers from the 1870s onwards when Robert Knight became secretary. Superficially, power in the Society seemed to rest with the branches, who had to approve most decisions, but since funds were centralised the reality was that Knight and his district officials made all the significant decisions. Popular election of a general secretary, far from restraining the tendency to increased bureaucratic power, generally strengthened it, for as Sidney and Beatrice Webb pointed out, it 'invariably resulted in permanence of tenure exceeding even that of the English civil servant'.[44]

By no means all unions were centralised, however. In Scotland centralisation was rarely attempted and rarely achieved before the end of the 1870s. With the Glasgow region, in population and in concentration of industry, so overwhelmingly dominant, there was generally a refusal by Glasgow societies to subordinate themselves to national decisions and by provincial societies to accept Glasgow's domination. Local autonomy within unions for long remained sacrosanct in Scotland and, as a result, nearly all the national Scottish unions had a federal structure, with money and power remaining a local responsibility.

No doubt his Scottish experience persuaded Alexander McDonald of the necessity of having a decentralised federal structure for the National Association of Miners, which he was responsible for bringing about in 1863, though it was also a recognition of the diversity of conditions and attitudes that existed in different coalfields. The national organisation was largely concerned with co-ordinating political pressure and day-to-day industrial policy was firmly in the hands of regional bodies, who pursued independent and usually unco-ordinated activities. An alternative centralised Amalgamated Association of Miners was formed with the aim of achieving co-operation on industrial tactics, but it was not particularly successful in doing this.

A decentralised federal structure persisted also in the Lancashire cotton unions. The 'amalgamations' that were formed were very loose federations of local societies to help co-ordinate industrial

B

tactics. Even after the appointment of full-time officials the tradition of local autonomy remained and although these officials encouraged co-ordination of action between local societies and a considerable amount of uniformity in dues and structures they did so within a federal structure. In the weavers' societies, for example, the secretary was principally appointed to calculate piecework rates. Co-ordination of activity was necessary only for purposes of collective bargaining and most other decisions were outside his ken and left to the local societies.

Other societies continued this variety and the wide variations in rules and structures of unions do not lend themselves to generalisations. Suggestions of a widespread adoption of 'new model' structure are inadequate and even within the A.S.E. there was opposition to centralisation. One can detect a trend towards national organisations and there were numerous pressures encouraging this. The development of a national market brought common problems to societies in different areas. Increased mobility of labour necessitated national links if union membership was to be meaningful and if pressure from cheap labour was to be lessened. In craft societies, where traditional 'tramping' in search of work continued well into this period, the need for an overall picture of the labour market encouraged national organisation and central control.[45] Where there was no desire to encourage mobility as in cotton or in mining or in Scotland the tendency towards centralisation was much less marked. Size was also important in encouraging concentration of power at the centre, since with large funds there needed to be some kind of responsible authority, and with the creation of a bureaucracy there was the tendency of all bureaucracies towards centralisation of power. But, the trend was a gradual one: unionists clung to local power and displayed intense jealousy and suspicion of national officials who tried to dictate policy.

III

The desire of workers to protect their job from the competition of outsiders is fundamental to the emergence and development of most trade unions. The first and ever-present threat was from workers who were willing to do work cheaply, often because they lacked the skill of the fully-qualified craftsman or just from the pressure of want. It was the expansion of industry to meet a rapidly growing demand that brought the threat of competition from cheap labour to the forefront of trade union thinking. From the early years of the century workers had seen, in such trades as shoemaking, cabinetmaking and tailoring, the creation of 'honourable' and 'dishonourable' sections of the trade. The former accepted the traditional customs and rates of the trade maintained by the trade societies, while the latter involved the production of goods as cheaply as possible, in non-society shops, with the work sub-divided among less-skilled workers.[46] It remained a major concern of unions: hence the stress laid on the payment of out-of-work benefit, to ensure that necessity did not force a man to do work too cheaply.

A second threat came from the steady migration into the cities, which brought the pressure of competition from the country-bred worker on the urban artisan. It too was an old problem. In the 1820s the Glasgow cotton spinners excluded from membership those who had not begun their career in the industry as piecers in the West of Scotland and the Grand General Union of Spinners of 1829–30 sought to restrict entry to the relatives of established spinners.[47] Throughout the century, however, most urban trades suffered from an influx of rural workers.

Thirdly – and of growing importance – was the threat to job security caused by technological change. In a number of industries the semi-skilled machine-minder threatened the demand for the services of the skilled craftsman. It was just such a threat which was a major factor in the strike of engineers at Messrs Hibbert and Platt of Oldham in 1851, which formed the background to the engineers' lock-out of the following year. The craftsmen found that planing and boring machines were being adapted to undertake more and more of the craftsmen's work and since the machines were operated by unskilled labourers then the skilled man's job was being steadily eroded. The engineers, therefore, demanded the dismissal of 'illegal men' on the machines and the restoration of the operating of the machines to craftsmen.[48] A further important aim of craft unions was, therefore, to delineate jobs as the monopoly of their members.

Primarily, then, the purpose of craft unions was to lay down and maintain rules of entry to the trade to prevent the encroachment on the craftsmen's position by the unskilled or the cheap. One measure of skill was the serving of an apprenticeship of five, sometimes seven, years, but in very few trades were workmen able to maintain a comprehensive apprenticeship system. Most crafts were expanding rapidly and there was a constant flow of workers, from the country into the towns, who had all the skills of the craft without necessarily having served an apprenticeship. By 1877, as George Howell calculated, less than 10 per cent of those admitted to unions had been properly apprenticed.[49] Where evidence of an apprenticeship was not possible, some societies, such as the A.S.E. or the Amalgamated Carpenters, would accept an alternative measure of having worked five consecutive years at the trade, 'be possessed of good ability as a workman, be of steady habits, good moral character, and earning the ordinary rate of wages in the district'.[50] Some craft societies, particularly in the building trades, accepting the limitations in their ability to impose an apprenticeship where none existed, asked only that an applicant for membership have his efficiency as a workman vouched for by two members of the society.[51]

It was common for a further attempt to restrict entry to be made by laying down limits to the number of apprentices who could be employed in a workshop. Such restrictions were usually based on custom and on local agreements and were not written into the society's rules.[52] An exception to this was the Flint Glass Makers' Society, which had a national rule of one apprentice to three groups of workers, or 'chairs' as they were called in the industry. Disputes on the issue were frequent, culminating in a three-months' strike followed by a three months' lock-out in 1858, which ended with a new agreement of one apprentice to two 'chairs'.[53] Another exception was the Provincial Typographical Association which tried to impose a maximum of three apprentices per shop. It was impossible to maintain such a restriction when the industry was growing rapidly, but it remained in the rule book.[54] There were many reasons for the attempts to restrict the number of apprentices. Many employers used apprentices as a source of cheap labour and cast them out into the labour market when their apprenticeships were completed. In part also, the restrictive policy was intended to maintain wages by limiting the supply of skilled labour: 'to prevent an oversurplus of labour in our market', as William Allan put it.[55] A third reason involved the more traditional concept of family right to the craft. Craftsmen were finding it difficult to get their sons apprenticed when they had to compete with the sons of farmers from the surrounding areas.[56] Fourthly, since it was the craftsman who was responsible for the actual training of the apprentice, he felt the need to have some control over who was to be apprenticed.

Restriction of entry into a trade was a policy applicable only where there was an hierarchical structure to the trade, with well-established lines of progress from apprentice to master craftsman. In some of the most important industries, particularly in mining and cotton, no such structure existed. In coal mining all men would work through various tasks, above and below ground, and eventually would graduate to working as a hewer at the coal face. Although there were frequent complaints at men, totally lacking in experience, being imported to work at the coal face there was no attempt to establish any kind of apprenticeship system and no hard-and-fast division existed between craftsman and labourer. Miners' unions were concerned with maintaining their level of piecework rates, not with limiting numbers.

In the textile industry, too, there was no division based on an apprenticeship system into skilled and unskilled. 'Skill' came from experience, while the actual training required for what was mainly machine-minding, was little. Nonetheless, there was restriction of entry. In cotton spinning, for example, the hand-mule spinners generally excluded the workers on the new self-acting machines through to the 1860s. When the self-actor minders came to predominate they adopted the exclusive tactics of the older spinners' unions of restricting the supply of labour. Minders could only be recruited, by order of seniority at the individual mills, from the piecers (the boys responsible for joining the threads) and the number of piecers was restricted to two per machine.[57] In weaving, on the other hand, any remnant of an apprenticeship system dating from handloom-weaving days had long disappeared and the unions of powerloom weavers appearing in the mid-century decades made no attempt to limit entry into the trade. As Professor H. A. Turner has argued, the weavers' societies anticipated the 'open' unionism of the next generation and like it was intent not on restricting numbers, but on negotiating uniform wage rates.[58] Both mining and cotton industries had some natural protection in that they were industries concentrated in certain areas and tending to draw their workers from the families of the mining villages or the cotton towns. There was a less intense and less constant pressure from outsiders, though it was certainly not entirely absent.

In addition to laying down rules for entry into the trade, the unions also endeavoured to maintain some control over the methods and level of payment. Many craft societies opposed the introduction of piecework, again usually by custom and tradition rather than by specific regulation, though some societies had fines for members taking work by the piece.[59] The A.S.E., the Ironfounders, the Amalgamated Carpenters, the Operative Bricklayers and the Plasterers all expressed opposition to payment by the piece. Traditional craft ideas of payment by time no doubt helped maintain this attitude, but opposition to piecework had more specific reasons. It was believed that piecework tended to reduce wages and reduce the quality of work, to increase the hours of work and demand increased exertion from workmen, if they were to maintain a reasonable standard of living. According to Edwin Coulson of the Bricklayers it encouraged employers to use poor quality materials and there were frequent complaints that employers would employ a workman as a 'chaser' or pace-setter to speed up the rate of work.[60] But behind all this was the desire of most craft societies to maintain some uniformity of hours and of wages. It was a constant source of criticism of trade unions that they sought to maintain a 'uniform rate of wages without regard to differences of skill, knowledge, industry, and character'.[61] In fact, as union leaders never tired of pointing out, the unions sought a standard *minimum* rate, with no restriction on higher payment for better workers.[62] The standard rate was local, not national, and there were substantial variations in these rates, though the tendency throughout the period was towards uniformity between districts. But, even within districts there could be differences of as much as 3s per week in the rate in different towns.[63]

Not all unions were opposed to piecework, however. The coal miners, the cotton spinners, the ironworkers, the tailors, the shoemakers, the flint glass makers and many others were traditionally paid by the piece. Piecework had generally developed where higher skill could be directly measured in terms of higher output. In cotton spinning, for example, the more skilled a worker was the more spindles he could control. It had developed in other trades where supervision of individual workers was not easily possible. This was the case in mining when the sub-contracting or 'butty' system broke down and a coal hewer was left to work at his own pace – similarly in trades like the tailors and shoemakers where there was a great deal of outwork.[64] It involved the complex process of working out rates for different tasks and required regular meetings of employers and workers to devise new rates and to take account of new processes.

Tradition and custom were probably the most important factors in explaining the different payment systems which societies chose to defend. However, the pressure from employers was generally towards piecework in order to increase productivity, and technological developments, bringing sub-division of processes, encouraged this tendency. The continuing opposition to piecework by societies like the A.S.E. and the Ironfounders had the effect of more and more new processes being done by non-unionists.[65] Most societies throughout the period were probably losing ground in their opposition to piecework and being forced to accept a compromise of both piecework and time-work. In some cases this reflected difficulties in working out piece rates. The printers, for example, generally accepted piece rates, but for complex type-setting jobs reverted to time rates. In newspaper presses, piece rates were paid, but the printing unions also insisted on payment for idle time. In shipbuilding, the Boilermakers' Society generally accepted piece rates in building new ships, but insisted on time rates for the less measurable task of ship-repairing.[66]

The actual level of wages was the subject of local bargaining and there were variations of as much as 10s or more per week between different areas. An engineering fitter, for instance, could earn 34s in London in the 1850s, in Manchester 30s, but in Newcastle only 24s. Most societies were at pains to deny that they insisted on uniformity of wages, though this was common accusation thrown against unionism. But they did have a concept of a standard rate. This was the level of wages that the average skilled workman would expect for his work. The rate for either time-work or piecework would be based on custom, on negotiated agreement or on what had been won by strike action. The standard rate was the highest rate that a considerable number of workers in a trade in an area, which might sometimes be a town or even part of a town or, at other times, might be a wider region, was able to get. Once a rate was won it was held on to as the norm. If an increase in wages was gained at a later date this new level became the standard. If, on the other hand, wage reductions were imposed, the aim of the union was to restore the 'standard rate' as quickly as possible. Unions regarded the standard rate as a minimum and insisted that any workman wishing to join the union had shown himself capable of earning this standard rate. They vehemently denied that a highly skilled man might not be paid more, but inevitably there was a tendency for employers to pay most of the workers at this minimum rate. There was also a very gradual tendency towards a national rate. It had not got very far by 1880, but the districts covered by a particular rate tended to become larger and unions did use comparisons between districts as an argument for wage rises.

Hours of labour, too, were generally left to local bargaining. But where union organisation was reasonably strong there was a tendency towards uniformity. At the beginning of the 1850s ten hours per day or a 60-hour week was fairly common, though there were many exceptions to this, most notoriously on the railways and in the 'sweated sections' of the piecework trades. During the early years of the decade a number of crafts succeeded in procuring early finishing on Saturday and a 58½- or even a 57-hour week. At the end of the fifties and throughout the sixties there was constant trade-union pressure, particularly in the building trades, for a 9-hour day. The builders' lock-out of 1859 and the strikes of 1861 in London were merely the best known of a number of local movements. The timing depended on local leadership and circumstances. For example, a 9-hour movement began among the Liverpool stonemasons in 1846; in London it gathered strength from the mid-fifties; in Edinburgh it came in 1861; while in Glasgow it did not take place until 1866. Success varied from area to area. Thus Leone Levi found in 1867 that a building worker in London worked on average 56½ hours per week, while in Cheshire he worked 55½ hours and in Derbsyhire 58½ hours. The Newcastle engineers led the way for a renewed demand in 1871 and their successful example was quickly followed in other areas and by other industries. In Scotland, in the 1870s, the engineers on the Clyde went even further and succeeded in winning a 51-hour week, though by the end of the decade this had been lost and 54 hours and, in some cases, 57 hours reintroduced.

In an increasing number of industries, hours of labour were regulated by legislation governing the working time of women and children. The Factory Acts of 1844 and 1847 had limited the hours of work of women and of young people under the age of 18 to ten hours per day. Although the hours of adult men were not covered by legislation, in an industry like cotton, where the men were dependent on the assistance of women and children, it had the effect of limiting the hours of men. This was even more the case when further Acts of 1850 and 1853 stipulated the 'normal day' for women and children (i.e. the hours during which they could be in the factory) and prevented their use in relays to keep up the men's hours. In 1860 the Factory Acts were extended to bleaching and dyeing works, in 1861 to lace factories, in 1864 to potteries, match-making, cartridge manufacturing and paper staining. The Factory Acts Extension Act of 1867 brought a large number of new industries under control – iron, copper, brass, steel and tin works, letterpress printing, bookbinding, tobacco works among others. The Workshops Regulation Act of the same year, though not particularly effective, covered smaller manufacturing establishments with less than fifty workers. Again, all these measures dealt only with the hours of women and children, but they almost invariably brought about a reduction in men's hours.

In 1867 a number of cotton unions began pressing for a further reduction of hours. Influenced by the still active Joseph Rayner Stephens, they demanded an eight-hour act for *adults*, females and young persons. At the beginning of the 1870s they decided, however, to limit their demands to nine hours and, in January 1872, societies of both spinners and weavers in Lancashire formed the Factory Acts Reform Association. Once again they focused on the hours of women and children, but made little secret of the fact that it was adult male hours they wanted shortened. A nine-hours bill, introduced by A. J. Mundella in 1873, was withdrawn because of strong Liberal opposition, but the following year, the new Conservative government passed a Factory Act which gave women and children in the textile industry a week of 56½ hours (instead of Mundella's 54). A further consolidating measure of 1878 largely removed the distinction between factories and workshops.[67]

Accustomed to government intervention, the textile workers used their unions as political pressure groups to press for shorter hours 'behind the women's petticoats'. The miners too, having successfully brought about government intervention on safety in the pits, occasionally looked to the state to legislate on hours. The policy of the National Association of Miners in the 1860s was for an eight-hour day by legislation, though this brought some opposition from the Durham miners, some of whom had already procured an even shorter shift by trade-union action. In the 1870s the miners in many areas began to deliberately reduce their hours in an effort to restrict output and thus raise prices.[68]

Whatever the variations in hours of work there was agreement that once established they should be maintained. The excessive and systematic use of overtime was generally frowned upon, though no society actually forbade overtime. It was something to be discouraged as harmful to health, but also as likely to keep other workers out of a job. The main concern of most societies by the 1860s and 1870s was to ensure that any overtime was paid at higher rates of time and a quarter or time and a half.

Just as in the structure of their organisations so there was among unions tremendous variations in methods of attaining their aims.

The ultimate objective of protecting their members from encroachments on their wages, hours, customs and status was the same. The best way to achieve this depended on tradition, on the circumstances of the trade or on conditions in a particular locality. The ideal of craft unions was to regulate their trade by what has been called 'autonomous regulation'.[69] In other words, they wished to lay down a code of rules as the practice of the trade, which employers would accept. Wages would be maintained by strictly controlling entry and through payment of adequate unemployment benefit. The practice fell far short of the ideal and craft unions involved themselves in collective bargaining. Indeed, one of the most successful unions of the period was the United Society of Boilermakers and Ironshipbuilders, which while restricting entry into the trade also negotiated detailed collective bargaining agreements. At the other extreme the weavers, having learned from the vain attempts of their handloom predecessors to control entry into the craft, sought to maintain their wages by means of the negotiated uniform list. Tradition played its part, but there was a great deal of pragmatism. If a union felt it was possible to restrict entry into the trade it did so; if conditions seemed favourable to a wage demand it would be made. But, there was no set way of acting, though each union was influenced by the activity of other unions in the area. A successful strike for higher wages or shorter hours by one union was likely to stir others to action. Conversely, the failure of one union was likely to discourage a 'forward movement' by others. On both hours and wages it was very much a question of playing it by ear.

IV

Among the most important developments of the mid-nineteenth century were the successful attempts at drawing together societies in different trades into both local and national organisations. There was a long tradition of co-operation between different societies, dating back probably to the eighteenth century. A major local crisis was likely to result in a local committee of delegates from different trades to deal with it. Its function might be to raise money to assist striking workers or it might be intended merely as a forum where the strikers' case could be put before the public. These committees would be organised on an *ad hoc* basis, but there was probably continuing contact between the leading unionists in a town. From 1818 there were recurring attempts to organise a general union of workers on a permanent basis, culminating in the Owenite Grand National Consolidated Trades' Union. The extent of federation in such bodies varied, but all sought to present a strong and united front to employers in time of dispute. Yet a further cause of united action in a particular town might be for political purposes: to provide witnesses for a parliamentary inquiry affecting unionists or to take part in a reform campaign. On occasions national links between different committees were achieved. For example, the activities of the various trade committees of 1834 in support of the Tolpuddle martyrs produced some measure of national co-ordination as did those three years later in support of the Glasgow cotton spinners. Early in 1843 a union of Sheffield trades was formed 'in order that such measures may be resorted to as shall tend to place us artisans in a better condition',[70] and the following year this body summoned a national conference out of which arose 'the National Association of United Trades for the Protection of Labour', established in March 1845. It sought to bring about a 'general confederation or union of trades', but its aims were much more limited than its Owenite predecessors and the affiliated societies retained their autonomy. Delegates from trade societies were formed into districts and intended to meet monthly. For a time the Association published its own newspaper, the *Labour League*, which was distributed as far north as Aberdeen[71] and in 1856 the secretary claimed a membership of five or six thousand. Three permanent officials were based in London and their main function was to act as mediators in disputes and to lobby members of Parliament. Although it continued in existence until the mid-sixties, it was of little importance after 1851. In that year the officials, together with a number of Wolverhampton tinplate workers, were indicted on charges of conspiracy and intimidation. The Association had not the money to defend them and the task was left to a defence committee appointed by the various London trade societies.[72]

There were a number of other attempts by trade unions to band together in the late 1840s. A 'Delegated Committee of Sympathy' was formed in Aberdeen in the summer of 1846 to 'support each other in the event of a strike of any of them, or when any general movement was required in support of trade unions'.[73] It survived for about three years. In Sheffield a committee of trades delegates recommended the formation of a 'general Trades Council' to face a hostile Manufacturers' Protection Society.[74] In Liverpool the Trades Guardians' Association was formed and has had a continuous existence, under a variety of titles, to the present day. Throughout the 1850s meetings of such bodies became more and more frequent. During the lock-out of engineers in 1852 a conference of Metropolitan Trades met regularly and affirmed the need for co-operation between trade societies: '. . . our safety lies in union, wider spread and more closely knitted – union which shall apply not to one trade only, but to all trades – union which shall take in all existing societies'.[75]

A similar body met weekly during the Preston strike of the following year[76] and there was a Metropolitan Trades' Committee on the Friendly Societies' bill of 1855 and the strike in the flint glass trade in the winter of 1858–9 quickly brought together a committee of sympathy in London.[77] According to a future secretary of London Trades Council, George Odger, there were regular publications of a 'general London trades report' from about the 1830s. By the end of the 1850s, therefore, there was a well-established pattern of action in time of crisis among the trade societies of London and a tradition of mutual support, which was not confined to disputes in the metropolis. In most other towns of any size there was a similar pattern of development. The timing and the form it took depended upon local circumstances, but as trade unionism grew during the prosperity of the years of mid-century, so too did efforts to draw together separate unions. From 1858 these efforts began to come to fruition in the establishing of permanent trades councils.

Two trades councils were formed in 1858, in Glasgow and in Sheffield, and the following year brought the preliminary steps that led to the London Trades Council. The Glasgow Council grew out of a series of meetings and demonstrations in support of the unemployed during the bitter winter of 1857–8. The Council met weekly and consisted of two delegates from each affiliated trade society, whose task it was 'to examine, devise and execute the best means of improving the condition of the working classes morally, socially and politically'.[78] A permanent organisation in Sheffield followed a dispute in the office of the *Sheffield Times*. When the local printers' society published an attack on the proprietor of the paper he sued them. A committee of local trades was formed as usual, partly to support the printers, partly to mediate and partly to draw up rules for a trades' organisation. The outcome was the Association of Organised Trades of Sheffield and Neighbourhood. The secretary was the secretary of the local branch of the Typographical Association, William Dronfield and the treasurer was the soon-to-be-notorious publican-secretary of the saw-grinders' society, William Broadhead. Unlike the Glasgow Council the main work of the Sheffield Association was carried on by an executive committee of thirteen, one of the first members of which was Robert Applegarth, secretary of the local society of carpenters and joiners.[79]

A trades council in London was formed as a result of the strike and lock-out in the building trades during the winter of 1859–60. Early in 1859 the flint glass manufacturers in the Midlands, banded together as the Midland Employers' Association, introduced the 'document' in an attempt to carry out their expressed aim of destroying the Flint Glass Makers' Union. This had been resisted by the men and their appeal for assistance was answered from all parts of the country. As they had done frequently in the past, the London trades' delegates met at the 'Bell Inn' by the Old Bailey to collect funds for the locked-out men.[80] When, therefore, a few months later the Central Association of Master Builders in London introduced the 'document' in response to a demand for a nine-hours' day by a committee of building trade unions, the reaction was the same. The introduction of the 'document' raised the dispute into a national issue affecting all trade unions. The 'Bell Inn' committee re-formed. From the work of this committee two main weaknesses were manifested: the lack of co-ordination between trade societies and the lack of means of informing the public of the unions' side of the case. To combat these weaknesses in the future the London Trades Council was formed and the *Bee-Hive Newspaper* was established. Early in the struggle, William Allan, general secretary of the A.S.E., urged 'that a standing committee of all the trades of London should be maintained in order to meet crises like the present',[81] and when the strike was over a committee remained to devise some plan for this purpose. In July 1860 the first Council was formed consisting of seven members elected by a general meeting of trades delegates. The following year it was enlarged to fifteen members and the young and ambitious bricklayer, George Howell took over as secretary.[82]

Either spontaneously or in imitation of the pioneers other councils began to appear. By March 1859 the United Trades Delegates Association of Edinburgh and its Vicinity was holding regular fortnightly meetings.[83] In the autumn of 1859 there was a Newcastle and Gateshead Association of Trades.[84] Nottingham seems to have taken Sheffield as its model and an Association of Organized Trades was formed there in 1861. The Liverpool

Trades Guardians' Association revived in 1861 as a result of a protracted, but successful, struggle against an attempt by the master builders to introduce payment by the hour. It merged into a new United Trades Protective Association with Charles Williams, soon to be general secretary of the National Association of Operative Plasterers, as its secretary.[85] Bristol, Bolton, Halifax, Leeds, Greenock, Barrow, Preston, Warrington and many other towns and trades councils in the early sixties. Some of these survived while others were extinguished after a short burst of activity. The years 1865 and 1866 brought a new flowering with the formation of important councils in Wolverhampton, Birmingham and Manchester. Wolverhampton Trades Council arose as a result of a dispute between the plate-lock makers of the town and their employers. During the struggle a group of the strikers formed a co-operative production company and it was to support this company that a conference of local trades' delegates was formed in May 1865: a conference which inaugurated a permanent trades council in July 1865.[86] A bitter strike and lock-out in the building trades persuaded the Birmingham unions to form their trades council in June 1866.[87] Three months later the Manchester and Salford trades formed a Council based on the Sheffield model.

By the end of 1866 trades councils had established themselves as an integral part of the trade-union movement. Between 1858 and 1866 at least twenty-four trades councils or similar bodies had had some kind of existence. Bristol, Greenock, Halifax, Hull, Dundee, Barrow in Furness, Warrington, Newcastle, Dublin, Preston, St. Helens and Darlington each had an organisation that existed for a short period and then succumbed to apathy, trade recession or to personal squabbles. Most of them were re-formed in the early seventies only to collapse again. In the nation's most populous towns, however, London, Birmingham, Manchester, Glasgow, Edinburgh, Sheffield, Nottingham, Liverpool, Wolverhampton and Leeds a permanent organisation had been established. The expansion of trade unionism in the prosperity of the early 1870s brought renewed trades council activity. By 1875 there were about forty of them, but few of the councils formed in the early seventies survived the decade. By the early 1880s their numbers had been reduced to about twenty.

Trades councils depended for the core of their membership on the small craft societies and the larger national societies tended to hold aloof from them. In part this was because the large societies were jealous of any body that seemed, no matter how slightly, to threaten their authority and were unwilling to let the smaller societies participate with them in decision making, especially as they regarded the smaller societies as rather irresponsible; in part it was recognition that trades councils had little to offer to the large society. A council's main function was generally to organise mutual support during strikes and the national societies had little need of this kind of assistance. The Amalgamated Carpenters' Society withdrew from the London Trades Council in 1867 and although local branches of the society were free to affiliate to trades councils any expenses had to be met by the membership, not from the society's funds.[88] The A.S.E. was somewhat similar. With the death of William Allan in 1874 the executive disaffiliated from the London Trades Council and till 1885 hardly a single branch of the A.S.E. was represented on any trades council. Neither the boilermakers nor the miners bothered with councils. Where some large societies were present they sometimes tried to dominate a council. This happened in Birmingham in the mid-1870s when the Amalgamated Brassworkers' Society tried to steamroller its view through the Council. Faced with the united hostility of the smaller societies, however, it eventually withdrew.[89] In Lancashire the cotton spinners' unions were usually powerful enough to ensure that their views were attended to.

For a brief period in the 1860s the London Trades Council did attract to it the leading unionists in the country – the Webbs' famous 'Junta'. 'By 1864', they wrote, 'the new organisation was entirely dominated by the Junta . . . the Council became in effect, a joint committee of the officers of the large national societies.'[90] But matters were never as straightforward as the Webbs suggest. The Junta of the Webbs consisted of Applegarth of the Carpenters, Allan of the Engineers, Daniel Guile of the Ironfounders, Edwin Coulson of the Bricklayers and Odger, secretary of the Council. Coulson was a member of the first full council in 1861 and Applegarth was co-opted on as Carpenters' representative in 1863. Daniel Guile came in in 1864 along with Danter, president of the A.S.E. There was considerable opposition within the London trades to the increasing domination of the large amalgamated societies in the Council and George Potter, manager of the *Bee-Hive Newspaper* tried to organise the discontent. During 1864 and 1865 the Trades Council was rent with disputes which became focused on the rivalry between Applegarth and George Potter. Personal animosities and jealousies played a very large part in the quarrels, but Potter was able to draw support from many of the small unions, particularly the carpenters' societies, who had suffered a loss of members to the Amalgamated Carpenters. In the dispute Odger and Coulson were usually to be found aligned with Applegarth, but Guile was as often as not on Potters' side. In 1865 the Ironfounders withdrew from the Council in the belief that 'the ill-feeling which had been established during the past twelve months is calculated to do more harm or injury to trades' unions than all the good they can ever do (under the present system) will be able to repair'.[91] It was probably symptomatic of the distaste that many felt for the quarrelling that at the annual delegate meeting of August 1865 neither Potter nor Applegarth nor Coulson was elected to the Council, though one or two of Potter's supporters were elected. Not until the end of 1865 was Allan co-opted on to the Council. Never at any time, therefore, were all the members of the Webbs' Junta on the Trades Council together and, although the Council's reports in these years did tend to reflect the views of the amalgamated societies, the Council never functioned as a 'joint committee of the officers of the national societies'.

Trades councils were essentially local bodies dealing, in the main, with local problems: they were at their most effective when acting as forums for the discussion of matters of local interest. They played both an industrial and a political role. In their industrial role they would give assistance and advice during strikes: they would, where possible mediate in disputes between employers and a member union or in demarcation disputes between rival unions; they could, on occasion, lead a local agitation for shorter hours or better conditions in particular trades; a few performed the role of organiser and assisted in the formation of new unions. Their political role was carried on at two levels: by directly involving themselves in both local and national politics and by acting as a political pressure group on issues particularly concerning trade unions. The amount of activity on these issues varied greatly between councils, but one thing all had in common was that they were weak organisations often balanced precariously between survival and extinction. They were particularly vulnerable to economic fluctuations since dues to a trades council were usually the first economy a union would undertake when times were difficult. The councils had no executive power and were dependent on getting at least some measure of consensus before they could take action. However, despite all the limitations many councils were in the 1860s and 1870s speaking for the organised working class in their localities.

V

The same pressures that pushed trade unions to co-ordinate their activities at a local level brought about national organisations. A national trade-union conference in 1845 produced the National Association of United Trades for the Protection of Labour, but the first really representative national conference was in 1864 when the London Trades Council called a meeting on behalf of the Glasgow Master and Workman Acts Reform Committee to promote a national campaign against the Master and Servant Acts. It was widely attended but made no provision for future meetings and passed the leadership of the campaign back to the Glasgow Committee.[92] The increasing incidence of lock-outs during 1865 and 1866 caused many unionists to think about a national defence organisation. During a major lock-out of Sheffield file grinders in May 1866 the Wolverhampton Trades Council suggested the calling of a national conference in Sheffield 'to take action conjointly to rebut the lock-out system so prevalent with the capitalists'.[93] The Sheffield Association of Organised Trades took up the idea and the conference opened on 17 July 1866 and sat for five days. The result of the conference was the formation of the short-lived national organisation, the United Kingdom Alliance of Organised Trades,[94] which had by the end of the year more than sixty affiliated societies with 60,000 members. Its object was to provide mutual support in the event of lock-outs and over the next year it received considerable support in the North of England. However, it shared its officers with the Sheffield Association and when the treasurer, William Broadhead, admitted to the Royal Commission Inquiry into the Sheffield Outrages his deep involvement in the outrages most societies speedily dissociated themselves from the Alliance.

It was the setting up of a Royal Commission to inquire into the activities of trade unions that occasioned the next national conference in March 1867. At the end of 1866 trade unions found themselves under attack from a number of directions. Employers, in the eyes of unionists, seemed to be becoming more militant in their opposition to trade unionism and there had been a whole series of lock-outs. In October an explosion in the house of a Sheffield non-unionist produced a tremendous public outcry against unions, with a section of the press talking of the need for unions to be 'stamped out as a public nuisance'.[95] Hard on the heels of this came the court decision of Chief Justice Cockburn in the case of Hornby *v*. Close, declaring trade unions to be 'in restraint of trade'. He dispelled the illusion that the funds of unions whose rules were deposited with the Registrar of Friendly Societies were secure from dishonest officers. The outcry against unions, together with Cockburn's ruling, presented the greatest threat to the large amalgamated societies. The former jeopardised their image of moderation and respectability, the latter threatened the very basis of their strength, their large funds. As a result they decided to work together to undo some of the damage in a 'Conference of Amalgamated Trades' which held its first meeting in January 1867.[96] The conference made no secret of its intention to act purely in the interest of the large societies and at no point consulted the other unions. It was to remedy this that George Potter, ever vigilant for an opportunity to embarrass Applegarth, called a conference in St Martin's Hall in March 1867. The London Trades Council and the Conference of Amalgamated Trades boycotted the conference, but in doing so they found themselves at variance with most of the rest of the country. Much to the surprise of the 'Junta' (for with the setting up of the conference of amalgamated trades such a group now did exist) Potter's conference proved a great success. Delegates from thirty unions and nine trades councils representing almost 200,000 unionists attended.[97] It was not that all the provincial unions were sympathetic to Potter in his battles with the Junta, but his conference offered the provincial unions a say in dealing with the crisis. A committee was formed to keep an eye on the proceedings of the Royal Commission, but no provision was made for future conferences.

The initiative for summoning what is usually regarded as the founding conference of the Trades Union Congress[98] came from the Manchester and Salford Trades Council. In the light of the public hostility to trade unions, S. C. Nicholson, the President of the Manchester Council had been impressed by the effective platform provided by the 1867 conference and urged the necessity of an annual congress of trade-union delegates. To some extent the annual meetings of the National Association for the Promotion of Social Science had been used as a platform by some unionists, but on a number of occasions the published reports of its proceedings had revealed an anti-union bias. When it published in its report of the Sheffield meeting of 1865, a strong attack on trade unions, but failed to include William Dronfield's defence of them,[99] Nicholson and his colleague W. H. Wood had come to the conclusion that working men would have to depend on their own organisation[100] if they were to overcome 'the profound ignorance which prevailed in the public mind with reference to the operations and principles of trade unions'.[101] They therefore persuaded Manchester and Salford Trades Council to call another national conference. Thirty-four delegates representing 118,000 unionists met in June 1868 and made arrangements for a further conference in Birmingham the following year. It was very much modelled on the meetings of the Social Science Association: delegates read long papers on the advantages of trade unionism, on conciliation and arbitration, on trade unions and politics. The London Trades Council and the Conference of Amalgamated Trades were conspicuously absent from the Manchester Congress but they made a point of being at Birmingham in 1869. Given the task of calling the next conference, the London Trades Council failed to do so until March 1871. This London Congress met while the controversial Trade-Union Bill, with its accompanying criminal clauses, was going through Parliament and in these circumstances the nature of the Congress altered. It became less a forum for the reading of formal papers and much more a discussion centre for the outstanding issues facing unionism. Resolutions began to be passed and votes taken. To continue its work a Parliamentary Committee was elected consisting of Alexander McDonald, Lloyd Jones, George Potter and George Howell 'to co-operate with the London Trades to watch over the passage of the Trade-Union Bill'.[102] Given this special position, the London Trades, represented by the Trades Council, sought to maintain it, while the Parliamentary Committee sought to increase its power. At the end of 1872 the London Trades Council was suggesting that there was really no need for a further committee and a few provincial delegates should merely be appointed to co-operate with the London Council. Congress would have none of it, however, and the Parliamentary Committee continued. The London delegates had to get themselves elected to it.

From 1871 the annual meetings of the TUC were firmly established. The Mayor of Nottingham gave the delegates a municipal reception in 1872. The following year the first printed report of the proceedings was issued and a set of standing orders had been drawn up. By the end of the decade membership of the affiliated unions had risen to over half a million. George Howell acted as secretary from 1871 until 1876 when he was succeeded by the stonemason, Henry Broadhurst, who was to dominate the Congress through the Parliamentary Committee until the end of the 1880s.

Despite the great variety in their size, their style and their structure trade unions were, by the 1870s, acting together on a host of issues. In their trades councils and at the Trades Union Congress they were generally speaking with a united voice. Something that could fairly be called a trade-union movement was in existence, whose interests and activities were not confined to industrial disputes but had been widened to include the whole field of social policy.

Chapter 2

Trade-union Strategy

The principal objectives of trade societies in the mid-Victorian decades were the defence of the wages and the rights of their members and, where possible, the gradual improvement of their conditions. This has always been the aim of trade unionism, but there is more than one way in which this can be done. Broadly, there are two alternatives: trade unions can adopt a policy of confrontation with their employers and with the rest of society or they can adopt a policy of conciliation, of seeking a *modus vivendi*. By the mid-nineteenth century the former policy had given way to the latter as the dominant philosophy of unionism. The alternatives were never mutually exclusive and at any moment and within the same group of workers could exist side by side. But it was the policy of conciliation that came to be the most important.

Contemporaries tended to see the change as a sudden one, with a discontented, hostile and often very violent working class giving way as a result of the prosperity of the 1850s, to a contented, moderate working class who shunned the violent methods of their forefathers. There was more than a hint of regret in the words of the old chartist Thomas Cooper as he viewed the transformation of the working class in twenty-five years.

In our old Chartist times, it is true, Lancashire working men were in rags by thousands; and many of them often lacked food. But their intelligence was demonstrated wherever you went. You would see them in groups discussing the great doctrine of political justice – that every grown-up, sane man ought to have a vote in the election of the men who were to make the laws by which he was to be governed; or they were in earnest dispute respecting the teachings of Socialism. *Now*, you will see no such groups in Lancashire. But you will hear well-dressed working men talking, as they walk with their hands in their pockets, of 'Co-ops'

(Co-operative Stores), and their shares in them, or in building societies. And you will see others, like idiots, leading small greyhound dogs, covered with cloth, in a string![1]

Even inveterate enemies of the unions admitted that there had been a marked improvement in the behaviour of the working classes since 1848, but despite their belief it is clear that the transformation had not taken place overnight.

The earliest trade unions had come into being as a result of the far-reaching changes brought about by industrialisation. As with any group in society, the workers were hostile to developments which caused a fundamental alteration in their way of life, in their status and in their standard of living. The unions that emerged in the eighteenth and early nineteenth centuries were, by and large, therefore, concerned with resisting change. Resistance took many forms. Most notorious of all was the machine-breaking that reached its peak in the Luddite unrest of 1811–12, when the Nottingham framework knitters took forceful action against the new stocking machines. Resistance could take a more intangible form of rejection of the new industrial disciplines through drunkenness, absenteeism and bad time-keeping. With the appearance of organisation among the workers spontaneous expressions of discontent gave way to more formal strikes against changes in conditions, often accompanied by violence against property, employers and blacklegs. The Owenite and the chartist movements of the 1830s and 1840s both attracted groups of workers who were feeling the impact of changes in their industrial situation – hand workers competing with machine-made goods, artisans competing with cheap semi-skilled labour, building craftsmen competing with large general contractors. In both Owenism and chartism there was an important element of looking back to a pre-industrial society or, at any rate, of seeking an alternative to the existing industrial system. There were, therefore, within the working class, substantial sections who were alienated from the prevailing values of society and this alienation was reflected in a series of confrontations with that society in the form of strikes against employers or demonstrations against the government.

Not all workers, however, suffered displacement, dispossession and deprivation as a result of industrialisation: some gained from change. The skill of the engineer and the iron founder was at a premium in a period of expanding new industries. Scarcity brought its rewards and few machine builders were to be found in the ranks of the protesters. For yet others, time brought a reconciliation with industrial change. The second and third generation in the factories had no alternative way of life to which to look back. Regular wages brought their compensations in the form of material possessions. Even as the Owenite bodies planned their new society and as the chartist marchers filled London's clubland with terror of impending revolution, there was a growing groundswell of commitment to industrialisation by more and more groups of workers.

By the 1850s alienation had given way to harmony with the prevailing system. The prosperity of the 1850s, with expanding trade and industry bringing rising real wages, did not create the new attitude of the workers, it merely strengthened currents that had been flowing in the direction of conciliation. Industrialisation was coming to mean improved standards for increasing numbers of workers. Fewer were seeking an alternative system and a majority were concerned with making the best of the existing one. Of course, hostility to industrial change did not disappear, for the progress of industrialisation is not an even one. Even in the 1850s and 1860s some industries were just embarking on their industrial revolutions and in those industries the response of the workers was still violently hostile. The shoemakers of Northamptonshire reacted to the introduction of the sewing machine into their trade in the 1850s not so differently from the Luddite stocking-makers. The brickmakers of the North of England had little to learn in the 1860s from machine-breakers of half a century before when it came to dealing with the new brickmaking machines and those who worked them. And Sheffield unions maintained a tradition of assassination, maiming and sabotage into the 1860s that was every bit as violent as the vitriol throwing of the Glasgow cotton spinners in the 1820s. But these were exceptions, the remnants of a dying philosophy. By the 1850s, the dominating working-class philosophy, as expressed through their trade unions, was one of acceptance of the prevailing values of society.

Foremost of these values was the belief in progress – faith in the possibility, and indeed inevitability, of ordered change for the better. In industry it meant growth and expansion, which could only be good since it brought Man greater control over his environment. It brought power and it brought prosperity. Progress could come through individual exertion and the progress of each individual would, in aggregate, bring mankind's progress. The individual was vitally important. He had to be responsible and committed to the idea of progress. Hence that second great belief, self-help, 'the root of all genuine growth in the individual' and 'the true source of national vigour and strength'. Progress could not come through institutions or through legislation: it was 'the sum of individual industry, energy and uprightness'. The role of government was to help and stimulate men 'to elevate and improve themselves by their own free and independent individual action'.[2] The good society was, therefore, the free society, unrestricted by archaic measures giving protection to particular groups, and allowing each individual the liberty to shape his own life as long as that life was committed to elevation and improvement.

To the hostile observer in 1850 trade unionism still seemed to stand against these values. It was still associated in the bourgeois mind with the hostility to ordered progress reflected in Owenism and chartism. It still seemed to have within it Luddite tendencies of opposition to technological change. It seemed to reject individual liberty in favour of protectionism, putting greater faith in institutions, in restrictive regulations and in protective legislation than in individual progress through self-help. Only gradually throughout the 1850s and 1860s did sympathetic observers elucidate the ways in which trade unionism now fitted into the values of a modern society and convince a sceptical world that unionism could indeed strengthen these values.

For the unionists who believed in the policy of conciliation it was essential to elicit some response from employers and from the rest of society, for conciliation meant compromise on both sides. It was, therefore, necessary for them to persuade the middle classes that they did accept their values, while at the same time trying to modify the system and to ameliorate the worst abuses. The history of trade unionism in the mid-nineteenth century is, therefore, a history of a struggle for acceptance on the part of trade unionists. At the forefront of this struggle were the groups who were most committed to the industrial system – engineers, ironfounders, boilermakers, cotton workers, later joined by miners and building workers. When the policy showed signs of success other groups followed.

I

The first necessity was to show that they were committed to improvement. Unions were not just to protect the rights of their members but 'to promote their physical, intellectual, moral and social improvement'[3] and to 'elevate' their character.[4] When he took over as general secretary of the Amalgamated Carpenters' Society in 1862, Robert Applegarth saw his task as being 'to raise so far as I knew how to do it, the whole tone and character of trades' unionism'.[5] There were various ways of doing this. The printing unions had their libraries in many towns, containing useful and elevating texts. Trades councils ran lectures for the intellectual improvement of the working class. The Glasgow Trades Council, for example, had as its first guest lecturer Sir Archibald Alison, the former Sheriff of Lanarkshire, whose determined pursuit of unionists twenty years before had led to the trial of the Glasgow cotton spinners in 1838.[6] The Amalgamated Carpenters' organised science classes for their members at the end of the 1860s.[7] In 1878 the London Trades Council was offering French classes. Unions were to be found supporting the demands for free public libraries and in Halifax, the branches of the ironmoulders and of the A.S.E. offered one day's wages towards the free library fund.[8] Elevation could come also from improved surroundings and it had been a favourite line of attack on unions that their meetings were associated with the ale house. Gradually, therefore, meetings were moved out of the public house. The London Society of Compositors moved into private premises in the 1840s;[9] Applegarth persuaded his Sheffield union to move from the pub to a reading room in 1858[10] and there were a number of trades halls built to provide meeting rooms. Rules were introduced by societies excluding any one from meetings who was under the influence of drink – with such effect in the Ironmoulders' Society that publicans no longer found it profitable to rent rooms for their meetings. As a result it was possible at the Royal Commission to claim that unions had acted as a curb on drunkenness and to contrast the moral stature of the unionist with the dissipation of the non-unionist. The union man was hard-working, honest and provident, said Daniel Guile, while 'most of the men . . . who are non-society men in a locality are drunkards, idlers and very often improvident men, that do not care for their wives, or children, or themselves, and I lament to say that very often they are defrauders'.[11] It was thanks to trade-union organisation, claimed the Bricklayers, that the London bricklayers of 1861 had been transformed from the 'drunken, dissipated, half-clad and therefore careless body of men' they had been in 1848.[12]

The second step was to show commitment to the ethic of self-help. This was easy for the great amalgamated societies that combined the role of trade union and friendly society. The A.S.E. regarded itself as 'a great Assurance Association' whose funds were 'a general voluntary rate in aid of the Poor's rate',[13] a point repeated by many other unions.[14] By subscribing to such a union a man was fulfilling all that Samuel Smiles could have wished in looking to the future and taking precautions against the hazards of old age, sickness and unemployment. As Thomas Brassey told the House of Commons in 1869, by their benefit side, trade unions 'encouraged a noble spirit of self-help'[15] and Applegarth reminded his members in 1870 that 'to teach workmen the practical lesson of self-reliance, to provide during the term of prosperity for the hour of need, is one of our great objects'.[16]

A third essential that unions had to get across to the middle class was their moderation and to do this they had to refute accusations that they were strike organisations. This the union leaders tried to do constantly, repeating time and time again the refrain 'we are averse to strikes', 'the executive council does all it possibly can to prevent any strike', 'the members generally are decidedly opposed to strikes'.[17] 'Strikes are to the social world', declared George Odger in a much quoted statement, 'what wars are to the political world. They become crimes unless they are prompted by absolute necessity'.[18] The way to resolve disputes was by negotiation, by conciliation and if necessary by arbitration. This was the rational way to settle matters and trade unions were intent on stressing how rational they were. Increasingly unions adopted rules that insisted that all attempts at conciliation must be exhausted before a strike took place. Only thus would it be possible 'to remove the prejudice which many employers entertain against your union', John Kane of the Ironworkers warned his members, since the prejudice had largely resulted from the actions of members 'who love strife more than peace, and who disregard the strict injunction against continuing work without legal notice, which is opposed to the principle of Arbitration and Conciliation'.[19] Even when strikes did by some misfortune break out the union leaders were at pains to stress that it was organisation that prevented their getting out of hand and succumbing to bloodshed and rioting. It was the trade union which ensured that the struggle was pursued with 'order' and 'dignity'.

Moderation could be shown in other ways. The Liverpool Tailors guaranteed the efficiency of their members and paid for spoiled work. The Bookbinders paid the employer if one of their members left his work unfinished,[20] as did the Boilermakers'

Society. The latter society had a fining system if an employer were 'injured by the misconduct of any member'.[21] Wage demands were reasonable. Owenite claims of 'the right to the whole produce of labour' had given way to 'a fair day's wages for a fair day's work'. Boilermakers were instructed 'not to make unreasonable demands on employers'[22] and to remember,

> Capital and Labour seem
> By our Maker joined;
> Are they not like giant twins
> In the world of mind?
> What can Labour do alone?
> Grind its nose against the stone,
> Turn a gristless mill!
> What can Capital indeed
> By itself? but hoard its seed
> Eat a golden pill.
>
> Up the hill of progress bright
> March we on in tether,
> Making difficulties light,
> Pulling all together.
> So we shall in concord joined
> Show to wondering mankind
> Capital and Labour
> Are our oars to pull the boat,
> Are our wings to soar aloft,
> In our high endeavour?[23]

Finally, there was the creation of a whole aura of respectability around the unions in all kinds of ways. There was the sartorial respectability of the frock coat and top hat. There was order and parliamentary dignity in the proceedings of conferences. Union leaders attended the right meetings and supported the right causes of Italian liberation, educational reform, temperance and a host of others, which showed they were in tune with the liberal 'spirit of the age'. If their advisers were not as moderate as some would have liked there was no doubt about their respectability and Applegarth maintained that 'if the policy I have pursued has been wise and beneficial, it is not due to myself alone, but in the first place to Professor Beesly, Mr Harrison, Mr Ludlow, Mr Hughes, M.P., Mr Lloyd Jones, Mr H. Crompton, and to such friends of the working classes who have been at my back with the best advice and counsel'.[24] Edinburgh Trades Council went one better and invited the Lord Advocate, the past Lord Advocate and an M.P. from each party to become honorary presidents of the Council.[25] Trade unions no longer represented the ragged masses who, marching in the rain to Kennington Common in April 1848, seemed to threaten progress and order, but sat with the leaders of opinion and worked for the same order and progress as the middle classes.

The essence of the policy was a very deliberate appeal to middle-class public opinion which had to be won to the unions if they were to get the acceptance they so desired. Thus, the carpenters were told,

If they had any grievances they should write to their employers, and if the employers refused to agree to their terms, or took no notice of this appeal, the best thing to do was to lay their claims before the public. . . . If the public agreed with the employers it was of no use for the men to press their case any further, and if the public was with the men it would be no use the masters to hold out any longer . . .'[26]

In all the major struggles of the period the sympathy of the public was sought and by demanding shorter working hours rather than pay rises, as many of the most important strikes of the period did, the unions could once again argue that it was all in the cause of improvement. When unrest among the Lancashire engineers boiled up in 1851 on the issue of who was to man the new planing machines – craftsmen or labourers – it was not an issue that was likely to attract much public sympathy. The executive of the A.S.E. switched the focus of discontent to piecework and systematic overtime, particularly the latter, for this was an issue that could be 'sold' to the public. Overtime was injurious to health, but worse, it deprived the workers of leisure for the 'cultivation of their mind'.[27] During the ensuing lock-out the A.S.E. courted publicity, issued circulars for public consumption, did not resort to picketing, gave financial assistance to the labourers caught in the middle of the dispute and on more than one occasion offered to submit the issue to arbitration. It was the employers who were put in the wrong. In the Preston cotton strike of 1853 there was the same appeal to public sympathy. The union welcomed the attempted mediation of a committee of local gentlemen; the employers rejected it.[28] There was a remarkable reduction in the violence and intimidation that had for long been associated with cotton strikes and even the strike breakers were treated 'with friendliness and cordiality'.[29]

The London building workers strike of 1859 was one of the most important struggles of these years in catching the public interest. Again it was a demand for shorter hours and much could be made of the desire of the workers for time to pursue elevating studies. Letters were sent to the press, public meetings put the workers' case, prize essays on the advantages of the nine hours were published. When the employers instigated a lock-out the nine-hour claim was abandoned and attention was focused on 'the odious document', which threatened the very right of combination. The nine-hour demand was revived in 1861 and similar tactics were employed. The stress was on moderation: 'But while we wish to advocate the *reasonable* claims of our class, it is with a sincere wish to do so respectfully in relation to the position of capital, and to the proper observance of social order.'[30]

One of the most effective uses of press publicity that influenced the course of an industrial dispute was in the Newcastle nine-hour strike of 1871. During that strike John Burnett, the leader of the striking engineers engaged in a debate in the letter columns of *The Times* with Sir William Armstrong, the leader of the employers. Burnett's theme was that the Nine-Hours League had constantly sought to negotiate with the employers, while the employers had refused compromise and dealt with the men only through a firm of solicitors. It contrasted favourably with the boast of Sir William Armstrong on how successfully the employers had been able to recruit foreign labour to break the strike. Undoubtedly, Burnett's articulate statement of the case was an important factor in rousing public sympathy for the strikers and forcing concessions from the employers.[31]

It was the feeling of the London unionists in 1859 that the existing press was inadequate for getting across the trade-union case that brought about the publication of the *Bee-Hive Newspaper*. It was the creation of George Potter, who had been secretary of the committee of the London building trades that co-ordinated the nine-hours movement in 1859. During the strike and lock-out only the sensationalist Sunday paper *Reynold's Newspaper* had given consistent support to the unions and Potter had reason to complain bitterly of a press 'in the hands of the capitalist who pays well for any denunciations against labour'.[32] The new paper was launched in October 1861 as a trade-union newspaper and although, during the next sixteen years, it reflected the frequently idiosyncratic views of George Potter it was, nonetheless, one of the most important vehicles for the publicising of unionist activities, not only in London but in all other parts of the country.

The annual reports which most societies of any significance began to publish in the 1850s and 1860s seem also to have had an eye on a wider readership than merely the members of the society. In the 1860s both the A.S.E. and the Amalgamated Carpenters often had their reports reviewed in middle-class journals and newspapers. In both 1866 and 1868, *The Times* went through the Carpenters' report in great detail and not unfavourably.[33] Trades councils regularly sent reports of their activities to local newspapers and the Trades Union Congress from the start welcomed reporters. The publication of rules, accounts and reports contrasted with the secrecy that had often existed in the past and was deliberately intended to refute the claims that were still made from time to time that unions were secret conspiracies.

The same desire for publicity brought trade unionists to meetings of the Social Science Association where they read papers on the value of unionism and refuted criticisms made. They welcomed the publicity of inquiries into trade unionism, such as that organised by the Social Science Association in 1859–60. The committee of the Association remarked particularly on 'the cordial manner in which this society has been met upon the part of trade societies throughout the island'.[34] When in 1866 an M.P. called for a House of Commons inquiry into 'the dangerous increase of Trades Unions', Applegarth hurried off a letter to Gladstone '... that this Society will regard with pleasure any enquiry that may result from the "motion" of the Hon. Gentleman, and will gladly furnish every information respecting the "increase in our organization" and as far as possible will render assistance with a view to ascertain how far the "increase" of "Trades Unions" is "dangerous" or otherwise.'[35] The Royal Commission in Trades Unions which was eventually appointed in 1867 was an ideal opportunity for the unions to put across their case to a wide public audience and this they did with considerable skill, working closely with their two friends on the Commission, Frederic Harrison and Thomas Hughes, to ensure that the right questions were asked to produce the right answers. And lest people were unwilling to plough through a parliamentary blue book, Applegarth's and Allan's evidence was published separately in pamphlet form.

In their evidence the unionists carefully reiterated the points they had been making over the years: their moderation, their respectability, their aversion to strikes, their encouragement of 'industry, energy and uprightness'. Daniel Guile of the Iron-founders summed it all up:

Now if all men were society men, and asked a fair day's wage for a fair day's work, and all masters were willing to abide by that rule, then all the masters could go into the market on the same footing; not only that, but the union encourages a man to become proficient in his trade. He knows that if he would be a respected member of society he must be at least above the common rank, and it gives him a stimulus; and another thing is, that it enables the working man, who is looking on with some degree of anxiety 40 or 50 years, to see that there will be something at the end of that time to rely on; superannuation money, sick pay, accident money, and all those things are in his favour, and make him a provident man.[36]

The strategy of the unionists involved a very deliberate process of image building. Most successful at it were the leaders of the large amalgamated societies like Allan, Applegarth and Guile. A number of questions do, however, arise. Firstly, to what extent were these men representative of rank and file opinion in their own unions? Secondly, to what extent were the attitudes and policies of the amalgamated societies supported by other smaller unions? And thirdly, how great a gap was there between the public image of the unions and the reality?

II

There are few things more difficult for the historian of trade unionism to do than to decide what was rank and file opinion on any particular issue. Like any voluntary organisation, no matter how democratic its constitution, trade unions tend to oligarchy, and the larger the organisation the more pronounced the tendency. Unions are the classic example of Roberto Michels' 'iron law of oligarchy': 'It is organisation which gives birth to the dominion of the elected over the electors, of the mandataries over the mandators, of the delegates over the delegators. Who says organisation says oligarchy'.[37] It is the oligarchy that controls the means of communication the reports and the journals. It is the oligarchy that organises the meetings and brings out the issues to be discussed. Therefore, it is not enough to argue that because Allan and Applegarth remained in office over a large number of years then they clearly had the support of a majority of their members. The history of unionism is full of examples of leaders who have lost touch with the membership and yet remained firmly entrenched in office through the passivity or the mistaken loyalty of the membership, or through an organisational machinery designed to perpetuate oligarchic control. Robert Applegarth was, in fact, one of the few general secretaries who had to face an annual ballot of all the members of the society. Most other general secretaries were appointed by the executive committee. Really, all that the historian can do is to examine how rank and file membership acts on particular occasions and whether these actions are in accord or opposed to the policies of the oligarchy.

The secretaries of the large societies were quite open in stating that the executives of the unions were likely to be more moderate than the bulk of the membership and that they acted as a restraint on militancy. Before any strike action could take place with union support it had to be approved by the executive committee, therefore it was possible for a policy of moderation to be imposed on the union by the executive. In all the large unions there were, on occasion, revolts against what was regarded as too moderate a policy. Applegarth faced this in 1865 when the Birmingham joiners struck against the 'discharge note'. The strike had the support of the executive, but when the employers withdrew the 'note' the men still refused to return to work until details of new working rules had been settled. Such obduracy Applegarth found unacceptable and he hurried to Birmingham to press for a resumption of work. When the men refused to heed his advice the executive withdrew financial support from them. With voluntary aid, the Birmingham men were able to stay out for a few more weeks and there was a great deal of hostile comment against Applegarth. Nonetheless, on the evidence of resolutions in the Society's *Monthly Report*, his action generally received approval from the membership. The Battersea branch thought it would help 're-establish the confidence the public have lost for Trades Unions' and the Borough branch felt that 'such moderate and reasonable views cannot fail to advance our Society in public estimation'.[38] Applegarth had no difficulty in being re-elected a few months later, and even the Birmingham branches voted for him.[39] Members of the A.S.E., also, often showed signs of greater militancy than their executive. The London patternmakers were very critical of the A.S.E.'s failure to support their strike in 1865, and thought 'that the A.S.E. was getting too Conservative, owing to its large funds, and that its officers, having well-paid, easy berths, did not wish to be disturbed by the trouble and annoyance of strikes'.[40] In 1871 when the Newcastle members, together with a large number of non-unionists, took unofficial action for the nine-hour day, they received the support of individual branches of the Society long before the executive belatedly stepped in with aid. George Howell gives an example from the Stonemasons' Society of a strike in Bristol in 1876 when one of the lodges resorted to intimidation. The employer contacted the executive of the union and an officer was sent to investigate. 'He met the men; and denounced their conduct, and strike pay was refused.'[41]

When, in the 1870s, a number of unions became committed to a policy of submitting all disputes to formal boards of conciliation and arbitration, rank and file members generally showed a much greater unwillingness to submit to arbitrated wage reductions than did the executive members of the boards. In the Ironworkers' Union, whose president, John Kane was one of the strongest advocates of boards of conciliation and arbitration, there were numerous revolts against official union advice and a refusal to accept arbitration decisions.[42] Most of the leading supporters of arbitration were agreed that it was a *sine qua non* of success that there should be a strong union for only thus could arbitration decisions be imposed. One sign of growing discontent with moderate official policies in the large unions was the formation in 1875, in Manchester, of an Association of Trade Union Officials whose chief object 'was to protect an official who was unjustly dealt with by the members of his society because he sought to prevent strikes when a minority were clamouring for extreme action'.[43]

However, usually, the rank and file revolts were over the question of tactics on particular occasions rather than a rejection of the whole policy of moderation. It is true that many of the leaders probably sought to obtain middle-class approval for unionism with greater avidity than did the average member. Many of them were motivated by personal ambition to mix with the great or to get into Parliament or to be praised by middle-class sympathisers. Others no doubt were fascinated by the sheer accumulation of large reserve funds and were unwilling to put them at risk. But it is doubtful if there was any widespread opposition to the philosophy of the leadership. The circumstances that produced cautious leaders intent on working within the system produced cautious, moderate members. The members too liked the security of large

C

funds. As William Allan told the Royal Commission, 'a man who expects to get a certain amount of money as superannuation or sick benefit will be very careful about proceeding as far as a trade dispute'.[44] And in the Carpenters many of the expressions of moderation emanated from the branches rather than the executive. In 1864, the Pimlico branch was congratulating the secretary of the Plymouth branch 'for the judicious manner in selecting his language, by avoiding that noisy declamation which too often raises a barrier rather than smooths the way towards the working man elevating himself in Society'.[45] Two years later, the Borough branch was proposing that unionists should refute the charges of selfishness made against unionists by starting a fund for a lifeboat, the *Amalgamator*, to be presented by the Society to the National Lifeboat Institution.[46]

III

Some of the smaller societies had reservations about a policy that put moderation above all things though certainly the success of the amalgamated societies encouraged imitation. The secretaries of many small provincial societies were talking the same language as their counterparts in the large unions. Thus in 1860 the United Joiners of Scotland were telling the Social Science Association, at its meeting in Glasgow, that unions should give full publicity to all their proceedings and were advising their fellow unions 'to lop off from their constitution or rules any of the restrictive measures that are often the means whereby their action is retarded, and a tool put in the hands of opposing parties to damage them and their cause in public estimation'.[47] There was not a trades council that did not at some time pass motions in favour of the settlement of disputes by conciliation and arbitration. Nevertheless, there was some opposition. Not all unionists favoured the linking of a large friendly society side with trade unionism and many of the smaller unions saw the dangers of being too open about their financial position. T. J. Dunning, the secretary of the London Bookbinders, and not in any sense a militant, attacked the policy of registering under the Friendly Societies Act. Those unions, like the A.S.E. and the Amalgamated Carpenters who had done so 'have ceased, by enrolment or registration, to be trade societies, having by that process become simply benefit societies'. In their trying to impose their policies on other unions is found 'the singular burlesque of the emasculated pretending to govern the virile'.[48] Others agreed with Dunning that interest in friendly benefits could be carried too far. William MacDonald of the Manchester Painters' Alliance pointed out that a union 'that does everything else but interfere with wages is not a trades union at all, but a sick and burial club, or a sanitary association'.[49] And William Matkin, London secretary of the General Union of Carpenters, spoke for many unions when he opposed registration in 1871: . . . we shall destroy our objects as a trade union, because by registering *we shall expose the whole of our financial position* – a course I entirely disapprove of as it might prove very disadvantageous to us at times, for our employers would have every facility at all times for ascertaining our exact position, and we know too well that they are ever ready to take advantage of our weakness.'[50]

The most forceful critic of the amalgamated societies was George Potter, the manager of *Bee-Hive*. He, on occasion, seemed to be advocating a policy of greater militancy. In 1865, in the pages of his newspaper, Potter attacked the actions of Applegarth in urging the Birmingham workers back to work before they had got all their demands. A few months later, he was encouraging the iron puddlers of North Staffordshire in their refusal to submit their case to arbitration, which Applegarth, Allan and other leading figures had been urging them to accept. Potter was attacked as 'mischievous and untruthful',[51] as 'irresponsible' and as 'a strike jobber'.[52] But Potter's position was not as simple as it seems at first glance or his critics tried to make out. Applegarth was attacked by Potter, not because he was advocating a generally moderate policy, but because, in Potter's opinion, he had undermined the position of the strikers. Potter believed that once a strike had been embarked upon support should continue, no matter how much developments might be regretted. He consistently argued that those on the spot understood the situation much better than a central executive. It was the structure of the amalgamated unions of which he was critical, rather than the policy. His was the world of the small local society, where decisions were made at a mass meeting of members rather than by the 'clique' of the executive council. His support came from the small local societies who disliked central control and who disliked the manner in which the amalgamated societies attempted to impose their views on the trade-union world. Potter sought more democracy, rather than more militancy. He bowed to no one in his support of conciliatory policies. He defended himself from attacks in 1865 by comparing his own record on conciliation and arbitration with that of others:

'No man has perhaps been concerned with more strikes than Mr Odgers, secretary of the London Trades Council, but never a word about arbitration publicly escaped his lips until recently.'[53] At the Sheffield conference of July 1866, Potter's representative, George Troup, pressed that 'as a matter of agreed policy . . . no workers who refused arbitration would be supported'.[54] At the St Martin's Hall conference of March 1867 Potter was at pains to stress the importance of getting across to the public 'our wish to be moderate in all our demands'. In courting the support of middle-class allies Potter was just as adept as Applegarth and, from the end of the 1860s, there is little to distinguish his views from those of Applegarth or Allan. His articles and speeches ring with the familiar phrases: 'A strike of the present day differs as much as light and dark from a strike of half a century ago'; 'Trades' Unions, as now organised and conducted, are among the foremost proofs of the improved mental training of the working men, and, at the same time, of their increased power of self-control and self-restraint'; 'under their action and influence the self-respect of the working man was cultivated, his capacity for enjoyment expanded and his character morally and intellectually elevated'.[55]

Potter was able to attract widespread support from provincial societies at the St Martin's Hall conference, but this was in no sense a protest meeting against conciliatory policies. Alexander McDonald of the miners, the most powerful union leader at the conference, was thoroughly committed to moderation, as was John Kane of the Ironworkers, W. H. Wood of the Manchester Trades Council, William Dronfield of the Sheffield Association of Organised Trades, and many of the others who attended. They were not protesting at the policy of the amalgamated societies, but at being excluded from the decisions being made concerning possible legislation by the actions of the London-based general secretaries in forming their exclusive Conference of Amalgamated Trades. Once again, Potter was protesting against an oligarchic system and seeking to democratise the trade-union movement. He was not questioning the fundamentals of the policies.

There were still a heterodox few who seemed determined to shatter the image that was being so carefully created. The methods used in Sheffield against those who failed to pay their union dues were in a tradition that died hard and were not entirely disapproved of in the area. The confessions of William Broadhead to the Commission of Inquiry into the Sheffield Outrages brought a denunciation of such violence from unions, large and small, up and down the country, but the saw grinders welcomed him back into the society.[56] Strikes, especially in the coal and iron areas, could still degenerate into riots of the most violent nature. Five miners lost their lives in one such fracas in Denbighshire in 1869 when troops opened fire. In Blackburn the chairman of the local employers' association had his house burned down during the 1878 strike. But, in general, the policy which held sway was that of stressing moderation and responsibility, of courting public sympathy and of impressing on the public just how much a part of a modern liberal society were the unions.

IV

This was not, however, the only policy. Nor was it a policy to which all others were sacrificed. One can over-stress the 'respectability' and the 'moderation' of even the amalgamated societies. Applegarth, at the Royal Commission specifically intervened to make the point that with all the talk of the social aspects of unionism there was a danger of losing sight of its main purpose: 'pure and simple ours is a trade society'.[57] Despite all the talk of unions being like a great 'assurance association' it was a point that was never entirely lost sight of by the unionists. The policy of conciliation was persisted with because it was working – in the industrial field. Unions were getting as much, if not more, from negotiation as from confrontation. The A.S.E. or the Amalgamated Carpenters could make great play of the very few strikes in their societies, but this was because the employers were making concessions. The large reserve funds may have encouraged caution in the officials, but they also encouraged caution in the employers. Publicity of accounts helped build a good public image while at the same time ensuring that the employers knew exactly what they were up against. Striking was never abandoned as a policy of last resort. The introduction of piecework was still being fought by the A.S.E. in 1876 as it had been in the early fifties and with similar lack of success. In many strikes the A.S.E. proved a useful ally. Between 1853 and 1866 the society gave 179 grants to other unions on strike, including £3,000 to the London building workers in 1859.[58] In 1874 a levy raised £1,105 to support locked out agricultural labourers and the following year £1,000 went to the striking colliers of South Wales.[59]

One can see a similar attitude in the trades councils. Each was committed to a policy of conciliation and arbitration, but, as the secretary of the Manchester Trades Council put it they were not 'peace-at-any-price men': 'They believed first in conciliatory measures, and if these did not meet the difficulty, then they said, "Let us unite together for the mutual support and protection of the combined unionists as unionists".'[60] The first activity of trades councils was to organise financial support for trades on strike by issuing appeals and organising meetings. Even the London Trades Council, influenced more than most by the thinking of Applegarth and his associates, devoted more time to this than to any other activity through the 1860s. The belief in the necessity of the strike weapon was always there and this was why societies of all shapes and sizes joined in the campaign against the Criminal Law Amendment Act in the 1870s and in defence of the right to peaceful picketing.

There were frequent declarations of support for the 'principles of amalgamation' throughout the period, but this, as often as not, resulted from admiration of the strength which the amalgamated societies had as much as from respect for their moderate policies. In 1852 there was a call for a union of all the London trades: 'With such a union strikes would cease with the necessity for them and fairness would be secured by the power to assert that as a right which we are now too often compelled to sue for as a boon.'[61]

In the 1860s both the Glasgow and Edinburgh Trades Councils proposed schemes for the 'amalgamation' of the Scottish unions, despite the warnings of the Glasgow secretary, George Newton, who feared 'that the masters might throw all classes of workmen on the street, and cause bloodshed'.[62] In June 1872 a United Trades Confederation of Scotland was formed to combat 'the disposition of employers to unite for the purpose of frustrating the just demands of labour', and to assist 'trades in the throes of a lock-out, or strike that could not be prevented without loss or degradation'.[63] It failed, however, because the large societies refused to come in, fearing that it might in fact 'encourage strikes'.[64] However, by the end of 1874 even large unions were becoming concerned at the more aggressive views that a body like the National Federation of Associated Employers of Labour was expressing and began to consider plans for their own federation. John Kane of the Ironworkers, J. D. Prior, Applegarth's successor at the Amalgamated Carpenters and Robert Knight of the Boilermakers and Ironshipbuilders drew up a scheme for a federation of large unions 'in order to successfully meet the wealthy and influential combination which capitalists have now formed' and to establish 'a fund available in any important trade struggle in which the course pursued by the workmen merits the sympathy and assistance of the trades thus combined for mutual protection'.[65] Significantly, however, they deliberately excluded small societies and trades councils, because, 'the large and wealthy societies, with important interests at stake, can never submit to having their members levied at the discretion of local and irresponsible bodies'. Nothing came of the proposals. Most societies too jealously guarded against any infringements of their autonomy. But the fact that such proposals were made is at least an indication that even those arch-conciliators, John Kane and Robert Knight could envisage a situation in which unions would have to fight to defend their rights.

It is also possible to exaggerate the extent to which the unionists were really committed to the whole gamut of mid-century values. While the contribution made by trade unions in leading workers away from the evils of drink was a useful point to make at a Royal Commission, in practice most societies continued to hold their meetings in public houses.[66] Trades' halls were built, but it was found that the workers did not care 'for the books, the quiet games, the instructive lectures, the improving talk, the large national views, the tea, coffee, buns, and bread and butter', but preferred 'the stronger drinks and, as they think, the more vigorous style of talk and lines of action they find elsewhere'.[67] At the same time as they were working hard to earn the plaudits of the middle class, Odger, Applegarth and other leading unionists were finding common ground with Karl Marx and with European socialists in the International Working Man's Association, committed to the 'economical emancipation of the working classes'.[68] It is probable that for most British unionists the main attraction of the International was as a possible means of curbing the importation of foreign labourers as strike breakers, coupled with an often rather vague internationalist sentiment. But as late as 1873, when the revolutionary aspirations of the International were clear to all and most British unionists had scurried clear, the Birmingham Trades Council continued to subscribe.[69]

There were very clear limits also to how far unionists supported the individualist ethic. As was frequently pointed out by their critics, unionism, by its very nature, was opposed to individualism. Unions were class organisations and their members 'consent to debase themselves individually in order that the class to which they belong may be aggrandised collectively'.[70] Smiles and his followers talked of the individual genius; unions were concerned with the average workman. For all that he sought to picture unions as part of the liberal *milieu*, Applegarth saw his society as the opponent of 'that system which gives Praxiteles his due and Arkwright, Brunel and Stephenson "full scope for the exercise of their extraordinary skill" but leaves the thousands of less skilful to scramble through a selfish world as best they can'. Its task was to apply a 'humanising influence' to society and 'to lift up the less fortunate to a proper position'.[71] Most unionists envisaged some kind of co-operative commonwealth as much nearer their ideal society than the *laissez-faire* one of the middle classes and like the Glasgow unionists regarded trade unions as 'but simply a passing phase of the present so-called civilisation, a stepping stone towards a higher development of industrial life and societarian arrangements'.[72]

The conciliatory policy adopted by trade unionists in the mid-century does, therefore, need to be seen in perspective. It was a strategy that was still concerned with achieving the traditional aims of unionism. The strategy grew among workers who were committed to industrialisation and who were concerned to procure as much as possible from it. It worked for those workers who were in trade unions, because in the favourable economic conditions that existed through most of the period their standard of living was rising. As long as it was successful it was persisted with. In order to make it work it was imperative that enough employers and others of the middle class were also persuaded to accept a conciliatory policy and to make concessions to the workers' demands.

Chapter 3

Enemies and Friends

Not everyone was convinced by the image-building efforts of the trade unions. A number of persistent critics continued to believe that, despite their protestations, there had been little change in the real nature of unionism. W. R. Greg,[1] one of the most unrepentant of unionism's enemies saw little improvement: 'The working men of 1875 (taken in aggregate and allowing for large exceptions) do not appear to me less easily misguided, less unwise in the pursuit of their own interests, less blind followers of mischievous agitators and leaders, and assuredly neither less brutal nor less intemperate, than those I lived among in 1850.'[2] He found a ready platform for his views in the influential Reviews, the *Quarterly*, the *Edinburgh* and *Blackwood's Magazine*, which, although not quite the great opinion formers of a few decades before, were nonetheless widely read by politicians and other leaders of opinion. The *Edinburgh Review* constantly attempted to link the unionism of the 1850s and 1860s with the violent days of the 1830s. All that had happened in the intervening years, according to Harriet Martineau, writing in 1859, was that unions had become 'more intricate, more stringent and more secret'. They were still seen as dangerous secret organisations whose 'most stringent laws were unwritten', whose 'most significant usages are unrecorded', whose 'committees cannot be fixed with responsibility' and whose 'punishments are inflicted by invisible hands'. They were the creation of the inferior workmen who wished 'to stint the action of superior physical strength, moral industry, or intelligent skill', thus robbing the individual, the manufacturer and the nation.[3] Eight years later there was little change in the views being expressed and opinion in the *Edinburgh Review* had, if anything, hardened. 'We must grapple, firmly and fearlessly, as in a struggle for life or death, with the lawless and overbearing despotism of the Trades' Unions,' it declared, and 'the conflict between the law of the land and the law of the Unions must be brought to an issue.'[4]

The *Quarterly* got Robert Lowe to review the evidence to the Royal Commission in 1867 and he, too, was not particularly impressed. He accepted that there was a difference between an association such as the Amalgamated Carpenters and one like the Sheffield Saw-Grinders, but both contained within them 'the germs and elements of crime', since they were 'founded on the right of the majority to coerce the minority, on the absolute subjugation of the one to the many'.[5]

For those who preferred a wider audience the national press provided a forum. One persistent publicist throughout the 1850s was Thomas Fairbairn, son and partner of the great Manchester engineer, Sir William Fairbairn. Writing above the pseudonym 'Amicus', he sent scathing denunciations of unionism to *The Times* during the engineers' lock-out of 1852, during the Preston strike of 1853, and again during the London builders' lock-out of 1859. In all the message was the same. Unions were 'unjust, mischievous and tyrannical bodies', created 'for the protection of the dunce, the drunkard and the unskilful', run by a 'small band of professionals' who were intent on becoming 'rulers of the destinies of the trade'.[6] At the end of the 1860s, Edmund Ashworth of the great Bolton cotton firm used *The Times* for a series of letters on 'The Injurious Effects of Trades' Unions'. There was less talk of 'dangerous agitators', but because unions now effectively controlled many industries they were destroying the competitive position of British industry. High wages were driving up prices so that it was now cheaper to import locomotives from Belgium than to build them at home. Employers were unable to seek new orders because the rate of wages which unions required them to pay made it unprofitable. The classic example of what unions could do, according to Ashworth, was in the Thames shipbuilding industry where high wages had driven shipbuilding from the Thames to the areas of lower wages such as the Tyne and the Clyde.[7]

In addition to journals and newspapers there was a copious pamphlet literature on trade unionism, emanating from usually obscure provincial gentlemen who plagiarised their arguments from more erudite writers and who showed a woeful ignorance of the reality of unionism. The great public gatherings of the Social Science Association and the British Association were also used as platforms by unionism's opponents, and although they tried to balance hostile papers with contributions that were sympathetic to unionism, often read by leading local unionists, the unionists believed that the published reports gave greater prominence to their opponents.

Even the school books were not free from blatant antipathy to unionism. As late as 1879 a deputation of leading unionists was pressing the Archbishop of Canterbury to withdraw a standard five reading book containing selections from the works of Archbishop Whatley on political economy. Unions were attacked as tyrannies where 'the committee men' maintain power 'by intimidation and by violence to the persons and property of those who oppose them, or who refuse to join them'. Strikes only succeed because workers cannot go to work 'for fear of being assaulted and perhaps murdered by ruffians hired by their tyrants': 'No one who ventures to disobey the orders of a committee is sure of his life for a day.'[8] In fictional literature too they were attacked. Dickens and Mrs Gaskell, although both concerned at the plight of the working class, pictured unions as secret and often violent organisations futilely struggling against the law of supply and demand and Charles Reade, lacking any sympathy for a class he regarded as 'blackguards and blasphemous', portrayed unions in his novel of 1870, *Put Yourself in His Place*, as monstrous organisations for assassination and sabotage that could only be dealt with by a force of 'a hundred thousand special constables'.[9]

The grounds of attack on unionism were fairly limited, but constantly repeated. Firstly, unions were run by a small group of 'paid agitators', 'almost always the noisiest, idlest and most factious of their class',[10] who by intimidation and terror were able to control the mass of the workers, because the working classes suffered 'from a lack of individual will'.[11] By their secret rules and terrorist methods they were able to maintain themselves in power and to make the workmen 'slaves to an oligarchy'.[12] Secondly, they aimed at uniformity of wages, 'to equalise the payment of good and bad work, of easy and of difficult occupations'.[13] They worked only to the advantage of the poor worker, reduced every craft 'to the level of the commonest, most ignorant and most stupid of the persons who belong to it'[14] and were a barrier to individual enterprise and advancement. In this way they were opposed to the values of a society which held freedom to compete to be the greatest freedom. Against this, unions offered 'all the fallacies of the Protective system'[15] and threatened to push industry 'back into the old guild system of the times of Elizabeth'.[16] Thirdly, unions imposed restrictions that were disastrous to the efficiency and expansion of industry. The bricklayers' society was a favourite example used to illustrate this. It was claimed that, in Manchester, it prohibited the use of machine-made bricks or of bricks made outside the city; it forbade the use of a barrow to wheel bricks; it insisted that every bricklayer should have one labourer to attend him whether there was work for him or not; it demanded that the bricklayers should use only one hand when laying bricks.[17] Conclusions about trade unionism as a whole were drawn from such examples. It was restrictions such as these that were causing the deterioration of the nation's competitive position and allowing other countries to take over Britain's overseas markets and even compete in the domestic market. Finally, trade unions were valueless when it came to trying to fix wages, because wages were fixed by the laws of supply and demand. If earnings had risen it was not due to trade unions for 'had there been no Unions, it is probable that the general prosperity of the country, to say nothing of the decreased value of precious metal, would have brought about a rise'.[18] Where, by sheer brute strength unions had succeeded in driving up wages beyond the level fixed by supply and demand, the rise could be only a temporary one, since the ultimate effect would be to drive out capital.

It is a measure of the success of the trade-union campaign for acceptance that while, in the 1850s, such views held widespread approval and were the orthodoxy of the period, by the 1870s they seemed the querulous utterances of a group of unrepentant individualists, who were beginning to appear reactionary in a society where the whole *laissez-faire* ideal was coming under critical scrutiny.

I

To combat such views, trade unions could not rely only on their own actions and on the publicity of their own journals. To make an impact on a wider public they required the support of middle-class sympathisers, men who had access to middle-class journals and were in touch with the legislators and opinion formers. There was a number of such sympathisers in the 1850s, 1860s and 1870s, who were ready to speak out as defenders of trade unionism and to act as advisers to the trade-union leaders. Their motives varied: for some there was a sentimental admiration of the simple life, an adulation 'of manual labour, fustian jackets, and weekly wages as the exclusive symbol of all that is noble and virtuous in man';[19] for others, support of trade unionism stemmed from a hostility to the competitive, capitalist system and to a system of social relationships based on the 'cash nexus'; for others, there was a desire to have the working class as allies for some particular cause; and for yet others, sympathy was based on a fear of working-class strength, a fear of what might arise if concessions were not made to this strength. In any group of sympathisers such motives were mixed, but one thing that all middle-class sympathisers had in common was a desire to shape trade unionism to suit their own particular philosophy or goals. Sympathy was rarely altruistic. The trade unionists welcomed the assistance of these middle-class allies as essential if they were to get their case across to the public. They welcomed also the assistance of men who could lead them through the tangle of legal and political complexities with which their movement was beset. They were less willing to allow their activities to be shaped in the mould their sympathisers decreed.

There were numerous individual propagandists of the trade-union cause, but the two main groups who most effectively worked with and supported the unionists were the Christian Socialists and the Positivists.

Christian Socialism grew out of the shock of chartism which had brought to public notice what Carlyle had called 'the condition of England' question. Its origin dated from 10 April 1848 when it seemed the revolutions of Paris, Berlin and Vienna might come to London. Its Christianity was shaped by Frederick Denison Maurice[20] and its Socialism by John Malcolm Ludlow,[21] but it attracted to it men of less decided views who, nonetheless, sought to offer to the working classes some alternative to the violence (or threatened violence) of chartism: Charles Kingsley,[22] the brash, muscular vicar of Eversley; Thomas Hughes,[23] a young barrister, fresh from feats on the cricket field, that had given him his Cambridge blue; and Lord Goderich,[24] the radical-republican son of 'Prosperity' Robinson.

Maurice had, at the end of the 1820s, rejected the evangelical emphasis on the individual way to salvation and come to believe in the importance of the fellowship of mankind in the 'Kingdom of Christ', which, to Maurice, was life on Earth, here and now. Christ was in all men and humanity was one. If wars and wretchedness existed within God's 'Divine Order' it was because the Gospel was not known and understood. The Christian duty was to bring an awareness of the need of love and sacrifice for one's fellow man through Christian work and teaching and through the example of

Christian fellowship.[25] Appointed as Chaplain to Lincoln's Inn in 1846, Maurice attracted around him a group of young Christian barristers and others who engaged in teaching and visiting in the slums around Lincoln's Inn Fields. They desired in some way to close the divisions between classes by revealing the sympathy that existed among members of other classes for the workers' plight. The day following the demonstration at Kennington Common they directly addressed the 'Workmen of England' in a placard expressing sympathy and understanding for the Chartist workers living 'in shameful filth and darkness', growing up 'in ignorance and temptation', and 'shut out from a Freeman's just right of voting'.[26] They began to publish a periodical, *Politics for the People* which called for spiritual, as well as social and political, regeneration, and to make contact with working men. A number of conferences were held which brought the group into touch with Christian chartists such as Walter Cooper and with Owenite socialists, in particular the Owenite missionary Lloyd Jones. These contacts, together with the development of the ideas of J. M. Ludlow, pushed the group from mere Christian philanthropy and proselytising to experiments in Christian Socialism.

John Malcolm Ludlow had been educated in France and his views were shaped from the profusion of religious, social and political ideas in which the Paris of the 1830s had abounded. On his return to England in 1838, when he took up law at Lincoln's Inn, he had furthermore, been influenced by the works of Thomas Arnold, who had warned of impending social catastrophe unless the upper classes accepted a Christian responsibility for the condition of the poor. Ludlow saw himself, at any rate at first, as a disciple of Arnold.[27] He undertook visiting work around Lincoln's Inn and made his first contacts with Maurice. His French experience – he was in Paris again during the 1848 revolution – made him open to new ideas and he was particularly impressed by the appeal of socialism to the working classes. This impression was confirmed by the contacts he made in England with people like Lloyd Jones. Influenced also by the writings on co-operative associations of Buchez, Louis Blanc and Lamennais, he began to develop ideas of Christianising socialism and to lead the group around Maurice into initiating schemes for co-operative associations in England.

To some extent socialism fitted into Maurice's hostility to individualism and his advocacy of Christian fellowship. As he was at great pains to point out, for Maurice, socialism was not intended to overthrow the existing property relations of society. What co-operative associations could do was to bring a spiritual awakening, a rejection of selfishness, and an education to brotherhood and fellowship.[28] For others, in the widening group of Christian Socialists, co-operative associations were seen as the possible basis of an alternative social structure to capitalism. For others, co-operative associations were a useful short-term measure to deal with unemployment or exploited workers. These differences of viewpoint existed from the start but tended to be blurred over in the early years. In the end they brought about the disintegration of Christian Socialism as a movement.

Between 1850 and 1853 numerous, though usually short-lived, working men's associations engaged in co-operative production were established under the auspices of the Christian Socialists. Associations of tailors, printers, shoemakers, builders, bakers, needlewomen, pianoforte makers were formed, not just in London, but in Edinburgh, Glasgow, Liverpool, Manchester, Newcastle, Southampton, Norwich, Aberdeen and many other towns.[29] How much of the activity was socialist without the epithet Christian, it is impossible to say, but undoubtedly the Associationists were building on a residue of belief in an alternative co-operative society that dated back to the Owenite movement of the late twenties and early thirties. Up until the autumn of 1850 the Christian Socialists, although in contact with individual trade unionists in London had had nothing to do with trade societies as such. Indeed they tended to regard them as reflections of the class conflict in society which they so much abhorred. However, in the autumn of 1850, Lloyd Jones and Walter Cooper made a bid for trade society support for the associations that were being established. At first response was cool, but early in 1851, Newton and Allan, the moving spirits behind the new A.S.E., which had come into existence in January 1851, approached the Christian Socialists for advice on how best to use their surplus funds.

Presumably Allan and Newton looked to the Christian Socialists because of their own belief in co-operative ideas. But, they were also representing views held by a substantial number of their society. In the early years of the A.S.E. one can still detect the dichotomy of views which trade unionism had faced since its origin. Firstly, there were many in the society who believed that the long-term aim should be the development of a new economic order based on co-operative productions. They saw it as the purpose of trade unionism to free the workers from the shackles of the wage system. There had, for example, been opposition to the proposals for amalgamation of the engineers' unions when originally mooted, precisely because they seemed unconcerned with offering an alternative to capitalist domination.[30] Secondly, there was the policy, which was eventually to gain the upper hand, of accepting the capitalist system and, within that system, working to procure maximum advantage for the members. Early in 1851, the former policy was prominent and, with the Christian Socialists, Allan and Newton drew up plans for purchasing the Windsor Iron works in Liverpool and running them on co-operative principles. Before these came to fruition, however, the industrial crisis over manning, overtime and piecework came to a head and the co-operative plans were pushed to one side. Nonetheless, co-operative policy was not abandoned entirely and, throughout the lock-out, Newton's paper, *Operative* was advocating co-operation. Partly, this may have been regarded as a useful threat to use against the employers and a means of taking some surplus labour out of the market, but mainly it stemmed from conviction. The violent response of the employers to the union's demands – to its efforts, in other words, to improve conditions within the capitalist system – pushed the union into more seriously considering the co-operative alternative. With the support of 90 per cent of the branches, the A.S.E. decided to lay aside £10,000 for the establishing of co-operative workshops. In the event, the money had to be used for unemployment benefit as the dispute dragged on, but with the help of Christian Socialist money two co-operative workshops were opened at Mile End and in Southwark.[31] Such schemes could not save the Union from defeat and perhaps more useful was the £1,000 which Lord Goderich gave to keep the A.S.E. from bankruptcy during the last weeks of the lock-out. But the effect of the failure of their industrial policy on the leadership of the union seems to have been to push them even more strongly into advocating co-operative production. This was the only way to 'prevent the possibility of such a catastrophe again occurring', wrote Allan. 'We have learned that it is not sufficient to accumulate funds, that it is necessary also to use them reproductively; and if this lesson does not fail in its effect, a few years will see the land studded with workshops belonging to the workers. . . .'[32]

The Union's delegate conference later in 1852 amended the rules to include 'the promotion of co-operation in the iron trades' as one of the Society's aims. In the end little was achieved beyond talk and discussion. One major obstacle was the legal position of trade societies which prevented their holding property. But the most important reason was the pressure of a growing section of the union who, encouraged by the union's ability to survive the lockout and by the improved economic conditions, wanted to concentrate on orthodox industrial action.[33] By the end of the 1850s co-operation had been dropped from the rules. Nevertheless, the vision of a 'land studded with workshops belonging to the workers' died hard and as late as 1871, during the nine-hours' strike on Tyneside some of the striking engineers attempted to set up a co-operative workshop.[34] In other unions too the idea remained. Robert Applegarth in the Carpenters, for example, regularly prefaced speeches to his members with the phrase 'as long as the present system lasts'. Co-operation was his alternative.[35]

It was the lock-out of 1852 which pushed the Christian Socialists into becoming defenders of trade unionism as such, though to some extent, they found themselves in this position against their will. The employers' association, with their able and vitriolic secretary Sidney Smith, attacked the A.S.E. as seeking socialism – 'a "New Moral World", "the organisation of labour", and an experiment of the dreams of Louis Blanc, embracing the visions of Robert Owen, without their catholicity'.[36] The press, following this lead, linked the A.S.E. with the Christian Socialists. Some of the group were hardly enthusiastic at this imposed role. Maurice shuddered at the prospect of a war between capital and labour.[37] Association was about 'love' and 'sacrifice' and 'fellowship' not about piecework and overtime. Kingsley believed that 'whatever battle is fought must be fought by the men themselves'. The engineers were not distressed needlewomen or slop workers in need of Christian philanthropy, but were 'the most intelligent and best-educated workmen, receiving incomes often higher than a gentleman's son'.[38] The Christian Socialist task was to show the workers the way to association not to support them in their struggles with their masters. In contrast, Ludlow, Hughes and Goderich were 'aflame for battle'[39] and took up the union case with vigour in their own *Journal of Association*, in letters to the press and in lectures and pamphlets. They were particularly critical of the uncompromising position adopted by the employers and their persistent refusal to submit the matter to independent arbitration, and warned of the 'darker and nearer symptoms of a social war, perhaps not unbloody, of a possible English revolution'.[40]

The differences of viewpoint on the Christian Socialist role came to a head in 1853–4, when Maurice, expelled from his chair at King's College, led the movement away from its co-operative work to purely educational work in the new Working Men's College of which he was first Principal. It was the end of Christian Socialism acting as a body, but as individuals some remained active. Ludlow demurred at the abandonment of a socialist role and underwent a personal crisis on whether or not to take the leadership of the movement from Maurice.[41] In the end he did not feel 'spiritually good enough for such a leadership'[42] and contented himself with individual action. But, as individuals, the Christian Socialists had still an important part to play in trade unionism. Ludlow, Hughes and Goderich especially continued to speak out on its behalf.

In 1855 Ludlow acted as adviser to the A.S.E. and to a committee of London trades on the issues raised by the Friendly Societies' Bill and drafted a clause which allowed unions to register under the Act and receive protection for their funds. Goderich, now M.P. for Huddersfield, acted as their spokesman in Parliament and got the clause introduced as section 44 of the Act.[43]

The influence of Christian Socialism was also carried into what was perhaps the most important breakthrough in the progress of trade unions towards acceptance, the report of the National Association for the Promotion of Social Science on *Trades' Societies and Strikes*. The Association was formed in 1857 to provide 'to those engaged in all the various efforts now happily begun for the improvement of the people an opportunity for considering social economics as a whole'[44] and a committee on trade unions was set up at the second conference at Liverpool in October 1858. It reported to the Glasgow conference of 1860. The Christian Socialists were predominant. Out of a committee of thirty-two at least eight had direct associations with Christian Socialism. Ludlow and Maurice were both on the committee and Hughes was one of the secretaries. In addition, there was Thomas Randle Bennett,[45] who lectured at the Working Men's College, Charles Buxton,[46] the liberal brewer and politician, who had been a member of Maurice's group in 1853, Richard Holt Hutton,[47] the assistant editor of the *Economist*, who was a friend of Maurice and had assisted in Maurice's social work in London, Godfrey Lushington[48] who with his brother Vernon had been involved with the Christian Socialists in the early fifties and had taught at the Working Men's College, and J. W. Parker,[49] son of the publisher of *Frasers Magazine, Politics for the People* and other early Christian Socialist tracts. This last was a close friend of Charles Kingsley and one of the main members of the outer circle of the Christian Socialist group. Two other members of the committee could perhaps also be included among those associated with Christian Socialism: Thomas Dyke Acland,[50] who had been at university with Maurice and remained his close friend, and W. E. Forster,[51] who was a friend of both Kingsley and of Lord Goderich. W. B. Ranken, another Lincoln's Inn barrister on the committee may well have come under Maurice's influence.[52]

Undoubtedly many members of the committee started from a position of hostility to trade unions, but their inquiries greatly modified their views.[53] The result was a report that had much to say in favour of trade societies. The 'cordial manner in which this inquiry has been met upon the part of trades' societies generally' was favourably contrasted with the obstructiveness of most employers.[54] It rejected many of the popular assumptions about trade unionism. Trade societies were not entirely in violation of the laws of political economy and acted within these laws by allowing the worker to hold out for a fair market price for his labour.[55] Far from causing strikes trade societies seemed on the whole to lessen the number of strikes and their leaders, far from being agitators – a view held by two-thirds of the committee before the inquiry took place – were likely to exert a restraining influence, taking 'a cool and moderate view of a question in dispute'.[56] The committee found that the leaders were 'for the most part quite superior to the majority of their fellow workmen in intelligence and moderation'. They could, in fact, be the means of leading trade societies into moderate and reasonable paths: 'They have the confidence of their own class. Through them prejudices may be dispelled and the laws of that political economy which, correctly understood is the workman's best friend, gradually acquiesced in and obeyed.'[57] Indeed, trade societies as such had an educational value in teaching workmen 'the art of self-government' and 'a habit of deliberation before action' from which society could only gain.[58] All in all, it was clear to the committee that trade societies had brought progress to the working class,

That the workmen belonging to these societies form a better estimate now than heretofore of the condition of their respective trades, that they are less unreasonable in their expectations of obtaining increased wages, that they understand better the necessity of submitting to reductions, that they have generally overcome the prejudices which they once entertained against machinery and that their leaders are men of higher character and intelligence.[59]

Finally, the report rejected calls for any legislative restrictions on trade unions and declared that 'the rate of wages must be settled between the masters and men'.

The detailed examination of particular strikes carried out by members of the committee confirmed these far-reaching conclusions. The unionists had successfully persuaded the investigators that unionism, moderation and respectability were generally synonymous. Ludlow, investigating the West Yorkshire miners found that at union pits there was a 'general air of comfort and respectability', that 'rectitude of conduct is seldom interfered with by vicious indulgences' and that the pig had taken the place of 'the bull-pup and the game-cock'. In contrast, the non-union pits were a sorry picture of vice: public-houses were 'well-frequented', where the conversation 'mingled with the rattle of dominoes' would 'turn on cock and dog fighting'.[60] J. W. Crompton found that, in the printing trades, society men were 'superior both in ability and steadiness to non-society men'. Thomas Hughes, who investigated the lock-out of the engineers of 1852, made the strongest call for acceptance. He argued that people were shutting their eyes to the truth when they continued to regard unions as unrepresentative bodies composed of 'designing and idle men'. The facts had to be faced and unions granted the recognition they had the right to expect. Only in this way could the influence and actions of unions be harnessed 'to the great common interests of the nation'. 'I believe', he declared, 'that the present disastrous state of feeling between employers and employed can never be improved, will only become worse, while the Unions remain unrecognised by the law, and misrepresented, hated and feared by all classes of society except that great one of which they are exclusively composed, and whose ideas and wishes they do, on the whole, faithfully represent and carry out.'[61]

The discussion on the report at the Glasgow meeting of the Association showed that not all members of the Association approved of the committee's liberal interpretation. Edmund Potter, owner of the largest calico-printing works in the world, 'had very great doubts as to the soundness of their economical views'.[62] For Potter, labour was 'a mere purchaseable commodity, like all other commodities' and therefore trade unions by their very nature were unsound and 'their moral effects . . . bad'.[63] But Potter's views were very much in the minority, if the discussion at Glasgow was a reflection of opinion in the Association. Two old opponents of trade unionism, Sir Archibald Alison, now retired as Sheriff of Lanarkshire, and Henry Ashworth, Lancashire cotton spinner, confirmed advocate of *laissez-faire* and life-long opponent of the protective nature of unions, both added their testimony to the opinion that unions 'were now conducted in a very different spirit from that which prevailed thirty or forty years ago'.[64]

The Social Science Association's *Report* was a major step in the road to acceptance. After rational examination, trade unions were found to have much to offer, even within the limits of classical political economy. The arguments used in support of unions were to be repeated time and again by the defenders of unionism during the next two decades, with little substantia laddition.

II

The presence of Godfrey Lushington on the Social Science Association Committee was an important link with the second main group of trade-union protagonists, the Positivists. The three most effective members of this group were Frederic Harrison, E. S. Beesly and Henry Crompton,[65] with others such as Lushington and J. H. Bridges playing a less important part. The English Positivists had their links with Christian Socialism: Lushington had been part of the group around Maurice in the early fifties and Harrison had lectured at the Working Men's College. Crompton and Beesly were both related by marriage to Rev. J. Llewelyn Davies, another leading Christian Socialist. The Positivists, however, rejected metaphysical religion and built instead a secular religion which rejected the conclusions of faith for those of scientific inquiry.

Many leaders of English intellectual life in the mid-nineteenth century were positivists, in the broad sense of the term believing in the application of the methods of the physical sciences – observation and experiment – to all branches of knowledge. But the group at the centre of English Positivism, in its narrow sense, consisted of young men who had come under the influence of Richard Congreve at Wadham College, Oxford, and accepted the philosophy of Auguste Comte. To Comte all true knowledge was based on the methods and discoveries of the physical sciences. He saw the pursuit of knowledge as passing through three stages: a theological stage when phenomena are explained in terms of the will of gods or God; a metaphysical stage, when God is de-personalised and replaced by abstract concepts of forces or powers; a positive stage, in which all powers and agents are abandoned and attempts to find the causes of phenomena are replaced by pure scientific description. He applied this to the science of society, sociology, and saw a parallel three-stage development. First, a theological stage, when authority was maintained by kings and priests through a mixture of force and myth. Secondly, a metaphysical stage, which he saw as beginning with the Reformation and reaching its height with the French Revolution, when authority crumbled and was replaced by the 'anarchy' of liberalism, which, forgetting the inter-dependence of mankind, made self-interest its highest value. A positive stage was the only alternative, where there would be agreement on intellec-tual principles and social and moral values, based on positive thought, creating a society with 'love for its principle, order for its basis and progress for its end'.

To make the transformation to the positive stage a body of secular priests was necessary who understood how society worked and developed. They were men who had first studied the workings of society and then used their knowledge to shape the future, by guiding society to a true understanding of itself. To assist them in their task, they must look to that element in society in which the hope for the future lay, the working class, because only in the working class was there the good sense and matter-of-factness to dismiss metaphysics and, only in the working classes was there the basic dislike of war to make them reject authoritarianism and, only in the working class was there a clear understanding of the mutual dependence of men.[66]

During the 1850s, the Positivists around Congreve, like many others, were mere critics of a system of government still dominated by the aristocracy. But, by the end of the decade, when they were all in London, they began to propound their ideas for a funda-mental social transformation and to look to the working class – and in particular to the trade unions – as the force to bring this about. As a result they took up the cause of trade unionism, while at the same time seeking to provide it with intellectual leadership. Like the Christian Socialists, the Positivists were particularly attracted by the alternative to individualism which trade unionism seemed to offer, 'the sentiment of fraternity and the subordination of the interests of the individual to those of society'.[67]

They made their first contacts with trade unionists during the 1859 and 1861 lock-out and strikes of London building workers demanding a nine-hour day. They joined the Christian Socialists Hughes, Ludlow and R. H. Hutton in a committee of inquiry into the strike[68] and took their first public stance on behalf of the building workers in two letters to the press signed by Harrison and Beesly together with Hughes, Hutton, Ludlow, T. R. Bennett and R. B. Litchfield.[69] Harrison and Beesly came to see that moment as the harbinger of a new age, standing 'in the same relation to the coming industrial regime, as the meeting of the States General in '89 does to the subsequent history of Europe', ushering in a radical alteration in the conditions of society comparable to the Reformation, the French Revolution 'or even the foundation of Christianity itself'.[70]

The arguments they used on behalf of unionism were no different from those of the Social Science Association committee. Unions were a means of limiting industrial strife and of institutionalising the discontent of the workers. It was, they argued, the development of trade unionism which had led the working class away from the use of violence and outrage, and to attempt to curb them would bring a convulsion in comparison with which 'the French Revolution would be a rose-water affair'.[71] They looked to the large amalgamated societies to give leadership to the trade unions and Beesly built up a close relationship with Robert Applegarth. In articles in the *Fortnightly* and other journals they constantly tried to get across the idea that the A.S.E. and the Amalgamated Carpenters were typical of modern unionism and that the larger a society was the better. As Frederic Harrison wrote, 'there would be no greater security for the employer and the public than that societies should be stronger and their leaders more trusted'.[72] Beesly devoted a whole article to the Amalgamated Carpenters as exemplifying 'all the modern improvements in organisation which are giving a new signification and importance to the Unionism of the present day'.[73] The Positivists did not reject classical political economy, but they did reject the vulgarisation of it, which regarded any attempt by trade unions to affect wages as futile. Unions could not, they accepted, alter the aggregate wages of the labouring classes, but they could affect wages in their particular trade. They were involved in the 'debatable ground' between the aim of the employer 'to diminish the wages of the men to the point beyond which it would cease to be worth their while to work for him' and the aim of the worker 'to share the profits of the master up to the point beyond which it would cease to be worth his while to invest his capital in the business'.[74] Harrison, drawing his conclusions from the experience of the amalgamated societies, believed that the most important role of unions was to prevent drastic fluctuations in wages which were the bane of many workers and to limit the worst effects of speculation, 'those spasmodic seasons of excessive production and sudden concession which form the glory of the race of industrial conquerors'. Trade unionism aimed at bringing regulation and security into the lives of workers.[75]

The articles in the reviews were for the benefit of the middle class but the Positivists were also concerned to make contact and influence the rank and file unionists. They were, therefore, frequent contributors to the working-class press, providing something like 300 articles to the *Bee-Hive* alone.[76] In these their aim was to encourage unionists to attain a proper perspective of their social position and their social role and to adopt 'correct' attitudes to issues such as the American Civil War or the parliamentary reform campaign. Yet because of their association with the amalgamated societies and their friendship with the leaders they tended to become involved in the internal wranglings of London unionism in the mid-sixties. In public they seemed to be trying to restore unity, but in private they were highly partisan, hostile to Potter and his associates on the *Bee-Hive*. Harrison's letters to Beesly are full of phrases like 'the endless rascality' of *Bee-Hive*, 'an animal like Troup',[77] 'that blackguard Hartwell'.[78]

In much of their activities in the early sixties the Positivists were working alongside the Christian Socialists, Ludlow and Hughes, who continued to publicise the unions' cause and to act in an advisory capacity to Applegarth and Allan. They were firmly united in their support of the North in the American Civil War, which aroused an enthusiastic response among trade unionists. But the Positivists increasingly began to supplant the Christian Socialists as advisers to the unions. Partly this was because they deliberately set out to give intellectual leadership to unionism and to influence its decisions, while the Christian Socialists had always stood slightly apart, but they also had the advantage of accepting unions as vital institutions in themselves. Ludlow and Hughes still tended to see unions as a first step to – and less important than – co-operation. Beesly made the point forcefully: 'Unionism distinctly recognises the great cardinal truth which Co-operation shirks – namely that workmen must be benefited as workmen, not as something else. It does not offer to any of them opportunities for raising themselves into little capitalists, but it offers to all an amelioration of their position.'[79] The Positivists were not, therefore, concerned with trying to alter the organisation of trade unions, but to make them more conscious of their power. They were a major factor in pushing the London unions into political activity in the reform campaign and Beesly worked hard to convince them that their efforts must not stop with the winning of the franchise, but be a first step in a campaign for widespread social reform. His concern was to instil in the workers a sense of their importance as a class and to convince them that 'the main object of government and industrial organisation should be *their* comfort and happiness'.[80]

The Christian Socialists were more restrained in their advocacy of reform and they never encouraged workers to march in the streets. They stressed, not the right of the workers to vote, but their worthiness to do so. This was the message of the important volume which Ludlow and Lloyd Jones produced in 1867 on *The Progress of the Working Class 1832–1867*. Most of the arguments were familiar: the tremendous improvement in the character of the working class and its unions; the high character of unionists and their leaders; 'the training in self-government' which trade societies gave. Trade unions were linked with savings banks, building societies, friendly societies and mechanics institutes as evidence of the progress of the spirit of self-help among the working classes, but, in addition, they revealed 'forethought and sobriety', 'mutual trust and confidence', and 'powers of organisation which, when rightly controlled and directed, make the will of the masses like the will of the one', while rejecting 'the noisy, the violent, the self-seeking'.[81] All in all, in thirty years, the working class in general and the unions in particular had developed those characteristics of self-improvement, of responsibility and of 'manliness' which made them worthy of the full rights of citizenship.

III

The value of middle-class allies was brought home to the unionists at the end of the 1860s when they came under attack from public opinion as a result of another of the frequent outrages in Sheffield against non-unionists. The Sheffield press led an outcry, linking unionism in general with the outrages and calling for an inquiry, which threatened to destroy the respectable image so painstakingly created by the unions over the previous decade. Three months later they found themselves threatened from another direction when the Court of the Queen's Bench confirmed the decision of Bradford magistrates, declaring the funds of trade unions unprotected by the Friendly Societies' Act of 1855, since their proceedings were in restraint of trade. The leaders of the London-based amalgamated societies came together in a conference of amalgamated trades to plan their response to this crisis. They consulted with Hughes, Ludlow and the Positivists and decided that public examination would best show their distinctiveness from the primitive methods of Sheffield. They succeeded in getting what had originally been intended as an inquiry into the outrages at Sheffield broadened into a Royal Commission to 'inquire into and report on the Organisation and Rules of Trades Unions and other Associations, whether of Workmen or Employers, and to inquire into and report on the effect produced by such Trades Unions on the Workmen and Employers respectively, and on the Relations between Workmen and Employers, and on the Trade and Industry of the country'.[82]

Trade-union pressure persuaded the Home Secretary to accept Frederic Harrison on the commission to represent the views of the working class.[83] Ludlow did not get the place on the commission for which he had hoped and had to content himself with a letter to the commissioners, in which, drawing on '17 years observation and reflection', he declared, 'there is no one which is doing so much to educate the great mass of English working men into the capacity for self government and the duties of citizenship as the trade society'.[84] But, the tradition of Christian Socialism was represented in the commission by Thomas Hughes, who since 1865 had been M.P. for Lambeth, to which position he had been elected with trade-union assistance. In the event it was Harrison who most effectively defended the unionist cause. Hughes was irregular in his attendance.

The friends of unionism could draw little comfort from the other nine members of the commission. The chairman, Sir William Erle,[85] a former Lord Chief Justice of Common Pleas, had not, as a judge shown himself sympathetic to unionism and had revealed inflexibility, if thoroughness, in his judgements. The business interests were represented by Daniel Gooch,[86] chairman of the Great Western Railway Company and by William Mathews,[87]

chairman of the Midland Iron Masters' League. John Arthur
Roebuck,[88] member of Parliament for Sheffield, had travelled far
from his radicalism of the 1850s, when as 'Tear 'em' he had flayed
the inefficiencies of government. He had led the outcry in
Sheffield against the unions after the 1866 outrage. Herman
Merivale,[89] a former under-secretary at the India Office, was a
regular contributor to that most anti-unionist of journals, the
Edinburgh Review. There were two other former civil servants,
James Booth[90] and Sir Edmund Head.[91] In Harrison's opinion,
only Lord Elcho and Lord Lichfield[92] approached the inquiry
with a certain judicial detachment. Elcho was a complex figure
who opposed the extension of the franchise to the working classes
and who was later to become an arch-opponent of trade unionism
as chairman of the Liberty and Defence of Property League. In the
1860s, however, he was not entirely unsympathetic to unionism
and had acted as Parliamentary spokesman for the Glasgow
Trades Council in its campaign against the Master and Servant
Acts. In addition, he had worked closely with Alexander McDonald
and the Miners' Association to bring about an extension of mining
regulation.[93] The second Earl of Lichfield, a brother-in-law of
Elcho, was a landowner in the Midlands with industrial interests
and had actively advocated conciliation and arbitration.

The Royal Commission which took evidence throughout 1867
and 1868 and submitted its report in the Spring of 1869 was the
second decisive breakthrough to acceptance by trade unionism.
Thanks to the careful planning of Harrison, working with Applegarth, Allan and other London leaders, what was probably
intended as a forum for indicting unionism proved to be a show-
case for the large amalgamated societies. For, just as in his
writings, it was the large amalgamated societies that Harrison took
to illustrate the union position. He persistently sought to show that
it was these that were setting the modern trend which was rapidly
becoming the norm. He – aided by the evidence of Applegarth,
Allan and Guile – was able to reject allegations of violence and
luddism made by hostile witnesses on the grounds that such acts
were archaic exceptions or carried out by non-unionists. The
unions, through Harrison, were able to present a coherent case to
the commission in a way in which anti-union witnesses were not.
He successfully combatted the sniping of Roebuck, perhaps the
most virulently anti-unionist on the Commission, and eroded the
testimony of a number of hostile witnesses by revealing their facts
as mere surmise or hearsay.

The tactics began to pay off. As in the Social Science Association, publicity had been to the unions' advantage. In the discussions on the draft report the Commission generally divided between Harrison, Hughes, Lichfield, Elcho and Merivale on the one side and Head, Gooch, Booth, Roebuck and Mathews on the other.[94] Erle when he used his casting vote usually came down against Harrison and co., but in his desire to get a report, he was willing to make considerable concessions. Also the death of Sir Edmund Head tilted the balance in favour of Harrison, who with Hughes whittled away the most hostile comments in the draft report drawn up by Booth, until Roebuck was complaining that there was nothing left.[95] Having moderated both the tone and the recommendations of the report, they then declined to sign it and produced their own minority report. Lichfield, to all intents, approved the minority report apart from a few sentences, but only Harrison and Hughes signed it. The influence of Harrison on the majority report is evident. In dealing with the relations between trade unions and strikes, for example, the argument is purely Harrison's.

> It does not appear to be borne out by the evidence that the disposition to strike on the part of workmen is in itself the creation of unionism, or that the frequency of strikes increases in proportion to the strength of the union. It is, indeed, affirmed by the leaders of unions that the effect of the established societies is to diminish the frequency, and certainly the disorder, of strikes, and to guarantee a regularity of wages and hours rather than to engage in constant endeavours to improve them.[96]

But, in its recommendations for legislation, the majority did not go as far as Harrison and Hughes wished. In a classic statement of *laissez-faire* it declared: 'The interest of the public will be best consulted by allowing each of these parties to do what he thinks best for himself without further interference of the law than may be necessary to protect the right of others.' To this end, they proposed that the legality of combination be recognised even when in restraint of trade, though the restrictions on picketing should remain and financial protection be given only when a union had no 'objectionable rules' such as limitation of apprentices or against piecework and non-unionists.[97]

The minority report became what Harrison intended, an 'armoury' of liberal ideas.[98] The now familiar defence of unionism was made. 'Unionism', as Hughes and Harrison wrote, had 'been carried'. It had within its ranks 'the superior class of workmen'. Taking the examples of the Engineers, Carpenters and Ironfounders, unions were now 'a stable institution', totally transformed from the 1840s. 'Violence and excess' took place only where unions were weak or non-existent. Effective organisation meant 'an increased sense of order, subordination and reflection'.[99] The report then went on to recommend the full granting of the right of combination to working men by the removal of the disabilities of the Combination Act, the law of conspiracy and the doctrine of restraint of trade. It went further, however, than simply urging freedom of combination and recommended that unions be given full protection for their funds under the Friendly Societies' Act, while at the same time being protected from legal action. They should have power to sue dishonest officials but could not themselves be sued. They were to have the privileges of corporate identity without the disadvantages.

The minority report gave the unions a programme for which to campaign. Harrison drafted legislative proposals. Hughes, now working closely with the new 'lib-lab' member who had defeated Roebuck at Sheffield in the 1868 election, A. J. Mundella, put the case in Parliament. Beesly kept attention firmly focused on the issue in his speeches and writings to trade unionists throughout the country. In the Home Office itself, Godfrey Lushington was involved in shaping legislation. The outcome, a Trade Union Act coupled with severe restrictions on picketing in the Criminal Law Amendment Act fell far short of the hopes of the unions and the campaign continued against what was regarded as 'class legislation'. Not until the fresh thinking of R. A. Cross came to the Home Office after 1874 did the campaign at last reach success with the repeal of the Criminal Law Amendment Act.

IV

In the 1850s and 1860s trade unions had to seek their allies among the unorthodox professionals of Christian Socialism and Positivism. As the mantle of acceptance came upon them in the 1870s they increasingly came to seek their allies among the orthodox politicians. Harrison and Beesly never gained that influence over the provincial unionists who predominated in the parliamentary committee of the TUC that they had had with Applegarth and his London-based associates. In part, this resulted from the animosity they displayed towards Howell, the secretary of the committee: an animosity returned in full measure. Harrison and Beesly were becoming disenchanted with a working-class leadership which, far from leading the unions to a class consciousness, with the power to bring about a social transformation, as the Positivists hoped, was docilely seeking the approval of the middle class. They now began openly to express opinions on the venality of some of the union leaders in terms that had formerly been confined to their private letters.[100] It was, however, more than a difference of personalities or of tactics. It was rather a fundamental difference of aim. Beesly's defence of the Commune in Paris and his implicit rejection of the Parliamentary system was out of tune with the views of a leadership that explicitly sought acceptance within the existing system. Throughout the seventies, Harrison and Beesly continued to seek in their writings to broaden the perspective of the working class but their place as chief adviser to the unions was taken by their more moderate and pragmatic associate, Henry Crompton. He limited his goals and was willing to accept the limitations of the organisation. He regularly addressed the TUC and was influential in focusing the attention of trade unions on the need for the reform of a wide range of legislation. It was at Crompton's prompting that Congress urged the codification of the criminal laws and kept up a campaign against the property qualifications for juries.

The Christian Socialists, too, suffered a certain disenchantment. Trade unionism and co-operation were drifting further apart and their interest lay with the latter. Although he loyally backed up Harrison in the Royal Commission, Hughes was already having some reservations about the potential violence of unionism. At the Social Science Association in Sheffield in 1866 he had accused the unionists of covering up for the perpetrators of outrages.[101] He welcomed the restrictions on possible violence made by the Criminal Law Amendment Act and refused to support the campaign for repeal. The final breach came in 1874 when he accepted a position on the Royal Commission on the Labour Laws despite the opposition of the unions to what was regarded as a delaying measure by the Conservative government. From then on he pulled out of any involvement with trade unions and consciously handed over to 'a new generation' and to 'new admirers'.[102] Ludlow, too, continued to hope that trade unions would become other than they were. From 1870 to 1874 he acted as secretary to the Royal Commission on Friendly Societies and seems to have hoped that unions would come to concentrate more on this side of their activities. In 1875 he succeeded Tidd Pratt as registrar and was responsible for framing the 1876 Trade Union Act Amendment Act.

Both Ludlow and Hughes lacked the inclination to give practical leadership to the trade unions and they retained a slight reserve in their relations with them. One important side-product of their association, however, was to give the unions a written history. Hughes in 1869 edited Le Comte de Paris' study of *The Trades' Unions of England*, translated into English by Nassau John Senior, Hughes' brother-in-law. Paris made use of the evidence to Royal Commission on Trades Unions and produced a very favourable account of trade-union development over the previous twenty years. Two years earlier Ludlow and Lloyd Jones had published *The Progress of the Working Class*, which traced the progress of the 'improvement' of the working class from 1832 to 1867. This work, in turn, influenced the young German economist Lujo Brentano to embark on a study of English unions, the first part of which was published by the English Text Society as 'On the History and Development of Guilds and the origin of Trade Unions'. Historical roots – even if tenuous ones – could only add to the respectability of the institution of unionism and Brentano's work convinced at least one important figure, Archbishop Manning, of the importance and necessity of unions and he sent a copy of the work to W. E. Gladstone.[103]

V

Some new allies of unionism came along in the early 1870s with the appearance of unions among previously unorganised workers. Both the railwaymen and the farm workers attracted support from unexpected quarters. In the case of some of these supporters sympathy was not extended to other unionists, but one is at least getting a recognition of the validity of organisation as a means of improving conditions.

The long hours worked on the railways, often as long as nineteen hours without a break, had been the subject of concern for politicians on a number of occasions in the past. A serious railway accident was likely to result in questions in parliament on hours of work. But little was done to alleviate the situation and the very peaceful industrial relations on the railways, created by a mixture of security of employment, relatively good pay and conditions and strict discipline, kept the matter out of the public eye. In 1870, however, workers on the Midland Railway approached the philanthropic brewer, M. T. Bass,[104] member of parliament for Derby and one of the Midland's largest customers, asking him to use his influence with the company to get a reduction of hours. Bass took up the matter with some enthusiasm pressing the issue in both the House of Commons and the letter columns of *The Times*.

Having created interest Bass now began to extend his enquiries and employed Charles Vincent, a clerk who had been involved in the earlier attempts at railway unionism, and James Greenwood, a journalist, to investigate conditions on other lines, to organise meetings on the issue and generally to publicise the situation. Their activities stirred the workers to organise and the Amalgamated Society of Railway Servants was formed. Other middle-class figures began to show an interest. Dr Baxter Langley,[105] a radical Liberal gentleman became president of the new society, and Samuel Morley and Thomas Brassey were among the vice-presidents. Although refusing office in the society Bass retained his interest in the union's development. He acted as the society's patron, giving financial assistance for the publication of the *Railway Service Gazette* and the opening of a railway orphanage in Derby. On occasion he exerted the pressure of a customer and shareholder on companies to prevent wage reductions, and to press for shorter hours.[106]

The cause of the railwaymen attracted people who were genuinely shocked by the revelations of long hours on the railways and concerned with the growing number of accidents. Those who were attracted by the agricultural workers' struggle were perhaps less altruistic. Here was a cause that could not fail to appeal to middle-class radicalism for it was in opposition to Tory farmers and landowners. There was hardly a single radical leader of note who did not declare his support for the farm workers' struggle. Joe Chamberlain, Jesse Collings, George Dixon, Auberon Herbert, Edward Jenkins, Samuel Morley all joined in demonstrations with the labourers.[107] If the views of another supporter, Bromley Davenport, Liberal member for North Warwickshire, are representative, most of them saw the labourers' movement as much more concerned with embarrassing the landed interest than with trade unionism. Davenport warned Joseph Arch, 'Don't let the movement be complicated by trade-union interference.'[108]

The movement also attracted unexpected support from churchmen. Canon Girdlestone, vicar of Halberton in North Devon, stirred up an agitation among the labourers of the West country at the end of the 1860s, and was active in encouraging the spread of unionism. Archbishop Manning took part in London meetings supporting the union. A number of nonconformist ministers from Birmingham joined Warwickshire demonstrations. These last, no doubt, saw it as part of the struggle against the established church, for the rural clergy on the whole aligned with the farmers and spoke out against 'agitators' who were disrupting the even tenor of village life. The Bishop of Gloucester suggested that the best place for such agitators was the village horsepond.[109] But the Church of England, too, provided supporters. Christian Socialist priests like J. Llewelyn Davies and Charles Kegan Paul were both active and Bishop Fraser of Manchester spoke up for Arch's union.[110]

As with other middle-class sympathisers with unionism the motives attracting churchmen and philanthropists to the new unions were not necessarily support for the aims and activities of the unions, but a recognition that here was a powerful force and a useful ally, who could help fight battles far removed from unionism.

D

Chapter 4

The Employers

When Alfred Mault, secretary to the General Builders' Association, gave his near-damning evidence to the Royal Commission on Trades' Unions in 1867, he summed up employers' objections to trade unions.

> First, that many of their objects are improper and contrary to public policy; in the second place, that those objects that may not be improper or contrary to public policy are pursued by improper means; and thirdly, that from the constitution of the societies, the natural result is that they exercise coercion over both masters and men, and tend to separate masters and men rather than to unite them in friendly feeling and for the promotion of the common good of the trade.[1]

Other employers took up the theme and condemned unions as disastrous to the workers, to the employers and to the nation. By insisting on uniformity of wage rates and by opposing piece-work, unions held back the better-educated, more skilful and more industrious workman. By restricting the number of apprentices, unions prevented employers selecting their own choice of worker; by limiting the amount of work performed and the rate paid, they restricted competition; by restricting the use of machinery, and, indeed, on occasion, by preventing its use altogether, unions threatened the financial stability of the firm. Together these were disastrous for the nation. The workman's skill was 'not fully developed'; the energy and capital of the employer were not used to the greatest advantage. Such restriction forced up the price of goods and 'the British manufacturer finds himself unable to compete with the productions of other countries whose labour is free'.[2] Employers particularly resented what they regarded as infringements on the prerogatives of management, by which they meant the right to fix wages, hours and methods of work, particularly if the infringements came from people who were not members of their workforce. The constant complaint was that trade unions set limits on the employers' freedom. The engineering employers in 1852 claimed that their lock-out was 'a purely defensive measure against the interference and dictation of a small but mischievous class of agitators'.[3] The Preston cotton masters in 1853 declared that the issue was not one of wages but 'a question of mastery', a rejection of 'the spirit of tyranny and dictation'.[4] Thomas Garnett, a Clitheroe manufacturer made the same point during a dispute in 1859. 'The real question,' he said, 'was whether an employer was to be ruled by an irresponsible committee sitting he knew not where and composed of he knew not whom.'[5] The London builders in 1859 argued that they could no longer accept the dictation of the unions. In 1865, Charles Markham, managing director of the Staveley Iron Co., wrote to Gladstone that 'the object and intention of the union was to become practically dictators in the management of our property'.[6] In 1871, the Tyneside engineering employers saw the issue of the nine-hours movement as 'a struggle on the part of the men for mastery'.[7] Nonetheless, in spite of these protestations, more and more employers were coming to accept the right of union officials to negotiate for their workers and to see the value of a structured system of industrial relations.

Recognition by employers of the right of unions to represent their workers was fundamental to the process of acceptance of trade unionism. It was clearly of little value for trade unions to lay down rules if there were no chance of these being accepted by the employers. The alternative policies were either to obtain concessions from employers by the use or threat of industrial action or to obtain a compromise solution to a dispute through negotiation. Both policies were adopted, sometimes in conjunction, but, as the value of the attrition of strike action began to be questioned, it was the latter policy, the desire for a system of collective bargaining, which steadily came to the forefront in the mid-century years. By the 1880s, over a substantial section of British industry a pattern of collective bargaining had emerged.

To some extent there was nothing new in this. In the older crafts, conducted in small workshops, rules laid down by the trade society had long been accepted as the custom of the trade. Price lists had always been negotiable in the craft trades, with representatives of the workers discussing with the masters the rates for new processes or any alteration of methods or prices.

With the emergence of unions among journeymen the process continued and small masters usually accepted the right of a union activist to speak for his fellow workers. Throughout industry where unionism had been strongly established since the eighteenth century, such as in the London printing and book trades, the unions had been accepted as a negotiating partner for decades. In some industries the acceptance of unions' rights went even further. Joseph Samuda, the shipbuilder, complained to the Royal Commission on Trades' Unions that, on the Thames, the shipwrights' union had steadily increased their power over the previous thirty years until, by the 1860s, the masters had 'no power whatever in fixing men's wages in all these departments in which they belonged to the unions'.[8] The rates were fixed by the union and were not negotiable. On the Clyde, the Greenock shipwrights operated a closed shop with the acquiescence of their employers from the 1840s to 1866.[9] In the Midlands flint-glass trade until the end of the 1850s, employers seeking new workers had to do so through the factory secretary. He, in turn, took the matter to the central secretary of the union who kept a list of the unemployed members and employers had to take the name at the top of the list.[10] As the industrial units grew larger, however, and as new industries developed, many employers had come to resent such restrictions and to fight against them. As the distinction between master and man, management and workers, became sharper as industry grew and competition intensified, employers had become more hostile to union intervention.

Nevertheless, the desire for industrial peace often forced recognition of unions on even the most recalcitrant of employers. Of forty-seven trade societies and branches who submitted answers to the Royal Commission in 1868, thirty-one claimed to have some measure of recognition from their employers[11] and examples of ad hoc negotiations taking place are legion. When John Platt of Oldham had trouble with his engineers in 1851 over the manning of new planing machines he discussed the matter with William Newton of the A.S.E. and together they worked out a compromise agreement.[12] The bitter dispute between the Flint-Glass Makers' Society and the Midland Association of Glass Manufacturers in 1858–9 ended in a negotiated settlement between the two bodies, which still largely maintained a closed shop in the industry.[13] By the end of the 1860s, in the Yorkshire coalfields, a number of the coal masters, as a general policy, settled matters at issue with union leaders.[14] The Greenock shipbuilders, although they had broken the closed shop in 1866, dealt with matters arising exclusively through the executive of the union.[15] In the building trades employers and unions in many towns negotiated to produce a set of working rules for the smoother running of their trade relations,[16] and as a future secretary of the Amalgamated Carpenters wrote, not the least important of the benefits to be derived from this was 'the recognition on the part of employers of the right of workmen to unite, in order to secure a voice in the settlement of the hours they are to work, and the rate of wages they are to receive'.[17] Successful industrial action by a union could often result in recognition, as happened, according to Henry Broadhurst, after the 1872 strike and lock-out of London masons. 'The practical capitulation of the masters on the men's terms induced many employers who had hitherto refused to recognise the Masons' Society to change their policy; some firms even going so far as to instruct their foreman to give the preference in taking on new hands to members of the society.'[18]

In many cases, no doubt, employers had little alternative but to negotiate with union representatives if their men were adamant and they wished the matter settled. But, throughout the period, one finds a growing positive acceptance of the value of union negotiators. The Clitheroe cotton master, James Garnett, put the simplest case of all. In 1860 he wrote, 'We have put an end to the strike at Low Moor, by having Mr Pinder, the Weavers' secretary. He is much better to do business with than the hands themselves because he can calculate.'[19] A number of the employers at the Royal Commission found the same. One iron-master thought union officials were better informed, 'know more about the trade of the country, and study more political economy' than the ordinary worker.[20] They found that union officials were more ready to reach a compromise settlement that were their own workers. When William Newton and John Platt negotiated on machine-manning in 1851 they could agree on a compromise that labourers would continue to man existing machines, but any new installations would be manned by craftsmen. Four-fifths of the rank and file members of the union were hostile to such an agreement.[21] This pattern was repeated in other industries and Thomas Brassey claimed in 1873 that 'the executive councils of the unions have entitled themselves to the gratitude of the employers of labour by accepting the use of machinery'.[22] As many employers came to discover, by negotiating with a union official a strike was likely to be prevented.[23] Indeed, the district delegates of the Boilermakers' Society were instructed by their executive 'not to make unreasonable demands on employers'.[24] The case put forward in both the Social Science Association and to the Royal Commission that unions encouraged a more reasonable and moderate attitude among workers permeated to the employers.

Many large employers of labour also welcomed the stability given to prices by union restrictions. Unions were seen as a means of eliminating excessive competition and undercutting by small employers. By fighting cheap labour, unions helped to prevent the cut-throat competition which threatened the sales of larger firms. This was one of the arguments that influenced Samuel Morley with his 5,000 employees in the Nottingham hosiery industry. As a result of union regulation he found that he could now build up stock in times of good trade – 'before I could not do that, because I was always afraid of some unscrupulous employer cutting me out with lower prices'.[25] In Birmingham the strongest allies of the unions were the large employers, who united with the unions in 'a deep hostility towards competition', which was to culminate in the Birmingham price-fixing alliances of the 1890s.[26] It was the large employers, particularly in heavily capitalised industries, who had most to lose from a stoppage that allowed machinery to stand idle. As Thomas Brassey pointed out, 'the disposition to be liberal towards workmen is developed, as a general rule, in proportion to the business and capital of the employer'.[27]

Many employers came to accept that they could only gain from an institutionalised system of industrial relations. The threat of the withdrawal of union support was usually – though by no means always – enough to discipline the workers and to prevent precipitate strike action.[28] Even when a strike did break out with union approval it was likely to be more restrained and disciplined than the violent 'industrial relations by riot', to use E. J. Hobsbawm's useful phrase, of former times. The comparison, as Thomas Brassey said, was between 'a standing army' and 'a guerrilla band'.[29] Trade-union leaders were also likely to be more amenable to innovation. For example, in 1873 the South Wales colliery owners were looking to Alexander McDonald and other union leaders to persuade the miners to allow a shift system of working, since McDonald and the other leaders were men 'whose superior intelligence will enable them to appreciate more readily the advantages of new and improved systems of working'.[30] For some employers, unions proved a useful supplier of labour. This too was a custom whose roots lay long in the past when local union offices acted as houses of call for unemployed members. It was, however, also an acceptance of the case put forward by the unions and their supporters that 'superior workmen' were unionists. As Applegarth said, employers and foremen knew that unionists were 'of good moral character'.[31]

Perhaps the strongest influence towards the acceptance of collective bargaining came from the extension of piecework. The multitude of different rates which this necessitated had to be negotiable if constant disputes were to be avoided. As a result, it was in the cotton industry that collective bargaining on piece-rates was most highly developed.

Piece-rates in cotton had been common from the earliest times and as in the older crafts, these were usually worked out by mutual agreement and accepted by the district. With a limited range of products and relatively static methods and techniques the process of settling prices was fairly simple. However, by the mid-century, technological developments had brought a diversity of products which made agreements on rates for particular jobs an infinitely more complicated matter, requiring careful calculation and complex negotiation. It was the weavers who were at first particularly concerned with getting agreed uniform piece-rates. The dozens of local weavers' societies, partly and sporadically linked in loose federations, made no attempt to limit entry to their trade, as did the spinners and other craft unions. The apprenticeship system in weaving had irretrievably broken down by the 1820s. Wages could only be maintained, therefore, by achieving agreed uniform rates for work. This had become, by the 1850s, and remained, the prime objective of the Lancashire weavers' unions. There were some earlier agreements, but the first major success came in 1853 when the Blackburn employers' association agreed on a list of piece rates with weavers' representatives. Under the Blackburn List, as it was called, a standard rate for a standard unit was laid down and then variations were calculated from this base. The variations were computed in each mill, but the standard list was subject to district and, later, industry-wide, bargaining. At both mill and district level, therefore, the need for agreement on piece-rates forced negotiation between employers' and workers' representatives. John Ward (John O'Neil)[32] a Clitheroe weaver, gives a number of examples of negotiations with his employers on piece-rates in the early 1860s, which on occasion had to be settled by calling in an umpire to settle differences.[33] At district level, the calculation of the standard rate required considerable mathematical ability and this forced the weavers' unions, federated in the North Lancashire Power Loom Weavers' Association, to appoint 'a skilled calculator of prices'. Thomas Birtwistle was appointed to the post of general secretary in 1860 after a competitive examination of his mathematical ability and negotiating skill. From the 1860s a group of professional negotiators appeared among the weavers' unions (there were twenty or thirty by the early 1880s), combining the task of union organiser with that of negotiator.[34]

The spinners, who had succeeded in controlling entry into their trade, and thus keeping up their wages by control of the supply of labour, were at first less concerned with obtaining uniform piece-rates. However, technical developments in spinning also brought variations in rates, which needed to be negotiated. Wage lists in spinning began to appear and in 1868 the Oldham union appointed its first full-time secretary. From 1878, the general secretary of the Amalgamated Association of Operative Cotton Spinners was also appointed by competitive examination.[35]

It was in the cotton industry that the fullest development of collective bargaining first emerged, but the pattern was gradually repeated in other industries. The existence of piece-rates steadily becoming more complicated as industry expanded and division of labour continued, forced other industries into accepting the need for negotiation on wage rates. It necessitated the emergence of a new type of union official who was more than an administrator of benefit funds, such as William Allan and Robert Applegarth largely were, and who could negotiate and bargain at the conference table with the employers. Even in those trades where day-rates, rather than piece-rates, were the rule, such as the building trades, union officials were more and more often called in to try to negotiate settlements, though usually on issues other than wages.

Full-time union officials welcomed this extension of their role since it encouraged the tendency towards centralisation of their unions, the perhaps inevitable concomitant of the development of bureaucracy. Concern for the society's funds as well as a desire for public acceptance made union officials actively seek alternatives to strike action. No doubt many officials relished the kudos of sitting down in terms of equality with the leaders of industry.

On the employers' side, the acceptance of union bargaining was assisted by the appearance of employers' organisations. Such bodies had existed since at least the mid-eighteenth century and Adam Smith's remark that wherever two or three employers are gathered together there one has a conspiracy against the public was much quoted. Usually they were temporary organisations, frequently called into existence to combat trade-union activities, such as the 'strike in detail' or the 'rolling strike' by which a union would strike against one firm at a time. They rarely survived the immediate crisis and in a highly competitive industry it was difficult for co-operation between employers to be achieved. However, by the 1850s some permanent bodies were coming into existence. The large engineering employers had united to counteract the power of the A.S.E. in 1851 and maintained their organisation after their successful lock-out. The Midland Glass Makers combined to curb the power of the Flint-Glass Makers' Society in 1858. The Master Builders' Association of London continued to function after the nine-hour struggles of 1859–61. In the Midlands there was a general builders' association under the able secretaryship of Alfred Mault. In Yorkshire there were associations of coal owners and of iron masters. One of the most powerful associations was that of the Staffordshire iron-masters. These bodies were in general hostile to trade unions. The numerous lock-outs in which they engaged in the 1860s were often intended not just to defeat a strike but to crush combinations of workmen.[36] Paradoxically, however, the existence of employers' associations to a great extent helped the development of bargaining. A constant fear for an employer was that he would be out-manoeuvred or undercut by a rival or that the financial position of his firm would be made public. The development of employers' associations, frequently accompanied by price-fixing arrangements, broke down some of the obsession with confidentiality and allowed more open discussion of prices and wage rates. This could have the effect of hardening employers' attitudes and making them even less willing to negotiate on wages. On the other hand, it often made it more possible for employers to agree to concessions on wages since they knew that their fellow employers were going to have to pay the same rates. In addition the development of district-wide and even industry-wide associations fitted in with the desire of most unions to achieve district or industry-wide standardisation of wage rates. Once employers had come round to accepting that negotiations with unions might be to their advantage the existence of employers' associations greatly simplified the development of bargaining.

I

While there was then a growing tendency for negotiations between employers and unions to develop on a voluntary and often *ad hoc* basis there was a great deal of public pressure for a more formal system of negotiation based on boards, councils or courts of conciliation and arbitration. The projects for conciliation and arbitration systems seem to have been based on a belief that in a modern civilised society industrial strife had no place. Alexander McDonald was reflecting widely held views when he told a House of Commons Select Committee in 1873 that 'I look upon strikes as a barbaric relic of a period of unfortunate relations between capital and labour, and the sooner we get rid of it by the more rational means of employer meeting the employed, and talking the matter over the better.'[37] If, as was believed, precipitate action leading to war between nations had generally given way to caution, moderation and negotiation, the same could be true in relations between master and man. There was also a belief that in a nation where the science of political economy was at its apogee haggling over wages could give way to scientific calculation.[38]

While the terms conciliation and arbitration were widely used in the mid-nineteenth century their precise meaning to contemporaries is often far from clear and when spokesmen both inside and outside of industry urged the establishment of a system of conciliation and arbitration it is not always certain what exactly they envisaged. Two of the strongest proponents of a system of conciliation and arbitration, the Nottingham hosiery manufacturer, A. J. Mundella[39] and the former trade unionist George Howell explained that, when they used the terms, they meant 'Come, let us reason together.'[30] Thomas Hughes made the same point to the Social Science Association. He instanced a Glasgow employer who, representing his fellow masters met with a deputation of workers 'to confer as to the rate of wages'. That, to Hughes, was 'arbitration'. 'At least, that was all he, and he believed the committee [on Trades' Societies and Strikes] meant by arbitration.'[41] As the Webbs pointed out, therefore, when the terms conciliation and arbitration were used in the mid-nineteenth century they frequently meant little more than collective bargaining and when union leaders called for a system of conciliation and arbitration they were really asking for consultation and negotiation, and the recognition of unions as bargaining partners by the employers. Thomas Winters, the secretary of the National Association of

United Trades, and for long a leading advocate of some system of arbitration, told the 1856 inquiry into the subject that eight out of ten unions had an arbitration clause in their rules and 'By arbitration they meant that when a case goes before their local committee, the local committee should appoint a deputation to wait upon the masters to see if they can agree.'[42] If, in order to achieve the right to negotiate, the intervention of a third party umpire was necessary unions were generally willing to accept this.

The call for arbitration certainly came from the unions. As Frederic Harrison told the Royal Commission, an analysis of the Social Science Association Report revealed that arbitration had been refused by the employers on nine occasions, in the disputes studied, while it had been refused by the men only once.[43] Most unions by the 1860s insisted that some attempt at 'arbitration' be made before strike action was considered and a number of trades councils had it as one of their major objects to substitute concilia-tion and arbitration for strikes and lock-outs. As one historian has said, 'If conciliation and arbitration did not pervade British industry to a far greater extent in the period it was not the fault of the trade unions.'[44] It was precisely because it was a demand for recognition of trade unions and for collective bargaining that many employers resisted the growing pressure for boards of conciliation and arbitration. They 'may possibly stave off a quarrel for a time, and here and there prevent a strike or lock-out', wrote the virulently anti-union James Stirling in 1869, 'but, in so doing, we lend the authority of public recognition to the pestilent principle of combination.'[45] Nonetheless, many unionists, politicians, employers, union sympathisers and do-gooders joined in demand-ing a formalisation of collective bargaining within a system of boards of arbitration and conciliation and various experiments were made in this direction.

From the trade union side the initial demand came from the National Association of United Trades for the Protection of Labour formed in 1845, under the presidency of the aristocrat-cum-chartist Thomas Slingsby Duncombe. It sought to recreate the general union of trades of the Owenite years, but with much more limited aims and with each society retaining its autonomy. One of its major objects was 'to promote the establishment of local Boards of Trade or Courts of Conciliation and Arbitration, for the purpose of adjusting disputes between employer and employed, empowering them to make bye-laws, rules, and regulations, and to take cognizance of all questions affecting the interests of labour and trade'.[46] By the early 1850s it had lost any semblance of influence as a trade union body, but its three permanent officials, especially the secretary Thomas Winters, remained active publicists of schemes for conciliation and arbitration and on occasion continued to act as mediators in minor disputes.[47]

In parliament the leading advocates of a system of arbitration were W. A. Mackinnon and Lord St Leonards.[48] The tradition of judicial intervention in industrial relations went back to the Statute of Artificers and beyond, and although the rights of Justices of the Peace to regulate wages had been abolished in 1812, the 1825 Combination Act still contained a section which allowed J.P.s to arbitrate or to appoint arbitrators for the settlement of disputes if requested to do so by both masters and men. The Act was, however, confined to certain trades and to disputes that were actually in progress. There was no provision for anticipating strikes and the Act was little – if ever – used. It was totally unknown to most of the witnesses to the Select Committee on Masters and Operatives in 1856. When W. A. Mackinnon took up the issue in 1855 he seems to have looked to the French *conseils des prud-'hommes*, where disputes were discussed by a joint board of masters and men. These Napoleonic creations existed in both France and Belgium and were concerned with interpreting contracts of employment. They made no attempt to fix wage rates.[49] A select committee on the matter was set up in 1856 under Mackinnon's chairmanship and it took evidence from trade unionists and others. One of the most effective members of the committee was Viscount Goderich who, since his Christian Socialist days, had been interested in the settlement of disputes by means of arbitration. Together with Hughes, Ludlow and others of the group he had worked out a scheme for arbitration modelled on the *conseils des prud'hommes*. The committee did little more than to recommend the principle of arbitration and they found little agreement among the witnesses on the particular form that arbitration should take. However, in 1858, Mackinnon introduced a bill to establish local councils of conciliation and arbitration. These councils would have been elected by all employers and workers within a five-mile radius. It aroused little enthusiasm. Firstly it was a permissive bill and the secretary of Glasgow trades council commented that 'if parties are not compelled to submit their case, he had little hope of any good arising out of the proposed bill'.[50] Secondly, it specifically excluded any arbitration on the matter of future wages. In this it followed the pattern of the *conseils des prud'hommes.* A further select committee on the issue met during 1860 and took more evidence. But, again proposals for legislation came to nothing.

From 1860 Mackinnon's role was taken up by Lord St Leonards, but not until 1867 did his bill for establishing 'equitable councils of conciliation and arbitration' become law. He had devised his measure in consultation with Odger, Howell and Thomas Winters of the National Association of United Trades, but it was never effective. Once again it was a permissive measure which could only be activated by a petition from a joint meeting of masters and men. It would deal only with existing disputes and had no power to anticipate trouble or to settle future wages. Even after a council had been established it still required joint agreement before an issue could be submitted to it for settlement.[51] Unions generally favoured an element of compulsion: that employers should be forced to negotiate if a dispute arose. An attempt to improve the measure was made in 1872 by A. J. Mundella's Arbitration (Master and Workmen) Act, but it proved as ineffective and unused as its predecessor.

Throughout the fifties and sixties there was considerable debate on the form that conciliation and/or arbitration boards ought to take. The legislation favoured general boards covering a locality, not one particular industry. The belief was that these would have an impartiality and freedom from the passions of those involved in the dispute that specialist boards could never have. This was an idea which had a particular appeal to trades councils. In May 1868 Peter Shorrocks, the general secretary of the Amalgamated Society of Tailors, proposed in the Manchester and Salford Trades Council that the council approach the chamber of commerce with a view to the two bodies forming a court of arbitration and conciliation.[52] William Gilliver, the secretary of the Birmingham Trades Council put forward a similar plan a few months later, at the Social Science Association, basing his suggestion on the experience of such joint action in Birmingham during a recent stonemasons' dispute.[53] Such a court was established in Manchester in October 1868, consisting of eight members selected from the trades council and eight from the chamber of commerce. It was meant as a court of last resort, 'only to be appealed to when the employers and employed had failed to effect an amicable settlement of any dispute by other means'.[54] Once a case had been referred to the court it was intended that both parties should be bound by its decision. The court met quarterly and was probably a useful forum for discussing general matters, but no case ever came before it for arbitration. The secretary of the trades council pinpointed the main reason when he talked of 'an extreme reluctance to place the disputed affairs of any well-organised societies at the disposal and settlement of those employed or engaged in entirely different trades from the case in hand, and who from the manner of their appointment would be entirely irresponsible to those affected by their decision'.[55]

Like the legislation, schemes for general boards achieved little or nothing. On the other hand attempts at voluntary and specialist boards, despite early reverses, were eventually remarkably successful. There had been some earlier attempts at developing a formal procedure in a number of industries. For example, in the Staffordshire potteries from 1836 to 1866, all disputes were supposed to be submitted to a committee of three masters and three men with power to call an umpire if they were unable to come to a decision themselves.[56] It does not seem to have been particularly successful in preventing strikes. A court of arbitration was established in the silk-weaving trade at Macclesfield at the end of the 1840s. Consisting of twelve members from each side, it was intended mainly to work out piece rates. When an attempt was made in 1853 to enforce a ruling unfavourable to the employers it collapsed.[57] The carpet-weaving trade of Scotland and the North of England had annual conciliation meetings from 1838, again to settle piece rates.[58] In the 1850s a number of such voluntary boards appeared. After a prolonged dispute in 1852 by the shipwrights of the Wear, a committee of conciliation was formed with a delegate and an employer from each shipyard. Its decisions were intended to be binding.[59] There were a number of *ad hoc* arbitrations in the printing trades. But the real breakthrough came in the 1860s.

After an eleven-week strike in the Nottingham hosiery industry during 1860, the three largest manufacturers, faced with a crisis at a period when demand for their goods was very high, decided to try to settle the outstanding issues by calling a conference with delegates of the workers. The workmen selected as their delegates the leading figures in the three unions in the industry and a dozen unionists met with A. J. Mundella, Thomas Ashwell and J. H. Lee. The outcome was the Nottingham Board of Arbitration for the Hosiery Trade consisting of first six and later nine members from each side of the industry. The employers were selected by the members of the Hosiers' Association and the workers' delegates by a general vote organised by the unions. The Nottingham Board was particularly significant: firstly, because it brought relative industrial harmony to an industry that had been notoriously afflicted by labour unrest; secondly, it had in A. J. Mundella an ardent publicist who wrote and lectured on the success of the board throughout the decade; and thirdly, it specifically recognised the crucial position of trade unions in such arrangements. Mundella regarded the support of the unions as essential to the success of his scheme. Only the unions had the necessary discipline to get the board's decisions accepted by the workers, and he found that the trade-union delegates were constantly a moderating influence, providing 'the greatest barrier we have had between the ignorant workmen and ourselves'.[60] The proceedings of the board were informal and its success was based on the willingness of both sides to compromise. After 1864 actual voting on the board was more or less abandoned and decisions were arrived at by negotiation. The decisions of the board were binding, but matters rarely came to such a point. A sub-committee of two employers and two unionists acted as a mediating committee and settled most disputes before they reached the board. At the board itself, the main discussions were on the different piece-rates for the 6,000 or so articles produced by the industry.[61] By the end of the decade, the board covered the hosiery industry of Nottinghamshire, Derbyshire and North Leicestershire, dealing with more than 60,000 workers.[62]

The essence of Mundella's system was voluntary negotiation, an 'arrangement for open and friendly bargaining'.[63] It grew fairly naturally from the necessity of getting agreement on a multitude of different piece-rates. A more legalistic system was devised in 1865 by Rupert Kettle,[64] a county court judge who was called in as a mediator in a dispute in the Wolverhampton building trades. Building was an industry where by the mid-1860s almost all payments were by the hour. The negotiable areas were not, therefore, rates for particular jobs, but rather the conditions surrounding the work, such as the time to be allowed to walk to a particular job or the number of bricks to be carried in the hod, or differences in the normal day between summer and winter. Informal working rules on these and many other matters had been accepted in most towns. Kettle proposed that these be made into formal written agreements, copies of which would be posted in each workshop and distributed to all new workers. These agreements would be binding on both parties and difficulties would only arise on the interpretation of the rules. Kettle, therefore, stressed the need for an arbiter from outside the trade – preferably a legal figure – who would interpret the code of working rules. There was, as in Nottingham a sub-committee appointed to mediate, but Kettle's system was much more a court than a negotiating forum.

Kettle and Mundella were the two leading figures in the 1860s in the campaign for a system of conciliation and arbitration. They wrote and lectured on the subject and influenced others to do likewise. The majority of the Royal Commission on Trade Unions singled out Mundella's scheme for praise and endorsed the need to bring 'employers and workmen together to discuss in a friendly manner the question of wages and other points of difference which arise from time to time'.[65] Boards, courts and councils began to multiply up and down the country some following the Nottingham pattern, others the more formal Wolverhampton system, and yet others devising what was really an amalgamation of the two. In 1867 Mundella's system was adopted by the Nottingham lace trade; in the following year, the Leicester hosiers followed. Kettle's plan was taken up in the Staffordshire potteries and in the building trades of Coventry, Leeds and Worcester and steadily spread to other towns.[66] The hope of both Mundella and Kettle was that their schemes would be adopted in the two great basic industries of iron and coal, industries that were the scene of numerous large and bitter disputes in the 1860s. Mundella worked closely with Lord Lichfield and Lord Elcho among the coal owners and with Normansell of the Yorkshire miners to secure the adoption of his system in the coal industry[67] and a pattern of negotiation did begin to emerge. Most coal fields had their Boards of Arbitration by the early 1870s.

In 1869 a Board of Arbitration was formed to cover the Teesside iron industry. The original impetus came from the Ironworkers' Union, under John Kane. After a series of disputes in 1866, he proposed the settlement of the issue by arbitration. The employers rejected his approach, but over the next few years, the ideas of Mundella and Kettle began to have their effect. Mundella impressed in particular David Dale, a director of the Consett Iron Company, and Dale and Kane succeeded in establishing a board in March 1869.[68] Its aim was first and foremost conciliation, but on the issue of wages an arbiter was frequently used. Kettle acted as arbiter in 1869 and again in 1873, Thomas Hughes in 1870 and 1871, Mundella in 1876 and David Dale, himself, in 1878 and 1879.

Other boards followed: in the South Staffordshire iron-trade in

1872; in the boot and shoe industry of Leicester from 1875; in the Northumberland and Durham chemical industries in 1875. In even more cases *ad hoc* committees were established to settle disputes, usually with power to call in an outside arbiter. A corps of such arbiters began to emerge – Mundella and Kettle, David Dale, Henry Crompton, who in 1876 produced a full study of conciliation and arbitration, W. E. Forster, Joseph Chamberlain, George Shaw-Lefevre and others. Sometimes they would offer themselves as arbiters in a dispute, such as Mundella did in the Tyneside nine-hours strike of 1871,[69] but usually it was a case of their being obvious names that came to mind who were likely to be acceptable to both sides, when an umpire was sought.

The difficulties facing an arbiter could be formidable, especially if he were unfamiliar with the technical details of the industry. Thomas Hughes found great difficulty in understanding the technicalities of the iron industry when he arbitrated in 1870 and 1871 and even greater difficulty at arriving at a compromise acceptable to both sides. One problem was to find a formula on which wages could be calculated. The favourite was the selling price of the product. Kettle, for example, believed that price formed 'the only legitimate fund out of which wages can be paid',[70] and employers generally favoured a sliding-scale related to selling prices. This was used in the iron-trade arbitrations between 1871 and 1875, and again after 1879, with quarterly meetings to fix the rate of wages. In the Durham coal trade a sliding scale was introduced in 1877. In this case prices were ascertained by two accountants, sworn to secrecy, one selected by the owners and the other by the men, who examined the account-books of various firms and agreed, on the average price.[71] The rapidly falling prices of the late seventies and eighties made this system less and less acceptable to employers who wanted to cut wages faster than the system would allow, and to workers, who found their wages falling drastically, and it steadily broke down in a formal system, though selling price was still used informally as a guide line in negotiations.

Other criteria apart from selling prices were never neglected by the union negotiators. In support of claims they would point to the condition of the labour market, wages paid in other areas and in other industries, the quality of management and the cost of living.[72] This last was frequently used by the unions. In 1874, the Durham miners argued that wages should provide 'a reasonable minimum of comfort',[73] and the ironworkers insisted to Shaw-Lefevre in 1878 'that there should be a minimum below which wages should not fall, whatever may be the position of prices'.[74] The Northumberland miners, on the other hand, explicitly declared that they did not seek a minimum wage.[75] Employers were unanimous in refusing to allow profits to be taken into account in the settling of wage rates. This would have been an infringement of the firm's dearest privacy which they were not yet ready to accept. One arbiter, W. E. Forster, did, in 1875, suggest to the Durham coal-owners that profits should be taken into account, but the employers refused to provide the necessary figures.[76]

Both employers and unions had much to gain from the development of a system of conciliation and arbitration. For the employers it brought an order and a discipline into relations with their workers, which in turn gave to the employers a considerable amount of security. It ensured reasonable undisturbed production which was vital for them at a time of good trade. It gave employers an indication of wage levels for some time in the future so that now they 'were not afraid, as they formerly had been, of going into markets, as now they knew what wages they would have to pay for a long time'.[77] Although at first many of the employers hoped to so organise boards of arbitration as to exclude full-time union officials from their proceedings, they fairly quickly came to accept that the presence of union officials was not only inevitable, but to be welcomed. Negotiations with union leaders were more likely to result in moderate compromises than were the battles of strike and lock-out. Union leaders were more likely to accept arguments for changes in work methods, such as the introduction of the shift system, than were the rank and file. And only the unions could exert the necessary control and discipline over the workers to ensure that agreements would be maintained. Indeed, Rupert Kettle generally required that, in those trades in which he arbitrated, unions should have a rule that bound members to agreements reached at boards.[78] For the unions, the development of a system of conciliation and arbitration meant recognition and acceptance. It gave to the union officials a status and a role for which they longed. But, more than that, the demand for conciliation and arbitration coming from the unions reflected a genuine desire to find an alternative to strikes and lock-outs, for these were expensive and often dangerously damaging to the unions. If union strength was to be measured by the financial reserves held by the union – and this was becoming an accepted measure – then these had to be protected from erosion by strikes.

Against this there were disadvantages for both sides. Since the system generally meant recognition of the union's right to negotiate on wages, employers had to sacrifice some of that managerial prerogative that they so valued. It required an open discussion of matters which at the beginning of the period were regarded as of the highest confidentiality. While, at a period of high demand at the beginning of the 1870s, boards of arbitration and conciliation provided a useful counter to union militancy when their bargaining position was strong, by the end of the seventies, the advantage was with the employers and many of them rebelled against the slowness of the system. At a time of rapidly falling prices many employers rejected the restrictions which a system of bargaining placed on their power to make frequent and substantial wage cuts. A number of boards began to fail in the late 1870s because employers were insisting on numerous wage reductions and because the boards were no longer able to control the price-cutting policy of some of the smaller employers.[79] For the unions, too, there were serious disadvantages. At a time of high demand, their acceptance of conciliation had often emasculated their bargaining strength. At a time of falling demand and falling prices, arbitration and conciliation were not able to prevent substantial wage reductions and therefore began to lose union support. Most destructive of all to union strength were the sliding scales, for these removed the main *raison d'être* of unionism, to actually negotiate on wage rates, since if wages were completely tied to prices there could be little argument on them. Mining unionism certainly declined during the period when sliding scales were in operation and this was largely accounted for by a belief among the miners that unions were no longer necessary if they had no influence over the issue of wages.[80] In some cases, the development of boards, may have prevented unions building up financial reserves. In hosiery, for example, the introduction of the board was seen, not as an opportunity for strengthening the unions at a time of industrial peace, but as a splendid means of keeping union subscriptions at a ridiculously low level.[81] In the potteries, too, the board was seen as an alternative, not a complement, to unionism and the men tended to desert the union.

Nonetheless, the 'arbitration craze', as the employers' association journal, *Capital and Labour*, called it, had its effect. It brought a substantial modification in the attitudes of employers, many of whom had been unremitting opponents of unionism in the early 1860s. When he addressed the Iron and Steel Institute in 1876, Mundella found that many former opponents such as Markham of Staveley, Schneider of Barrow and Hurst of South Staffordshire had come round to accepting the value of his proposals.[82] They had come to recognise what an employer like Thomas Brassey had been preaching throughout the 1870s: 'that the existence of trade unions must be accepted as a necessary consequence of the new phases into which productive industry has entered', and the only question was how to direct their activities 'into a useful channel'. It was idle to find fault with them since they were a fact of industry and it was better 'to recognise these organisations, and to make use of the facilities they offer for negotiation and agreement between employers and their work people'.[83]

Perhaps as important, however, was the effect that union acceptance of conciliation and arbitration had on public opinion. To the public it showed that unions were no longer a subversive influence concerned with fighting and overturning the existing system. Instead, they were accepting the institutions and the values of their society. They were accepting a common interest with their employers in the development of industry and they were contributing to, not threatening, the 'equipoise' which mid-century society sought. Often, indeed, it seemed to be the employers who were preventing the possibility of social peace.

II

Not all employers welcomed the trends of the 1870s. For many the unions, in the boom years of the early seventies, had become too powerful and had been altogether too successful in their public relations. 'A rampart' was needed to 'keep back an advancing army' of unionists[84] who not only threatened the national prosperity but whose demands smacked of the dangerous philosophy of socialism.[85] Trade unions had a 'well-paid and ample staff of leaders', they had money, organisations and their own press. In addition 'from the mistaken humanitarian aspirations of a certain number of literary men of good standing' they commanded a 'large array of literary talent' that had access to the leading London journals. They could influence elections; they could exert pressure on members of parliament, and they had 'the attentive ear of the Ministry of the day'. As a result the tide seemed to be flowing their way and their demands were about to be satisfied. Public opinion was coming to accept the need for the repeal of the criminal law Amendment Act, the conspiracy laws against unions, and the master and servant legislation. Nine-hours factory legislation, mines regulation and employers' compensation were all making progress in a euphoria of pro-union sentiment. A halt had to be called and a rival organisation to the unions needed to state the other side of the case and to hold back the 'advancing army'.[86]

These were the sentiments that resulted, in April 1873, in the formation of the National Federation of Associated Employers of Labour. It contained many of the leading names in British industry: from shipbuilding John Laird of Laird Bros, Birkenhead and E. J. Harland of Harland and Wolff, Belfast; from the textile industries, L. J. Crossley of Halifax, Stephen Marshall of Leeds, Henry and Edmund Ashworth of Bolton, Titus Salt of Bradford and Edward Akroyd of Halifax. There were engineering employers such as John Robinson, the president of Sharp, Stewart and Co., Manchester and Benjamin Peacock also from Manchester, David Greig of Fowler and Son, Leeds, Thomas Vickers from Sheffield and Joshua Field of the large London firm of Maudsley, Son and Field. The building trades were represented by the secretaries of the Yorkshire Builders' Association, the London Builders' Association and by Trollope of London. John Menelaus of Dowlais was one representative of the iron trade, as was E. Fisher Smith, the agent of the Earl of Dudley.[87] Also, somewhere in the background, was that ever-active opponent of unionism, Sidney Smith, who for twenty years had been trying to form and hold together associations of employers.[88]

The aim of the national federation was primarily to act as a political pressure group. As the employers themselves admitted, they had much to learn from the trade unionists when it came to lobbying ministers and members of parliament. Their first task was to halt the snowballing of opinion in favour of repeal of the anti-picketing legislation and they studiously matched trade-union meetings with ministers with meetings of their own. Mundella, Harcourt, Morley and others were always putting the trade-union case in Parliament, the federation's spokesmen, Sir Thomas Bazley[89] and Edmund Potter tried to counter them. Since the trade unions had their own labour press, the employers needed one too, and in January 1874 the first issue of *Capital and Labour* appeared. For the next eight years it kept up a relentless and frequently vitriolic assault on trade unionism. The charges against unions were the familiar ones, but they were steadily repeated: unions denied to capital its legitimate profits; they 'make rules for other men's businesses'; they 'dominate the workshops'; they 'dictate how the work shall be done, and who shall do it'; they 'fix the rates of wages'; they terrorise the non-unionist; and, indeed, they 'do all but take possession of plant and capital'.[90] Consistently the Federation denied that it intended to initiate a war of capital against labour. It was, it claimed, a defensive organisation, but if industrial peace were to be achieved capital had to be strengthened: 'the way to insure peace is to prepare for war . . . preparation for "industrial war" will be a new guarantee of industrial peace'.[91] Unionists certainly saw it as a threat and the formation of the Federation stimulated a number of schemes – all of them abortive – for a federation of trade unions.

For most of those employers who joined the National Federation their membership was no doubt little more than the natural response of employers who felt increasing trade-union limitation being placed on their freedom of action. For others there was a wider philosophical basis to their support. They saw many of the ideals of a *laissez-faire* society slipping away. In their place they observed the appearance of radical interventionist policies with – however mistakenly – the spectre of socialism behind them. Trade unions stood for protection and for increased regulation of industry. They were demanding not just a fair wage but a wage that would 'enable them to lead comfortable and respectable lives, "free from the anxieties" that destroy' – the German Social Democrats ideal of '*ein gutes Leben* – a good living'.[92] It was freedom of the individual that *Capital and Labour* set against the 'tyranny of the Trade Unions':

What we want is, that workmen should be isolated, as employers or tradesmen or professional men are, and no more. The middle classes are free; we wish to see the working classes equally free . . . A man has only his labour to sell. Let him take it to an open market, and get the most he can for it. If he can get more than others, or sees an opening in which it would be to his advantage to take less, he must be at liberty to make his bargain as he chooses; and he is not a free man, but a serf, if he cannot do this. . . . For our part, we claim for English workmen that individual liberty which is the most precious heritage of Englishmen.[93]

Noble as were the sentiments, the battle was already lost. The National Federation failed in its aims. Despite its protestations both in and out of Parliament, the criminal sections of trade-union legislation were repealed. 'Master and Servant' gave way to the less pejorative 'Employer and Workman'. Employers' compensation for industrial accidents may have been delayed by the Federation's activities, but it, too, came. Arbitration might be a 'craze', 'a confusion of ideas more flattering to the hearts than the heads of those' who took it up[94] but more and more of their fellow employers were taking it up. The Federation failed to successfully rebut the pro-unionists propaganda and after its failure to block the legislation of 1875 it declined in influence. The organisation seems to have collapsed even before the demise of its journal at the end of 1882.

III

Employers, like the unions, were faced with the alternatives of conciliation or confrontation. Some chose to fight and in the crisis years of the late seventies probably support for the diehards was increasing. With falling prices and shrunken export markets employers were probably less willing to make concessions. However, overall, the trend, as in the unions, was towards conciliation. Increased capitalisation in industry encouraged it. To blow out a blast furnace or to close down a large machine shop was expensive and the large employer found it cheaper to make concessions than to risk a stoppage. Public opinion insisted on industrial peace and condemned employers who refused to meet representatives of their workers. Once negotiations had begun employers generally found that these representatives were more amenable to compromise than a mass meeting of workers. Professional managers, who were spreading in most industries, found it more satisfactory to deal with professional negotiators. Protest that was institutionalised in unions and in formal procedures was much easier to handle than the guerilla warfare of previous decades.

On the workers' side, negotiation with union officials gave the recognition they sought, and most union leaders were willing to go to great lengths in order to prevent the breakdown of negotiating procedures. Some were so committed to making a success of the formal procedures that they were willing to put up with the often massive wage cuts of the late seventies rather than break with conciliation boards. Rank and file members were less committed to the formal structure, but, by the 1870s, most union's bureaucracies were powerful enough to deal with malcontents.

On both sides of industry, therefore, there were pressures that brought about conciliatory policies and with them came the development of a formal system of industrial relations.

Chapter 5

Trade Unions and Politics

Another major step in the progress of trade unions towards acceptance came with a recognition of their role in the field of politics. This was a twofold process, in part coming from a growing awareness by unionists of their importance as a political pressure group and in part coming from an appreciation by middle-class radicals that the leaders of the working class would be useful allies in their struggle against the continuing aristocratic domination of the British political system. Neither a consciousness of political power, nor an alliance between middle-class reformers and trade-union leaders came quickly: both were built up gradually during the 1850s and 1860s. The contentions within chartism and the extremism of some of the leaders had certainly convinced many unionists that politics were a source of dissension within the ranks of labour and that unions should concern themselves with building up their organisation and concentrating on limited industrial goals. That is not to say that belief in the essential rightness of chartist demands disappeared from among the unionists, rather it was a question of political demands taking second place to other issues in the order of priorities. It reflected also, a widespread apathy on the issue of politics among the ranks of the working class: an apathy, which it took many years for the political activists to overcome.

There were plenty within the ranks of the unions who continued to believe that the 'labour problem' was essentially political. Chartist groups continued to flourish and influenced a younger generation. George Howell recalled that he was 'often in contact with the chief leaders of the labour movement, and with those who still adhered to the Charter'.[1] Groups of unionists met at William Lovett's coffee house and at the 'Windsor Castle' public house in Holborn to discuss politics and to 'keep the old flag flying till at length they formed the nucleus from which sprang the Reform League'.[2] Other unionists were attracted to the extreme politics of the followers of Bronterre O'Brien who met regularly in Soho.[3] Unionists were to be found in most of the radical organisations and movements that appeared during the 1850s up and down the country, in support of the exiled Louis Kossuth or Mazzini, or in response to the Russo-phobia of David Urquhart. They were also to be found in the meetings of non-electors that were held at election times to encourage or frighten the candidates and their voters. But these were unionists acting as individuals and there was no official union involvement in such movements. It is always difficult to discern whether the presence of trade unionists and trade-union banners at a political demonstration actually indicated corporate involvement by a trade society in agitation. In the rules of many societies there was a clause expressly forbidding the discussion of political issues at society meetings and even where such a clause did not exist branch meetings were concerned with the every-day issues of the society, while national delegate meetings of unions usually confined themselves to the intricacies of rules' revision. Politics were left to a few interested individuals at meetings unconnected with the trade unions, but these individuals did not hesitate to declare themselves representative of their trade society.

This did not mean that, in any sense, trade unions regarded political action by their members as of no importance. The A.S.E., for instance, which as a body took no part in political movements, nonetheless urged its members through the *Operative* to participate in political activity. Social reform, it argued, could only come about with direct representation of labour in parliament;[4] special working-class grievances, such as the Master and Servant Act could only be removed if 'workmen had the power of making law as well as masters'.[5] The society's founding father, William Newton, stood as a working-class candidate at Tower Hamlets in the election of 1852, with a programme that contained most of the elements of the chartist platform.

In the minds of many trade unionists a sharp distinction was drawn between trade-union activity in political campaigns for specific measures, such as amendment to legislation affecting the working class, and wider political campaigns for issues not directly affecting unionists, such as parliamentary reform. The committees of trade unions were always active in the former, while they left the latter to the individual participation of their members. Thus, through their short-time committees, the cotton unions, continued to press for improvement of the factory acts. In 1852 and 1853 unions in the National Association of United Trades and others, after the leaders of the Association had been imprisoned under the Master and Servant Act and the law of conspiracy, pressed Parliament, through sympathetic members for amendment of these laws.[6] In 1855 the executive council of the A.S.E. used its influence with a number of M.P.s to get the Friendly Societies' Act of that year shaped to its wishes. This distinction between social measures affecting the working class and wide political reform movements continued to be made. A speaker at the Glasgow Trades Council, in 1859, made the position clear, when the Council was being asked to send delegates to a meeting in support of Garibaldi's struggles in Italy. He declared: 'As a lover of freedom [he] would do all in his power as an individual to promote the political freedom of Italy, but he thought it beyond their power to pledge themselves as representatives of the working classes, as the Council must not be considered the focus and arena of political creeds, but take up and defend every cause in respect of labour.'[7]

I

The appearance of trades councils at the end of the 1850s and during the 1860s brought into play an important new element. For these were forums, previously lacking, where trade unionists meeting together as representatives of their trade societies, could discuss wider political issues. It seems clear that many of the most politically conscious unionists, who were keen to encourage greater participation by the working class in politics, immediately grasped the significance of these new bodies as a means of involving the trade unions in political movements.

One of the first of such councils was in Glasgow, formed in the spring of 1858, and immediately it considered the question of involving itself in the parliamentary reform campaign which was reviving as a result of the efforts of John Bright. A number of old chartists in the Council, with some younger members, pressed it to declare for manhood suffrage. They came up against opposition from the delegates of some societies and when the Council did declare itself on the issue a number of these societies withdrew their affiliation. But those that were left were almost unanimous in supporting a demand for the extension of the suffrage. Time and again, however, when they took up the matter of parliamentary reform they found a general apathy among the rank and file of their unions.[8] A small group continued to press the matter and in October 1861 they persuaded the Council to issue *An Address to the Workingmen of the United Kingdom*, which was of vital importance in raising the question of trade unions and politics, throughout the country. It was a very moderate document. While declaring that 'no measure of reform will be final that does not embrace manhood suffrage', it argued that rather than wait for the election of a House of Commons willing to accept that, they should 'push for what is now attainable, a five-pound franchise for the Boroughs and ten pounds for the Counties'. Of more significance, however, was the final paragraph, which envisaged trade unions as the means of carrying out the agitation.

We would respectfully, yet confidently declare that the various trade societies of the country are the best means for carrying out a successful movement of this kind. We are aware that many are opposed to trades' meetings being mixed with politics; we cannot coincide with such views so long as trade societies are amenable to the law. There were several matters in law that affected them, such as the inequality of the law of master and servant; also how many times have they been baffled in the attempt to establish Councils of Conciliation and Arbitration? By what means are these measures to be rectified or obtained but by the possession of political power? – the want of which affects the whole labouring class. If these things be true how can it be that working men in their associated capacity ought not to enter politics?[9]

This was the first time that a trade-union body had specifically declared itself in favour of trade unions forming the base of a political agitation for parliamentary reform.

It was the address from the Glasgow Council which brought the issue of politics before the London trade societies. The elder statesmen of London unionism, who had formed the first London Trades Council in 1859, had given way, in 1861, to a younger group – George Odger, Edwin Coulson, Charles Murray, Randal Cremer and others. Most of them had worked together during the builders' lock-out of 1859 and were united in the belief 'that the working classes would get little advancement until they had political power'.[10] They wanted to use the Trades Council to lead the London unionists to a political consciousness, but their task was a formidable one. The slogan, 'no politics in trade unions' had become firmly entrenched in the minds of most unionists. The leaders of the Council, however, were as Howell, the secretary, said, 'ardent on the subject' of the Glasgow Address.[11] In the pages of their journal the *Bricklayers' Trade Circular*, Howell and Coulson urged unionists to take up the issue of parliamentary reform. They stressed that industrial issues could not be separated from political ones, citing as an example the use of sappers to break a strike of building workers at Chelsea barracks: 'The conduct of our present Government, in lending Sappers to a private contractor, while his own men were on strike, shows us plainly that we must reform before our voices can be properly heard in the House of Commons. Whilst Capital is heard on all sides of the House, Labour has no voice there; how then can we expect impartial laws from one-sided men?'[12]

With the publication of the *Bee-Hive Newspaper* in October 1861, another voice was added in favour of political action by unions. Encouraged by Professor Beesly and by James Stansfield,[13] the radical member for Halifax, Howell and his associates prepared to lead London unions into the arena of politics. Howell had been having meetings with Beesly and Stansfield on some trade outrages that had taken place in Sheffield and 'concerning steps likely to be taken by the Council in reference to politics'.[14] Despite their efforts, however, they failed to carry the delegate meeting of London trade societies. Even Odger's formidable oratory calling on the societies 'to take up the important question of reform and form a committee a thousand strong' did not move them. The A.S.E. executive wrote expressing disapproval of the Council's 'taking part in political matters'[15] and threatened to withdraw. Since fees from the A.S.E. made up almost half of the Council's annual income such a threat could not be treated lightly and there were probably other societies, like the London Bookbinders, who were also threatening secession.[16] As a result, Howell had to content himself with a statement that members of the Council would co-operate with other bodies campaigning for parliamentary reform, 'not as a COUNCIL but as individuals'.[17] Howell was criticised for the enthusiasm with which he had responded to the Glasgow Address and this, together with the difficulties he was having in getting employment, prompted him to resign the secretaryship.[18] His successor, George Odger, was, however, equally enthusiastic about politics and a group around him in the Trades Council continued to be active.

At the instigation of the tiny 'Silver Cup' Society of Carpenters, the possibility of a political initiative by the Council was again raised at the end of 1862. In an 'Address . . . to the London Trades Council and Fellow Unionists in London, on the necessity of combining the study of political and social questions', the Carpenters wrote: 'As a trade society we have no Political Union which we deem to be highly essential, and the Council appears to us to be particularly fitted for the accomplishment of that great object having within its means the power of drawing large bodies together in the shortest possible space of time.'[19] The pro politics members of the Council did not feel strong enough to take any initiative and Odger was instructed to reply that 'members of the Council individually sympathize' but that 'it was not within the province of the Council to move in agitations entirely political'.[20] Odger, however, pursued the matter further in a letter to the *Bee Hive* suggesting a separate association of unionists.[21] The result was the Manhood Suffrage and Vote by Ballot Association, formed 'for the purpose of obtaining our rights as citizens; or in other words our just share of political power.'[22] Odger was chairman, Petherbridge, chairman of the 'Silver Cup' Society was treasurer, and the committee included Howell and Applegarth.[23] As the reform agitation died down in the face of growing concern at possible British intervention in the American Civil War, the Association seems to have come to nothing, until it re-emerged two years later as the Trades' Political Union.[24]

As individuals, the leading members of the Council were active in a number of political causes that had the important effect of bringing them into contact with middle-class radicals. The three issues of Italian independence, the American Civil War and the Polish rising against Russian domination were particularly important in forging a link between radicals and labour leaders, not just in London but in other cities. One of George Howell's first acts as secretary of the Trades Council had been to send an address from the Council to the General Neapolitan Society of Workingmen of the Sections of Mutual Help, congratulating the Italians on their successful struggle for independence and urging them to show 'moderation and patience' in their demands.[25] The cause of Italy was dear to many working men and in all parts of the country it brought them into contact with the many Liberals who admired Mazzini and Garibaldi. The spontaneous working-class response to the visit in 1864 of Garibaldi to Britain cemented the links between working-class leaders and radicals. In London, for instance, Howell, Odger and other unionists worked closely on this issue with middle-class radicals like Stansfield, Professor Beesly and Edmund Beales.[26]

It was the Christian Socialists, Hughes and Ludlow, already acquainted with many of the London trade-union leaders, who first took up the cause of Lincoln in the American Civil War and campaigned against any possible British intervention in support of the Southern States.[27] The Positivists, Harrison and Beesly, quickly followed. Beesly approached the London Trades Council and pressed them to organise a meeting of trade unions in support of Lincoln. The famous meeting in St James's Hall was held in March 1863. This meeting was not called under the auspices of the Council, but, with Odger, Coulson, Applegarth, Howell and many other leading members of the Council attending, it became associated in the public mind with the Trades Council. To Howell and his pro-politics associates this meeting was of decisive importance in their 'endeavour to bring [unions] into the political arena'.[28] It was important also in that John Bright, as chairman of the meeting, made his first direct contacts with the leaders of the London unions. Again this was an issue that was not confined to London and there were meetings in many towns attended by unionists. In Edinburgh it was the Trades Council and the local branch of the Emancipation Society which organised a public meeting, a month before the St James's Hall meeting, to accord Lincoln 'its tribute and approbation'.[29]

The Polish revolution of 1863 was yet another important issue that brought together unionists and radicals. George Odger and Randal Cremer were two of the leading unionists in the National League for the Independence of Poland, which had Edmund Beales as president. The Polish issue also brought the London unionist into contact with some of the French workers who were taking advantage of Louis Napoleon's liberal phase to establish trade unions in Paris. A group of them had come across for a demonstration in support of Polish independence and they were entertained by the Trades Council. The meeting was followed by the issuing of an Address signed by Odger, Cremer and one or two other London unionists calling for the formation of a 'great fraternity of peoples', who in their congresses would 'discuss the great questions on which the peace of nations depends' and 'would clear the way for honourable men with comprehensive minds to come forth and legislate for the rights of the many, and not the privileges of the few'.[30] It was a short step to the formation, in September 1864, of the International Working Men's Association, which had Odger, Cremer and Howell on its first general council.

Odger's involvement in all these movements brought complaints from less politically active members of the Trades Council. Surprisingly, it was George Potter, now in the Trades Council, who suggested 'that the name of the secretary should not appear with every meeting he attended, as it gave them the character of having the support of the Council, which was not the case'.[31] Potter warned that it would cause some societies to leave and although Odger objected to the assertion that the Council did not recognise political action as forming part of its business, he felt it necessary to reaffirm, in his annual report of April 1864, that although it had been appealed to take part in 'the American, the Polish and the suffrage question', the Trades Council had taken no action, 'leaving members as individuals to do as they pleased in such matters'.[32] Nonetheless, at least one society, the London Bookbinders, withdrew 'on the ground that the council had indirectly, if not avowedly, engaged in politics of the most violent character', and Thomas Dunning complained that the Council 'had been made, if not the active means, most certainly the nucleus of the so-called political movements of the working classes'.[33]

This pattern of a few active leaders trying to arouse a hostile or apathetic majority was repeated elsewhere. It was a constant complaint of the leaders of the Glasgow and Edinburgh Trades Councils who were trying to organise trades' meetings in support of parliamentary reform that the majority of their members were uninterested, and, as in London, both Councils were weakened by the withdrawal of societies who objected to political discussions.[34] More support was forthcoming for issues that seemed to have a direct relevance for unionists, in particular the campaign against the Master and Servant Acts. These Acts were a long-standing grievance for trade unionists and there had been many complaints at the inequity of legislation that made breach of contract by a workman a criminal offence, that could be summarily dealt with, while breach of contract by an employer was a civil offence that could only be remedied by long and expensive litigation. It was the Glasgow Trades Council that initiated a campaign against them. The question of the reform of these Acts was first brought to the notice of the Glasgow Trades Council in January 1860 by Alexander McDonald, the miners' leader,[35] and in its political Address of 1861 the Council mentioned the Acts as one of the injustices which justified trade unions engaging in agitation for parliamentary reform. Eventually, in the spring of 1863, action was taken. One of the local Liberal members, Robert Dalglish,[36] was communicated with and he elicited from the government that in England and Wales alone there had been 10,393 cases under the Master and Servants Acts during 1861.[37] The Council then issued an *Address to the Trades Councils and Trade Societies of the United Kingdom*, putting forward their very mild proposals for the amendment of the Acts, and formed a Master and Workman's Act Reform Committee. Under the energetic secretaryship of George Newton this committee campaigned on the issue and, on its recommendation, the London Trades Council called a conference to co-ordinate the agitation. The conference was held on four days between 30 May and 2 June 1864. It was attended by delegates from the trades councils of London, Liverpool, Sheffield, and Nottingham and from the London Bookbinders, the Iron-founders, the Stonemasons, the Miners and the A.S.E.[38] The conference recommended that the agitation be pressed on with, by means of the introduction of a private members' bill into the House of Commons. Arrangements were left in the hands of the Glasgow Committee with the addition of Alexander McDonald.

A Bill was to have been introduced by J. M. Cobbett, but when he failed to get himself re-elected, the Committee turned to the 'liberal-conservative' Lord Elcho. To politically active unionists outside Scotland this was a choice of the greatest eccentricity since Elcho was a well-known and outspoken opponent of parliamentary reform. It is explicable only in terms of a close association that had grown up between Alexander McDonald and Elcho when they had successfully worked together for the Coal Mines' Regulation Act of 1860.[39] Although in their *Address* of 1861 the Trades Council had expressly accepted the link between social and political reform, they seem to have seen no inconsistency in working for social reform with Lord Elcho and for parliamentary reform with his political opponents the liberal-radicals. Newton and the Glasgow Committee, faced with protests from London Trades Council and other bodies, wanted Elcho's views on the reform of parliament to be separated from his views on the master and servant issue, refusing to accept that 'because a man was wrong in one point . . . he is wrong in all'. [40] The whole matter became tied up with the issue of parliamentary reform and created a bitter feeling and deep division within the trade-union movement in Glasgow.[41]

II

There was a number of reasons why trade unionists were reticent about linking their societies to reform agitations. There existed, on the part of the unenfranchised workers, a suspicion of politics and of politicians. To many, politics was little more than 'the scheming of schemers'. There was, in particular, a considerable suspicion of those radicals who most strongly advocated the extension of the suffrage, since these same men had frequently been leading opponents of factory and mines' legislation. Many workers believed 'that the hardest taskmasters and the greatest tyrants are to be found among those of the most advanced "liberal or radical" political opinions'.[42] Along with this went the continuing fear that political activity would cause division within a trade society and destroy the unity necessary for carrying out its primary task of protecting wages and conditions. But, perhaps the greatest barrier of all to political activity lay in the apathy of the majority of unionists, who were indifferent to the question. It was this barrier that the politically active unionist had to work hardest to overcome.

With the death of Lord Palmerston in the autumn of 1865 the 'quiet days' had come to an end[43] and the reform issue, dormant for the previous three years, revived. The campaign was slow to get under way and at first the moderate National Reform Union, under the leadership of John Bright, who favoured only a limited extension of the suffrage, made the running. From the formation of the Reform League in February 1865, however, the campaign for parliamentary reform among the working class gathered some momentum. But, it remains difficult to distinguish between the activities of trade-union leaders acting as individuals and acting as representative spokesmen of their unions. The first union to affiliate to the League was the Finsbury branch of the Amalgamated Cordwainers, and *Reynold's Newspaper* reported that delegates from the Operative Bricklayers', the Amalgamated Carpenters' and the Amalgamated Cordwainers' Societies attended a meeting of the League in December 1865[44] but it is not at all clear that they were officially appointed by their unions. By the middle of 1866, however, most of the leading unionists in London were identified with the reform movement, either in the Reform League or in George Potter's rival organisation, formed in February 1866, the London Working Men's Association. Odger, Applegarth, Coulson, Cremer and Howell were all among the

E

leading members of the League. T. J. Dunning, Thomas Connelly and Henry Broadhurst of the Stonemasons, and Joseph Leicester of the Flint Glassmakers' Society were members of the Association.[45] It was Potter's Association that first managed to get some of the smaller London unions out into the street in support of reform, when on 3 December 1866 more than 20,000 marched behind their societies' banners. The London Trades Council, whose leaders were all in the Reform League, had still remained officially uncommitted, but a fortnight after Potter's demonstration it declared its support for the League. William Allan of the A.S.E. moved the relevant motion and the League, working with delegates from the A.S.E., the Amalgamated Carpenters, the Plasterers, the Masons, the Bricklayers, the Bootclosers, the Hatters, the Shoemakers and the other societies, organised a further trades' demonstration.[46]

Outside London, commitment came earlier. The Birmingham branch of the League was formed in March 1865, after George Potter (at this time still a member of the League) had addressed a meeting of unionists, held to condemn the lock-out of Staffordshire ironworkers.[47] In July and August 1866, the recently formed Trades Council took part in demonstrations organised by the League,[48] and appealed to trade unionists to abandon their fear of political action and support 'those advanced independent Liberals who believe that the broader the basis of our institutions, the firmer they will stand'.[49] The secretary of the Council, Roger Bateson, was also secretary of the League branch. In Scotland, many of the politically active unionists restricted their demands to household suffrage, rather than to the manhood suffrage of the Reform League. The Glasgow branch of the Reform Union, of which George Newton, the secretary of the Trades Council was one of the secretaries, called only for the enfranchisement of male householders and lodgers rated for relief of the poor, with the proviso of carefully excluding 'any stipulation of finality short of manhood suffrage'.[50] There was considerable acrimony between the Glasgow reformers and the leaders of the Reform League in London. Howell wrote to Newton: 'We are not surprised that government should offer so little when the people are afraid to ask too much.'[51] The Glasgow Trades Council, itself, in grave danger of breaking up as a result of internal disputes, decided, in the summer of 1866, to erase 'that portion of its constitution, which permits the discussion of political questions', but most leading unionists were involved in reform movements and there was a remarkable display of unity at a great reform demonstration in October 1866 organised by the recently formed Scottish National Reform League. Moderates and militants stood together: John Bright, Edmund Beales and George Potter all attended and many of the Glasgow unionists, including Newton and Alexander McDonald spoke from the platforms.[52]

In Edinburgh, a meeting of unionists, in June 1865, pledged itself 'to support by all means in its power, these candidates who will support a liberal extension of the franchise' and contributed to the defeat of the sitting member and well-known anti-unionist, Adam Black.[53] The Trades Council organised a number of meetings in October 1866 and 'agreed on the principle of registered residential manhood suffrage and the ballot, as the basis of their agitation', though the secretary of the Council qualified this by saying, 'of course, it was not to be understood that, while they had adopted the principle of manhood suffrage, they would refuse to have anything less.'[54] The Council organised a trades' demonstration in the following month and out of this there emerged a branch of the Scottish National Reform League.[55]

From the end of 1866 trade unions increasingly identified themselves with the reform movement. Most of the Birmingham societies affiliated to the League[56] and, in London, societies of shoemakers, cabinetmakers and tailors.[57] The growth of trade-union support was helped by the Hornby v. Close decision of January 1867, which put the funds of many societies in jeopardy from fraudulent treasurers. According to Beesly, it was this that brought the Amalgamated Carpenters into the streets for the League demonstration.[58]

There were still, however, some reservations on the part of some unionists about an all-out commitment to political action and to association with the League. William Allan of the Engineers was still unhappy about making the 'societies channels for political agitation',[59] and one gets the impression of Howell and his fellow League members pressing rather reluctant trade societies. Some unionists continued to regard the League as dangerously extreme. In an important centre like Manchester, the position was complicated by the fact that both the president and the secretary of the Trades Council were active Conservatives. An invitation to take part in the League's demonstrations of February 1867 was rejected by the Council's executive committee, who considered it 'inadvisable to the interests of combination to identify with any particular class of partisans'. The full Council approved this decision, as one 'to be acted upon in the future'.[60] The radical element in Manchester, under William MacDonald, secretary of the Operative Housepainters' Alliance, after failing to win over the Council, formed their own Trades Demonstration Committee, which organised a successful demonstration in which only three unions failed to participate.[61]

III

The mass demonstrations at the end of 1866 and early in 1867 played a crucial part in convincing the politicians, and particularly the Derby–Disraeli government, of the vital necessity of settling the issue of reform with alacrity. In August 1867 the Second Reform Act for England and Wales, which had the effect of giving the vote to most male householders in towns, received the Royal Assent. The following spring, similar measures for Scotland and Ireland were passed and the country awaited the general election. Clearly there was a key question: how would the working class, organised in their unions and in the Reform League use their vote? The answer took the form of verbosity rather than action. At all stages Howell and the leaders of the League had consulted with their middle-class allies. They were dependent on the financial support of wealthy radicals and the election policy adopted by the League was to work in harmony with the radical wing of the Liberal party and to offer no encouragement to those unionists who favoured a more independent policy.

Talk in the Birmingham Trades Council of 'securing the return of a working man to Parliament as third member' received a 'mixed reception' from the affiliated unions and came to nothing.[62] At the same time, however, they declined to declare their support for the Liberal candidate, P. H. Muntz, in spite of an appeal from the Liberal Association. In Lancashire the strong Conservative element among some of the most politically conscious unionists prevented unions and trades councils from being used for radical agitation, and most radical working-class activity was carried on through separate political associations. In Manchester the Trades' Political Association, under William MacDonald's leadership, actively pressed the candidature of Ernest Jones, but Nicholson and Wood, the president and secretary of the Trades Council campaigned for the Conservative candidates and claimed that 7,000 working men had voted Conservative as a result of their efforts.[63] In Liverpool, as Howell reported to the Liberal whip, 'the secretaries of the principal trades are Liberal even Radical – but dare not act in consequence of the complex character of their respective trades'.[64] Members of the Bolton Trades Council dallied with a movement to bring forward 'a gentleman as a candidate who shall most nearly represent a majority of their own opinions',[65] but it proved fruitless, and they contented themselves with questions to the candidates on their attitude to protection of trade-union funds, the law of conspiracy as used against unions and 'any rash oppressive measure . . . that would operate to the disadvantage if trade unionists . . . designed to sever the sick, accident, or funeral benefits from the purely trades' unions'.[66] An attempt to include questions on the ballot and on compulsory education had to be abandoned when there were threats of withdrawal by the spinners' union – 'that being a political question'.[67] Before the election, two of Howell's agents formed a 'Liberal Trades Political Association' and the president of the Trades Council was chairman of this.[68] They failed, however, to elect a Liberal member.

In Yorkshire there was more radical activity. Since so many of the artisans of Sheffield had the vote before the extension of the franchise there was little incentive for them to take part in the reform demonstrations. However, in the election of 1868, the Association of Organised Trades combined with the Reform League to bring forward A. J. Mundella to oppose J. A. Roebuck, who had increasingly antagonised working men by his support of the southern states in the American Civil War and of Austria in Venetia; by his opposition to reform; by his change of mind on Irish Disestablishment; and finally by his manifest hostility to trade unionism, displayed at the meetings of the Royal Commission.[69] Robert Applegarth, who had been a founder member of the Sheffield Association of Organised Trades, worked closely with the Sheffield unionists to elect Mundella. Even here, however, the situation was complicated by the demand of several local unionists, including Broadhead, for the legal enforcement of payment of union dues. Mundella declined to support this, while Roebuck was reputed to be more sympathetic, with the result that the latter did receive support from some unionists. Mundella nevertheless successfully ousted him. In Leeds, the Trades Council, whose leading figures were all members of the Reform League, gave its backing to the League's candidate, Alderman R. M. Carter, and were willing to support him even if he had failed to get the backing of the Liberal Registration Association.[70] The

Council issued its own election platform, demanding the adjustment of the Master and Servant laws, protection of union funds, a national system of education, the return of working men to Parliament 'where practicable' and the settlement of disputes by Boards of Conciliation.[71] In Dewsbury, the Trades Council led the revolt against the Liberals and invited Ernest Jones to contest the seat in the interests of the working class. When Jones declined, they successfully nominated an unorthodox Liberal barrister, John Simon.[72] The Halifax Trades Council, on the other hand, refused to give any support to the co-operator E. O. Greening, who stood as advocate of a working-class programme. This was largely due to the influence of the Council's president who actively worked against Greening, canvassing for the Liberal manufacturer, Edward Akroyd.[73] In Bradford, E. S. Beesly had put forward a programme for trade unions and found considerable support among some unionists for independent action by working men. In the event, however, after some initial reticence, the Bradford Trades Council declared their support for the Liberal, Edward Miall.[74]

The trade-union movement in Glasgow was sharply split in 1868 between the Glasgow Trades Council and the Glasgow Working Men's Association: a split occasioned by the question of relations with Lord Elcho. The working-class reform movement was similarly divided between the Scottish Reform League and a group around the Trades Council leadership. The former, like their English counterparts, wished to maintain close relations with the Liberal party and brought forward, as their candidate for the new third Glasgow seat, a local merchant, George Anderson. The latter group, which was led by Charles Lang, the general secretary of the Associated Bakers' Society and chairman of the Trades Council, and by Alexander McDonald and was supported by Alexander Campbell in the editorials of the *Glasgow Sentinel*, made unsuccessful efforts to initiate a campaign for the return of a working-man candidate.[75]

One working-class candidate did come forward in Scotland in the election of 1868, Alexander McDonald. He offered himself as a candidate for the constituency of Kilmarnock burghs, a conglomerate constituency consisting of Kilmarnock, Dumbarton, Rutherglen, Renfrew and Port Glasgow. He stood as 'the people's candidate' and his committee appealed to working men to contribute one shilling each towards his election expenses.[76] He had the backing of the substantial community of miners in the constituency and of at least some of the shipwrights of Dumbarton, despite the hostile pressure being exerted by the main shipbuilder of the town, William Denny.[77] But McDonald had antagonised the Scottish Reform League by his opposition to the candidature of George Anderson, by his association with Lord Elcho and by his frequent criticism of Bright and other radicals. As a result he did not get the League's backing and instead was opposed by a League candidate, Edwin Chadwick, the father of the New Poor Law. Accusations of Toryism were thrown at McDonald, accusations which were to cling to him for the rest of his life.[78] But he made his position perfectly clear: 'He was called a Tory; he was not – neither was he a Liberal in the ordinary sense of the term; and he would be political hack to no man. He remained content to be one of the friends of Labour.'[79] The one outside source of support for McDonald came from the Positivist, E. S. Beesly, who had been warning English unionists against depending upon, or expecting too much from middle-class radicalism. He had been urging the working class to concentrate on social questions. Beesly regarded McDonald as 'one of the few representatives of Unionism I know who will be able to fight the battle with effect in such an assembly as the House of Commons'. His election, in itself, would solve nothing, as he would 'stand all but alone in the House', but it would be 'the first note of a preparation for the ensuing struggle, and everything must have a beginning'.[80] Beesly recognised in McDonald the spark of independence that he sought, largely in vain, among English trade unionists.[81] But, faced with the opposition of Chadwick and lacking effective financial backing, McDonald withdrew just before polling day. Thus the candidature of one whose whole career had been in the trade-union movement was sacrificed on behalf of Chadwick for the simple reason that McDonald, it was feared, would be too independent of the Liberal Party.

On the other side of the country, there was some division of opinion among the Edinburgh unionists. A small group of them – though including three of the executive committee – were expelled from the local branch of the Reform League for presenting an Address to Disraeli when he visited the city in October 1867.[82] Another group wanted independence of all political parties and one of their number declared, 'the working classes ought to be independent'. He had 'little confidence in the Whigs, still less in the Independent Liberals, and none whatever in the Tories. The working classes of Edinburgh should have one member of

Parliament to themselves.'[83] The bulk of unionists were, however, in the League and although its annual report of 1868 enigmatically declared that it was 'no party to politics' it was, in fact, firmly aligned with the Independent Liberals of Edinburgh, the party formed around Duncan McLaren,[84] Bright's radical brother-in-law. The Trades Council did, nevertheless, compile a list of questions on social and industrial issues for candidates in the 1868 election, dealing with protection of trade-union funds; extension of the factory acts; abolition of the 1825 Combination Act; master and servant laws; the establishment of courts of arbitration – in other words a fairly orthodox list of trade-union demands at this time, similar to a list which had been issued by other councils.[85] But the Edinburgh Council went further in its questioning and included additional matters of wide social significance – nationalisation of the railways; the establishment of a national library for Scotland; amendment of the patent laws; a 'national, compulsory, unsectarian system of education'; 'a system of legislation which shall make it compulsory to provide full house accommodation to those of the working classes who may be evicted from their dwellings in consequence of civic improvements, railway acquisition, or similar causes, previous to such eviction taking place'; and legislation for the prevention of deck-loading of ships. No group of trade unionists in the country went so far as that of Edinburgh in trying to relate its new political power to the whole field of social improvement or in demanding so much state intervention. The same points were made in an address presented by the Council to John Bright, when he visited the city in November 1868. Grateful though it was for the extension of the franchise, it wanted to ensure that parliamentary reform resulted in the adoption of legislative measures favourable to the working class, even if some of these measures were unpalatable to John Bright and other middle-class allies. But there was no effort by the Edinburgh unionists to bring forward a candidate of their own and the two Liberals were returned.

Generally, in the election of 1868, trade unionists failed to grasp their opportunity. There were, of course, difficulties in organising a campaign and in raising the necessary money. No union gave money for political purposes. The only position adopted by existing organisations like the Reform League and the London Working Men's Association was one of deference to the wishes of the radical wing of the Liberal party. In addition, however, it is clear that they were not dealing with a united trade-union movement: involvement in the campaign for parliamentary reform had been brought about by the strenuous efforts of a relatively small group of politically active leaders, with, behind them, a fairly apathetic membership that could only be roused to short bursts of activity. In the post-reform election they found a movement whose objectives were far from clear. Political views among unionists varied from Conservatism, through every shade of Liberalism, to independent working-class politics.

IV

The slight impact made by the new working-class electorate in the election of 1868 was widely noted. George Potter complained that working men had 'permitted themselves to be used as instruments of ambitious politicians, and allowed their cause to go by default'.[86] The *Daily Telegraph* exclaimed that the 'terrible dive – deep down – into democracy' had brought forth not 'a democratic lamb' but 'a rather old-fashioned Liberal Lamb'.[87] The politically active unionists, however, remained keen for further action and for working men to be elected to Parliament. George Odger was especially active. 'Rightly or wrongly,' he wrote, 'they want to be represented by men who live by labour',[88] and between 1868 and 1870 he offered himself as a candidate at Chelsea, Stafford, Southwark, Bristol and Preston. There was a number of political groups active in London that had leading unionists among their members. Potter still had his coterie and the support of a number of middle-class radicals. Randal Cremer had a group mainly of people associated with the International Working Men's Association. And, in January 1869, Allan, Applegarth, William Newton, Odger, Howell and Lloyd Jones formed a Working Men's Parliamentary Association.[89] The failure of the government to press forward with a trade-union bill confirmed their belief that 'class legislation' could only be removed by the working class having their own representatives. This is what the three groups were concerned to achieve and thanks to the mediating role of a radical barrister, R. M. Latham the personal rivalries between the leaders of the groups were smoothed over during 1869 and, in August, they united in the Labour Representation League, 'to procure the return to Parliament of qualified working men'. For the first time, the leaders of London unionism were united in a political organisation: Latham was president, Allan treasurer, and Lloyd Jones, secretary; the executive included Applegarth, Odger,

Howell, Coulson and Guile as well as Potter and his allies, Thomas Connolly and T. J. Dunning. There were also young men of the future like Henry Broadhurst and George Shipton.[90]

Inevitably such diversity produced tensions within the organisation and there were differences of opinion on how closely ties with the Liberal Party ought to be maintained. While the president of the League, Latham, was declaring that the aim was 'the harmonizing of working men's interests with those of the general community',[91] Odger was continuing to stress that it was 'highly desirable the working classes should have their interests represented in Parliament by men of their own order'.[92] Odger's independence went further than the now much-mellowed *Bee-Hive* liked and it felt it necessary to 'deprecate his appearing to use language not adapted to promote solidarity between middle and working classes'.[93]

Undoubtedly, the hope of most of the members of the League was that the Liberal party would find a place for a few working-class candidates. But, time and again, they were rebuffed. Odger's numerous efforts to get elected were always frustrated by an orthodox Liberal candidate; Applegarth withdrew from Maidstone in 1870 because of Liberal pressure; Howell did the same in the following year at Norwich as did Potter at Nottingham.[94] Amity with the Liberal Party was not helped by the appointment of Sidney Smith as secretary of the London Liberal Association.[95]

With the passage of the Criminal Law Amendment Act in 1871 disaffection with the government increased. The recently formed parliamentary committee of the TUC published division lists pinpointing those Liberals who voted for the harsh amendments to the measure, emanating from the House of Lords.[96] A few months later, the Labour Representation League was publishing lists of those who voted against a clause in the Ballot Bill which would have allowed election expenses to be transferred to the rates:

Gather yourselves in every constituency. Disregard meaningless party cries, and, as a first necessary step for the vindication of our claims, punish by exclusion from Parliament the men who by their political treachery, cowardice and vulgar worship of wealth have decreed that, you shall not cease to have branded on you the degrading stigma of political inferiority.[97]

Of course, discontent with the government was not confined to the trade unionists. Many middle-class radicals saw the high hopes they had from reform fading to nothing. The important nonconformist element was bitterly alienated by the Education Act of 1870 and could unite with working men in protesting at the actions of the Liberal government. The object of the protest was the same, but there was an essential difference. Almost all the main working-class leaders at this time saw their quarrel with the Liberal government in class terms. The middle-class radicals might protest that the Liberal government was betraying its principles, but, in practice, it was the working class who suffered from legislation by a parliament in which they were not represented. Many felt that 'class legislation' required a class response, but they also wanted to keep it a response within the spectrum of Liberalism. As Professor Hanham has said, 'the strength of the Liberal position was that Liberalism was something much wider than the Liberal party'[98] and there was little quarrel with the beliefs of Liberalism. While condemning the actions of the government, therefore, these same unionists were working with the radicals in the numerous leagues and associations that were at the heart of Liberalism outside parliament. Nonetheless, a revolt within the bounds of Liberalism left considerable room for manoeuvre.

Membership of the Labour Representation League was on an individual basis and there was no corporate trade-union involvement in these efforts to elect working men candidates. The London Trades Council, re-formed in 1872 after three years during which it had more or less ceased to function, took no official part in politics. The *Bookbinders' Trade Circular* had early warned it to tread warily:

. . . it will only be useful for good while it takes into consideration questions that immediately concern trade unionists as trade unionists. There are many questions that belong to them, and that it is quite right for them to discuss as citizens; but as trade societies, as there are men of all creeds, both political and religious, those questions only should be considered where members meet on a common platform.[99]

The Council heeded the advice and took no part in metropolitan politics.

The implementation of the Criminal Law Amendment Act and the continuing use of the law of conspiracy against unionists was an issue on which they could act. The five London gas stokers, recently released from Maidstone prison, had pride of place in the trades' demonstration which the Council organised on Whit-Monday 1873 and the trade-union delegates from all over England attended. The resolution passed at the demonstration contained no suggestion of the need for independent action by unionists. It did little more than condemn the Act and the injustice of the sentences under it. At the main platform, chaired by Odger, no mention was made of political action, though at other platforms a number of speakers took the line that 'every voter present should refuse his support at the next general election to the candidate who was in favour of a continuance of those obnoxious laws'.[100] In contrast, at the many other demonstrations against the Act in other parts of the country an altogether more forceful attitude was adopted: a West of Scotland trades' demonstration in November 1873, for example, resolved that only those candidates who favoured repeal would be supported in a general election.[101] Behind the scenes, the parliamentary committee of the TUC was lobbying members of parliament and the agitation against the Acts brought the trade unionists to an unprecedented awareness of their political power.

Although the Labour Representation League was intended as a national organisation – the successor to the Reform League – it achieved little success outside London. Perhaps, its very association with the Reform League made provincial unionists suspicious of it. The Birmingham unionists, for example, felt that to associate with the Labour Representation League would restrict their liberty of action.[102] But the sentiments being expressed by the London unionists were more than echoed in the provinces.

The Scottish unionists, in their first national conference in February 1870, demanded that 'the interests and rights of labour be represented both in municipal and imperial parliaments'.[103] In Birmingham the Trades Council decided that the 'obnoxious and unnecessary measures' would only be removed by the 'return of Members of Parliament who have a practical knowledge of the wants and intentions of working men, and the difficulties under which they labour, and especially trade unionists'.[104] They nominated a former president of the Council, William Gilliver, a cordwainer, as their candidate. Gilliver had been a vice-president of the Liberal Association, but at his adoption meeting, he 'disclaimed having anything to do with the Liberal Association . . . and if sent to Parliament to support Mr Gladstone, he would not do it, and he would follow no particular man or leader'.[105] Another member of the Council argued that since 'they had seen both parties fail . . . it now became their duty to start a party of their own'.[106] A Parliamentary Fund Committee was established to raise money for the election and for £300 per annum should the candidate be returned.[107]

Not all the Birmingham unions approved the Council's activities: the Brassworkers' Society and the Flint Glassmakers both ignored the advice of their leading members, and rejected a political role for their trade unions.[108] The Typographical Society complained that the Council was 'far exceeding its duty in introducing party politics'.[109] There was a great deal of pressure on the Council to withdraw its candidate, especially since a Conservative had decided to stand, and, at the last moment, Gilliver withdrew. As soon as he did so the Conservative candidate followed. This gave rise to speculation that Gilliver had been 'bought out' by the Liberals,[110] but there would seem to be little evidence for such an accusation. Clearly a great deal of pressure had been brought to bear on him personally, and on his committee, by the Liberal Association and by some of his fellow unionists. They found former middle-class sympathisers turning against them and the future of the trades council seemed threatened. Also Gilliver and most of his committee were Liberals. They were very discontented with much that the Liberal Party was doing or failing to do, but they viewed with alarm the prospect that their efforts would result in the return of a Conservative for a Birmingham seat. In other words, their protest against the Liberal Party's present policies was a protest within the limits of Liberalism. There would also seem to have been a half-promise by the Liberal Association, to put up a working-man candidate at the next election. A further reason was the perennial one of lack of funds, which became acute when the Brassworkers and the Glassmakers withdrew their support. Paradoxically, it was the secretary of the Amalgamated Brassworkers' Society, W. J. Davis, who, at the end of 1874, formed a Labour Association in Birmingham. The Association had a fluctuating existence for some years.[111] It supported Davis's campaign as an Independent Working Men's Candidate for the school board in 1875 and for the town council in 1880. Davis consistently refused to throw in his lot with the Liberal Association. He told Joseph Chamberlain, 'a Labour party must and would exist'.[112]

Unionists in other towns, before the election of 1874, expressed their dissatisfaction with the Liberal Party. The Bradford Trades Council nominated the President of the Bradford Stonemasons' Society James Hardaker, 'the leading representative of the working-class radicals in Bradford'.[113] He had the support of some of the nonconformist middle-class who were attempting to oust their *bête-noire* W. E. Forster, but he was decisively defeated. North of the border, in Glasgow, a group of unionists in the trades council was pressing for some action to bring about the election of a working man to Parliament. As always, the cautious argued that the time was not ripe for such a move, while religious differences created difficulties.[114] A committee was in fact formed to sound out the amount of support a labour candidate could expect, but their 'plebiscite' was overtaken by the snap election of January 1874. In Edinburgh the trade unionists, in their opposition to the Criminal Law Amendment Act, came up against Duncan McLaren, doyen of the Edinburgh radicals. He was outspokenly hostile to repeal of the Act and efforts were made by trade unionists to find an alternative radical candidate.[115] In the event they were unsuccessful and McLaren had no difficulty in being returned at the head of the poll. In Bolton, there was a report in 1871 of some moves by Bolton trade unionists to get a working man into Parliament,[116] but in 1873 the Trades Council decided that it was 'inexpedient in the present state of the political parties in Bolton to start a candidate in the Labour Representation interest'. For the election of 1874, however, it did resolve that unionists should 'vote for no candidate who does not promise at least to vote for the repeal of the Criminal Law Amendment Act, 1871, the Conspiracy Law and the Master and Servant Act'.[117] In Bristol the unions elicited a pledge from both the Liberal and Conservative candidates that they would support repeal and the pattern was repeated elsewhere.

At the general election of January 1874 fourteen Labour candidates went to the poll.[118] Two were elected: Alexander McDonald for Stafford and Thomas Burt for Morpeth. The miners were particularly active in this election,[119] because in some areas they had had to fight strenuously since 1868 to have their right to the franchise recognised, since their rents were usually deducted from their wages.[120] Besides Burt and McDonald, William Pickard of the Lancashire miners contested Wigan and Thomas Halliday stood at Merthyr Tydvil. In both cases they were opposed by Liberals.

When the election of 1874 was over, the Labour Representation League issued an address. After congratulating itself on the success of two working-class candidates, it continued:

The Labour candidates to a man were men of Liberal principles, who would have given an intelligent support to a really Liberal

Government; and yet the managers of the Liberal party, in nearly every constituency where they appeared, regarded them with suspicion, and treated them in an unfriendly spirit. Where a love of spirit and loyalty to a party should have operated, class jealousy prevailed. . . . The working men must, therefore, take their stand at once, and inform the middle-class managers of electioneering contests that their claims, both as to their men and their questions must be acknowledged. They must insist on being consulted as to who shall be brought forward, and the candidates of their own class must have as full recognition as those of any other class in the community. . . . If these conditions are frankly accepted, the working men should unite cordially with the Liberal men of their classes; but if the spirit that prevailed in the recent election is prevailed in, then the working men must fight their own battle in their own way, at whatever cost to a party which, whilst calling itself Liberal, makes prejudice and exclusion leading characteristics of its policy.[121]

The Address exemplifies the confusion of mind, the lack of direction, the frustration that are the hallmarks of the labour movement in politics in the 1870s. When the post-mortem on the 1868 election had been held there was considerable surprise at how little had been achieved by the working class. To remedy this there was talk in many parts of the country about bringing forward working-men candidates. It seemed only right that working men should join the other classes in the House of Commons. This seemed all the more necessary in view of the 'class legislation' from which the unions were suffering. But to bring forward a candidate required money and organisation, neither of which existed. A trades council was the obvious centre for such an organisation, just as it was the centre for the agitation, by petition and demonstration, against the labour laws. But, when a trades council did attempt to become the centre of a political organisation it was likely to face the wrath of many trade societies who continued to regard their function as an a-political one. It faced, also, the apathy of the majority of unionists and the issue was likely to be further complicated by differing and even opposing views of its political activists.

Many trade-union leaders were members of their local Liberal Association, or at least had associated with Liberal radicals in various campaigns. They could hardly conceive of working outside the ranks of the Liberal party. Yet, as the above address shows, when frustration with the Liberals was great, independent action was not ruled out. It was possible for the most cautious of unionists to envisage working men fighting 'their own battle in their own way'. That in almost all cases they failed to take the final step of bringing out candidates in opposition to the Liberals reveals not any betrayal or 'sell-out', but the size of the step involved. Their middle-class advisers gave little help in the matter. E. S. Beesly had pressed for a third party in 1869 and he and his colleagues urged the need for this up until August 1873. After that all was confusion. When Joseph Chamberlain announced his new radical programme, Frederic Harrison was enthusiastic[122] and a week before the election he was advising working men to vote Liberal.[123] 'The truth of the matter', writes Royden Harrison, 'was that the Positivists wavered between a conception of a third party organised *de novo* in the country and a reconstruction of the Liberal Party on the basis of Chamberlain's programme.'[124] With such advisers, the surprising thing is the extent to which trade unionists did take independent action in 1874.

It was in the general election of 1874 that there emerged 'the Conservative working man', that figure whom both the Liberals and the trade-union leaders had claimed to be mythical. In this first general election under the Ballot Act the voting behaviour of working men is not easy to discern, but contemporary observers were clear that substantial numbers of working-class votes had gone to those Conservative candidates who had committed themselves to repeal of the Criminal Law Amendment Act.[125] One such, R. A. Cross, became Home Secretary and was responsible for bringing in the required amendments to the legislation. Yet any gratitude for the labour legislation of 1875–6 was short-lived. With the Conservatives in power it was difficult for trade unionists to oppose the Government independently of the general Liberal opposition. Few wanted to. The crushing defeats imposed upon Liberals of all colours in the election of 1874 had come as a surprise to the radicals and unionists who had agitated against Liberal government policy in the years before the election. After 1874 there was a distinct closing of ranks within the Liberal party outside Westminster. Once the labour legislation was safely out of the way, trade unionists rallied to the ringing moral pronouncements of Gladstone against the wicked Turk and against the imperialist ambitions of the Prime Minister. The Labour Representation League was in the vanguard of the agitation and was once again advocating a policy of close collaboration with radicalism.

The demand for representation of labour was not given up entirely, however, and when Southwark Radical Club decided to bring forward George Shipton, Odger's successor as secretary of the London Trades Council, as a candidate, it received the approval of the Trades Council.[126] In Birmingham W. J. Davis of the Amalgamated Brassworkers was elected to the Corporation in 1879 as the candidate of the local Labour Association. By 1879, although independent of the Liberal Association, the Labour Association was in fact working in close co-operation with the Liberals and Davis eventually became a member of the Council of the National Liberal Federation.[127] In Manchester Slatter of the Typographical Association was elected to the School Board in 1879, but without official trade-union support. A suggestion by James Ashton of the Warpers' Society in Manchester that trade unionists had 'trailed too long at the coat tails of political parties' met with little response during the election of 1880.[128] In Scotland most unionists seem to have been quite content with their radical members and took no part in municipal politics. Only in Aberdeen was some discontent with the Liberal Association being expressed at the end of the 1870s. The Trades Council there disapproved of the manner in which the Liberal Association manipulated matters in the interests of 'an enemy of the working class',[129] and gave the warning that 'the Council had always striven in matters of this kind to act in harmony with the Liberal Association but that conduct of this kind by some of its most prominent members would be a lesson in the future'.[130] It was, however, a sign of the prevailing attitude that only six working-class candidates stood in the general election of 1880 and Broadhurst joined McDonald and Burt in the Commons, as the Liberal member for Stoke-on-Trent.

Chapter 6

Politicians and Pressure Groups

By involving themselves in political activities trade unionists came into contact with a large number of politicians, whose approval of trade-union activity in the political field helped to create a more general acceptance of trade unionism. The working classes had always had champions among the politicians, and a handful of members of parliament, like T. S. Duncombe, Joseph Hume, Col. Perronet Thompson and others, had spoken out in support of chartist demands. Outside parliament there were those who believed in the political necessity of an alliance between the middle class and the working class if power were to be wrested from the hands of the landed classes. In the early 1830s Thomas Attwood had managed to create an alliance of middle-class reformers and artisans in the Birmingham Political Union and it was in Birmingham that Joseph Sturge led the Complete Suffrage Movement of 1842, which sought to re-create the work of Attwood and to guide the workers away from the class aspirations of chartism. The Anti-Corn Law League had consistently tried to attract working-class support and within a month of the Kennington Common demonstration free traders like Cobden and George Wilson were arguing that the work begun by the League should be carried on through 'a union of the middle and working classes for the purpose of obtaining an extension of the suffrage, vote by ballot, equal electoral districts and a reduction of taxation'.[1] It was this tradition on which political radicals in the 1850s, 1860s and 1870s were building.

It was not an easy task to create an alliance of the middle and working classes in the mid-nineteenth century because there were deep suspicions on both sides. It had succeeded in Birmingham because the artisans in a town of small workshops 'served as the critical connecting link in a gently graded class structure to which the classic dichotomy between bourgeoisie and proletariat was unknown'.[2] But elsewhere class divisions were wider and sharper, with a middle class seeing among the workers a class consciousness which produced attitudes that were a threat both to property and to the individualist ethic, and with the working class seeing in the ranks of the radicals the same men who were destroying traditional work methods through industrialisation and who were resisting the attempts to bring improvements in working conditions by means of the Factory Acts.

There was a number of causes which brought different middle-class radicals and working-class leaders together, but one thing they all had in common was the belief that there was within the working class an elite who accepted the values of mid-Victorian society and who could, therefore, be used as allies in political struggles, without stirring up a dangerous class agitation which might threaten these very values. It was the Christian Socialists and later the Positivists who first put across the idea that this elite lay in the trade unions and it was they who formed the first links between trade unions and radicals: it was their publicity which propagated the view that the trade unions were in essence moderate, cautious and reasonable organisations that fitted in well with the radical idea of progress. Trade unions could, in fact, become the means of leading the working class as a whole to an acceptance of the dominating values of society. Like the Christian Socialists and the Positivists the radicals were trying to make of trade unionism something which it was not: to mould it into a preconceived pattern. They never entirely succeeded in doing this, but by associating with trade unionists they gave to trade unionism the nod of approval.

The socially-divisive decades of the 1830s and 1840s were too near for the attempts at alliance building between classes to have much success in the early fifties. The Parliamentary and Financial Reform Association organised in 1849 for this purpose was defunct by 1853, but, at the end of the 1850s and during the 1860s, new issues arose which brought working-class leaders and middle-class radicals on to the same platforms – Italy, America, Poland and, of course, reform. At the end of the sixties and in the seventies the links were being tightened by such issues as disestablishment, education and Turkish atrocities. Many of the radicals who associated with union leaders on these issues were really fundamentally opposed to most industrial activities of unions, but expediency made them seek the assistance of trade-union leaders in their desire to attract the support of the working-class elite.

I

A key figure in linking the working class and the middle class was John Bright.[3] A cotton master from Rochdale, spokesman of the Manchester School, Bright was always and remained strongly opposed to trade unionism. Their protective methods, their coercive nature, their antagonism towards employers went against everything the free society, in which he ardently believed, stood for. But necessity made them his allies. Bright's desire was to carry on the task that the Anti-Corn Law League had begun – the war against privilege (usually spelt with a capital P), which to Bright was the war against the continuing aristocratic dominance in the institutions of British politics. He was unrelenting in his hostility to the aristocracy and was willing to use whatever allies were necessary to pursue his cause. In curbing aristocratic power, he believed that the middle and working classes had a common goal. Directly opposed to this was the *ouvrièrisme* of chartism and from the 1840s Bright had been concerned to rebuild those bridges between middle- and working-class reformers which chartism had destroyed. The Parliamentary and Financial Reform Association with which he and Richard Cobden were associated made little progress and his persistent opposition to improvements in factory legislation confirmed working-class suspicion of him. The advent of the Crimean War, and Bright's unbending hostility to it, isolated him from both the middle and working classes and the election of 1857 drove him from Manchester into the political desert. In Birmingham, the oasis to which he turned, there were solid inter-class links which had been only a mirage in Lancashire, and it was from this new base that Bright launched his national campaign for parliamentary reform in 1858, 'a democratic crusade against the privileged orders'.[4]

It was not, however, democracy in any modern sense that Bright sought. In Birmingham, the artisans and craftsmen worked in harmony with the middle class, and it was to those, therefore, that Bright looked for support. His reform demands were limited. At the most, he wanted household suffrage and in 1866 he was quite willing to accept Gladstone's £7 borough franchise.[5] He had no desire to see the middle class overwhelmed by a working-class electorate that included not just the artisans but the 'residuum': there was a very distinct limit on admittance.[6] Like the committee of the Social Science Association, Bright found the elite of the working class in the trade-union leadership, as it was they who responded to his speeches and tried to link working-class demands to those of the middle-class reform committees. Inevitably, therefore, he had to turn to the trade unions. When the Glasgow Trades Council issued its political *Address* in 1861, Bright responded with enthusiasm:

> You have an organisation, more or less complete everywhere. Cannot this organisation for a single year, be made the instrument of your political deliverance? Is good or bad Government of no consequence to the millions who toil? I know how opinion has grown and accident and combination only are wanting to make it an omnipotent force on this question. Accident rarely fails a good cause, and combination is a weapon that may become invincible in your hands.[7]

This 'coquetting with Trade Societies' much shocked some of his associates,[8] but events pushed Bright and the union leaders closer together. His support for Lincoln and the Northern States in the American Civil War met with their approval and put him in touch with Odger, Howell and other London leaders. He chaired the St James's Hall meeting of March 1863 and his stirring defence of freedom was greeted with rapturous applause by the assembled unionists.

The common ground which they found on the issue of the Civil War more than anything helped to build the bridge that Bright so long had sought between himself and the working-class elite. Bright's stand against slavery dissolved, at any rate some of, the intense suspicion that many unionists had of him; the unionists' stand on the issue made an important contribution to the acceptance by the middle class of the point that had frequently been made by Hughes, Ludlow, Harrison and others, namely that the working class was no longer a danger to the constitution. For it was Bright and his supporters who perpetrated the myth that during the Civil War the workers of Lancashire had accepted the deprivation of the cotton famine with equanimity, rather than endanger the cause of freedom in the United States. The working class, too, put freedom above all. It was a fact that was referred to time and again by the supporters of reform as evidence of the political maturity of the working class. Yet there seems little doubt that it was to a large extent fictitious. As recent work has shown, there was much agitation in Lancashire against the Government's neutrality and in favour of its intervention in the war, preferably as a mediator, but not stopping short of support for the recognition of the independence of the South.[9] But the myth was more powerful than the reality and the belief that the working class had shown Liberal instincts towards the civil war was an important stimulus to reform.

Bright's relations with the Reform League in 1866 and 1867 were never easy. Its demand for manhood suffrage went further than Bright was willing to go, though he never lost touch with them. He sought, and to some extent achieved, a 'combined and friendly movement'[10] and the League leaders showed him a great deal of deference. He frequently appeared on League platforms and the League followed his lead in accepting – if reluctantly – Gladstone's bill of 1866.

Not all unionists were as deferential to Bright as Howell, Odger and the London leaders. His record was far from good. T. J. Dunning pointed to the doubts that many working men felt at the sight of advanced Liberals supporting the political aspirations of the working class while actively opposing measures of social amelioration.[11] Bright fell into this category. Alexander McDonald wrote in 1865 that the working classes had 'little sympathy with that class of Reformers who would as yet have had the factory children working all but interminable hours in the factories, who would still have the young engaged in bleaching and dye works, all but chained to the stoves, and who are at present totally indifferent to the long hours that the young are engaged in the mines of this country'.[12] Two years later, with the reform campaign at its height, he was still making the same point, specifically citing Bright as an example, and wondering why 'that gentleman . . . was tolerated as the leader of the Reformers of the country'.[13]

Bright himself never changed his views on the pernicious nature of unionism in industry. In the 1870s he attacked unions in more than one speech and George Howell believed that Bright was the major obstacle within the Liberal cabinet to repealing the Criminal Law Amendment Act after 1871.[14] Unions reflected – or perhaps exacerbated – a war between capital and labour and this Bright abhorred. Political reform, he believed, would break down the division between capital and labour and make trade unions unnecessary.[15] While courting the union leaders in the 1860s, he prosecuted some of his own workers for picketing.[16] But, just as in the 1840s, Bright feared a situation in which the working class was isolated, 'condemned to remain a separate and suspected order',[17] and to prevent it he was prepared to work with the union leaders.

Other radicals, too, swallowed their dislike of unionism and sought the unionists as allies in their campaign against the aristocratic establishment. Among the most important of these were the Nonconformists, who were campaigning for the disestablishment and partial disendowment of the Church of England. Edward Miall, editor of the *Nonconformist* had, as early as 1841, urged 'The reconciliation between the Middle and Labouring Classes' in a series of articles that were the inspiration of Sturge's Complete Suffrage Movement,[18] and he had used his paper to advocate manhood suffrage as a means of breaking the class consciousness of the working class, which exclusion from the franchise produced.[19] With the formation of the Liberation Society in 1853 the Nonconformists, acting as a powerful and vocal pressure group within the Liberal Party, brought disestablishment to the forefront of politics. The Liberation Society attracted to it a group of wealthy manufacturers from the industrial towns: Samuel Morley in hosiery; Robert and Samuel Kell in worsted; Titus Salt in alpaca; Peter Rylands in iron and Peter Taylor in silk.[20] As employers they had no great affection for trade unions. S. C. Kell looked on 'the sad spectacle of ignorance, folly and selfishness' which he saw in the annals of unionism.[21] But the elite of the working class was necessary to them in the struggle against the established church and the elite could be guided to an understanding of 'political and politico-economical science' and were too 'intelligent' to wish to destroy property.[22] Just as in industrial relations these same employers were coming to see unions as a brake on the more violent class attitudes of their workers, so in politics, they could be the means of leading the working class to an acceptance of the values of a reformed society. At first there was some attempt to by-pass the unions and to make contact with the respectable working class through mechanics institutes, temperance societies and all the paraphernalia of 'self-help', but by the mid-sixties there was a realisation that real links could only be created through the trade-union leaders who were involved in the parliamentary reform movement. Links were forged with the national leaders in London and there was some judicious subsidising of the working-class press. The Kells gave financial assistance to the *Miner and Workman's Advocate*, much to the disgust of one of the paper's directors, Karl Marx.[23] As the general election of 1868 approached financial help came to the *Bee-Hive* (which at times seemed to be threatening a dangerously independent line), from Morley, Salt, M. T. Bass, Charles Reed (M.P. for

Hackney and son-in-law of Edward Baines) and Daniel Pratt, the Nonconformist publisher, who obtained a controlling interest in the *Bee-Hive* between 1868 and 1873.[24] Morley was the most lavish in his contributions and, during the autumn of 1868, gave at least £1,900 to the Reform League, 'specifically to win a number of seats from the Tories'.[25] James Stansfield, the radical member for Halifax arranged for further financial help from Morley, Salt and others to establish the Adelphi Club in the premises of the Reform League, where middle-class reformers and working-class leaders could meet 'to bridge over the gulph [*sic*] that now exists between different classes'.[26]

Stansfield was one of a number of radicals who had made contact with working-class leaders in the 1850s through their support of the cause of Italian freedom. With Joseph Cowen[27] in Newcastle and P. A. Taylor in Lancashire he was a devoted friend and admirer of Mazzini and he had helped rouse working-class support for the Italian cause. In the early 1860s, he had communications with the London Trades Council through George Howell and had pressed the Council to take up political issues. His association with the London leaders was strengthened in the sixties by Garibaldi's visit in 1864, of which Stansfield was one of the organisers and, as with so many other radicals, by his support of Lincoln's cause and of Polish independence. Stansfield attended the London Trades Council meeting of April 1863 to meet the French unionists who had joined the Polish demonstration. He was an important link between the trade unionists and the inner circle of the Liberal party, acting as a liaison between Howell and the Chief Whip during 1868, arranging financial support for the League and generally ensuring that its policy remained firmly in line with that of the Liberal Party.[28]

W. E. Forster was another influential figure within the inner ranks of the Liberal Party who courted the trade-union leaders. His concern with working-class problems pre-dated his election in 1861 as member of parliament for Bradford. He had been influenced by Maurice and the Christian Socialists and in his turn, had helped to make Ludlow aware of the importance of trade unionism.[29] He widened his contacts with unionists in the 1860s, both in the reform campaign and in his outspoken championship of Lincoln. Forster was always quite explicit about his aims in courting the working-class leaders: he was concerned only with the elite and sought no more than household suffrage. As he told the Leeds' reformers in 1861, 'he doubted whether in England they would ever be able to go further than that'.[30] He expanded his argument in the Commons in 1865: 'If they are excluded as a class, they will agitate as a class and demand admission as a class. Assuredly the wise plan would be to admit the élite among them, the leaders of their movements.'[31]

In the Italian, Polish and American causes, in the disestablishment movement and in the parliamentary reform campaign there was overlapping membership. In London and in all the other main towns the same radicals were meeting the same politically active working-class leaders. Within the fairly narrow economic creed of most of the radicals, trade unions had no place, but within their political spectrum the leaders of the unions were essential as leaders of the working-class elite whose help was sought in the struggles for radical causes.

The American War and the reform movement also brought the union leaders in London into contact with intellectual radicals, like John Stuart Mill and Goldwin Smith,[32] who believed in the value of democracy. Mill's relations with working-class radicals went back to the 1820s but it was in the 1860s that he turned to the active participation in politics which associated him with the London unionists. He was a member of the Emancipation Society in 1863, and in 1865 at his election for Westminster he had the active support of Odger and other union leaders. He returned this with financial and literary support for working-class candidates in the 1868 election. Mill believed that a political transformation to democracy was a prerequisite of the intellectual transformation which he felt it necessary for Victorian England to undergo if it were to move towards the more perfect society of his ideal. The American Civil War was important in the development of his thought in causing him to have doubts about the liberal protestations of the upper classes[33] and he looked to an educated working class to help build a more rational and liberal society. As the nation's best-known philosopher and as the author of *The Principles of Political Economy*, whose precepts were so often flung against trade unionism, his association with the leaders of the unions in the reform campaign was invaluable in their struggle for acceptance. He acted as an important restraining influence on the Reform League during 1866, when it seemed bent on a further confrontation with the government on the question of admission to Hyde Park. While censuring the government for its actions, he persuaded the working-class members of the League to desist from a policy of confrontation unless what they were after was revolution and unless 'they thought themselves able to accomplish one'.[34] Mill's relations with the leaders of London unionism may well have influenced his thinking on political economy and made him more amenable to accepting the criticism of his chapters on wages as made by W. T. Thornton in 1866 and 1867. Mill announced his rejection of the wage-fund theory in 1867, but, perhaps significantly, he never altered subsequent editions of his *Principles*.

By 1867 trade unions were at the forefront of the debate on political reform. They were discussed at some length in the collection of *Essays on Reform*, which a group of intellectual liberals produced in 1867. The arguments were the familiar ones. G. C. Broderick suggested that the Constitution could be strengthened 'by subtracting a portion of the besieging force and adding it to the garrison': 'As we cannot expel from our population those elements which form the strength of Trade Unions it may well be less dangerous to incorporate them in our representative system than to leave them outside it.'[35] R. H. Hutton returned to the Christian Socialists' arguments of the value of voluntary association. Trade unions indicated 'a sense of the value of organisation', 'a distrust of mere scattered individual energies' and 'an appreciation of the value of true government'.[36] Even that essentially conservative figure, Leslie Stephen, believed, that despite their 'tyrannical practices', the 'power of organisation among working men' made it essential that they be incorporated in the constitution.[37]

Perhaps the most important contribution of all made by trade unions in the debate on reform was to the conversion of Gladstone to the view that 'every man who is not presumably incapacitated by some consideration of personal unfitness or of political danger is normally entitled to come within the pale of the Constitution'.[38] It was one of the most significant factors in stimulating the reform campaign. He had come to this position from a conviction 'that the fixed traditional sentiment of the working man has begun to be confidence in the law, in Parliament, and even in the executive Government'.[38] This conviction had been brought home to him as a result of his contact with deputations of trade-union leaders. In March 1864 George Potter organised a meeting of trade societies in opposition to Gladstone's Government Annuities Bill, which he regarded as a threat to friendly societies.[40] The meeting roused Gladstone to attack trade societies as bodies whose business it was 'in some way to coerce often minorities, but sometimes even majorities, through the medium of an artfully constructed system, which, pretending to consult the individual will of the members, in fact deprives them of all free agency'.[41] It was 'to disabuse the mind of the Chancellor of the Exchequer' of its belief that there was real opposition to his Bill from the trade societies and to explain to him that Potter was not 'the far-famed secretary of the trades unions', as he had described him, that Odger, Applegarth and Coulson went as a deputation from the London Trades Council to Gladstone. During the deputation they raised the question of the suffrage.[42] Two months later a further deputation from the A.S.E. asked that the rules of post-office savings banks be amended to allow trade societies to deposit their funds there. The following day Gladstone cited this request as a 'very small but yet significant indication, among thousands of others, of the altered temper' of the working class.[43] Such sentiments as they had expressed made them 'worthy and fit to discharge the duties of citizenship'. It was from 1864 that the cult of the 'Grand Old Man' began to appear. In the working-class mind he always remained distinct from his party and the adulation which large sections of the working class came to feel for him was to prove a major barrier to those who wished to lead the working class away from their attachment to the Liberal party. Yet, it is doubtful if he ever had anything but the deepest suspicion of some of the activities of trade unions.

It was not just at the level of national politics that the movements of the 1860s brought trade unionists into contact with middle-class radicals. In almost all the major towns the leaders of the working class were mixing with radical members of the Liberal party. At pro-Italy meetings, at pro-Lincoln meetings and most particularly at reform meetings, trade unionists were sharing platforms with the middle class. In many cases these were employers and such contacts no doubt had their effect on industrial relations. John Kane, for example, recalled frequently standing on the same platform at reform meetings with his employer in Gateshead, Crawshay, one of the great dynasty of ironmasters and they 'often conferred together on social and political questions'.[44] Suspicions must have remained, but both sides were keeping these in check in the interests of political unity.

Trade unions were also dragged into the other side of the argument and opponents of parliamentary reform used the example of unionism as evidence that the working class was not ready for the franchise. Robert Lowe, profoundly hostile to democracy as a result of his experiences in Australia, the United States and at the hustings in Kidderminster,[45] opposed giving the franchise to the working class precisely because they had trade unions. The unions and their leaders would awaken the working class to 'a full sense of their power' and they would dominate parliament.[46] Just as trade unions were hostile to 'superiority', 'skill', 'industry' and 'capacity', so they would be used against the independence of members of parliament. Lowe was totally unimpressed by the case made by Applegarth and his allies that trade societies like the Amalgamated Carpenters had to be clearly distinguished from the archaic unions of Sheffield and Manchester who engaged in 'rattening' and outrages. Lowe opposed trade unionism for the same reason as he opposed democracy: it sacrificed intelligence to mere numbers. The object of government was good government and rule by the majority was unlikely to provide this. Trade unionism was based on the 'false and dangerous' principle that the minority had to be coerced for the good of the majority. Lowe was, as he understood it, a Liberal, and trade unions were opposed to what was the essence of his Liberalism, *laissez-faire*. They created a 'monopoly of labour', based on 'a gigantic miscalculation' that they were doing something that the laws of supply and demand were not already doing.[47] To Lowe, the existence of trade unions was not proof that the working class was ready for self-government, it was proof rather that workers acted from class motives and still rejected the accepted values of the age. If progress was towards a freer society, where everything took second place to the rights of the individual, then unionism was the antithesis of it.

Other opponents of reform followed Lowe's one. The Conservative, Viscount Cranbourne, chided Gladstone for allowing himself to be influenced by his 'friend', Odger.[48] General Peel believed that the working man in the boroughs could not be trusted 'because he was always engaged in strikes' that would 'send our capital and business to foreign countries'.[49] The argument of Gladstone and the reformers, that the working class would not vote as a class, but would be as diverse in its political views as any other class, was rejected by Lord Robert Montague: 'the existence of trades unions was a sufficient proof of the fact'.[50] But, within the ranks of the Conservative Party also, there were those who regarded it as imperative that the working class should cease to be excluded and should have 'exponents of their views in the councils of the nation'.[51]

In the end Disraeli's reform measure went further than the

radicals had sought. He rejected the idea of admitting only 'a certain and favoured portion of the working classes' who would act as a 'Praetorial guard' to keep the rest of the working class out. This to Disraeli was a highly dangerous policy and only by admitting 'the great body of those men who occupy houses and fulfil the duties of citizenship by the payment of rates' was there a chance of 'touching the popular heart' and 'of evoking the national sentiment'.

The policy of the radical wing of the Liberal Party paid dividends in 1868, when, with the active help of the Reform League leadership, the Liberals were returned with a majority of 112 seats. But Gladstone's government contained few radicals and disillusionment with the Liberal Government followed closely on the election. Once parliamentary reform had been achieved there proved to be no radical programme, instead there was a plethora of ideas and reform and the efforts of the radicals were dissipated in a multitude of groups. As Joseph Chamberlain complained to John Morley, the editor of the influential *Fortnightly Review*, 'There are Leagues and Associations and Unions but no party.'[52] In the National Education League, the Liberation Society, the Land Tenure Reform Association, the Temperance Alliance, the Peace Society the anti-Contagious Diseases Acts Association and in many other such groupings, radicals sought to influence government policy. It was in these bodies that the politically active trade-union leaders maintained and extended their contacts with middle-class radicalism in the years after 1868.

From its formation in 1869 the National Education League was one of the most influential of these pressure groups. Run from Birmingham, it was in this that Odger, Howell, Applegarth, Daniel Guile and other unionists came into contact with the up-and-coming Birmingham radicals, George Dixon, Joseph Chamberlain and Jesse Collings.[53] It campaigned for a national system of free, compulsory, non-denominational education. When in 1870, Forster's Education Act shattered the hopes of the League by maintaining, and indeed strengthening, the denominational schools, it embarked on a campaign of great bitterness against the Act and against Forster personally, and it did not stop short of splitting the Liberal vote in by-elections. Applegarth was one of the most active of its working-class members and on his resignation as secretary of the Amalgamated Carpenters he acted for a time as secretary to Edward Jenkins, one of the League politicians. George Howell, in 1870 lectured all over the North of England on

the League's policy. In the first school-board elections under
Forster's Act a number of unionists stood as League candidates.
In London Potter was elected and in Aberdeen, Glasgow and
Edinburgh the trades councils co-operated with the Scottish
section of the League to present a list of candidates.[54]

John Stuart Mill retained his links with unionists through the
Land Tenure Reform Association, which called for the abolition of
primogeniture and the end to restrictions on free transfer of
property. Howell and Applegarth were both members, though
they failed to bring in the more militant workers of the Land and
Labour League, who were demanding nationalisation of land.[55]
One of the members of the executive of the Land Tenure Reform
Association was Charles Dilke, the newly-elected member for
Chelsea, already with a reputation for extreme radicalism, and
destined to be right into the twentieth century, one of the firmest
friends of trade unionism in the House of Commons.[56] At the
beginning of the 1870s Dilke's republican protestations found little
sympathy with the more moderate union leaders, but through
George Odger, one of his most outspoken supporters, Dilke was
introduced to the trade-union world.

The Liberation Society set out to strengthen its appeal to the
working class with the formation, in 1871, of the Working Men's
committee for Promoting the Separation of Church and State.
That ubiquitous pair Howell and Potter acted as chairman and
secretary and it included Applegarth and Guile among its members. Working-class committees were formed in a number of
towns and meetings were held attacking the Anglican clergy as
opponents of social reform.[57] Leading liberationists were to be
found in the Society for Promoting Universal Peace and here too
there were links with the working class. Many trades councils
petitioned Parliament in favour of regular motions proposed by
Henry Richard, secretary of the Peace Society, in favour of a
system of international arbitration.[58] In 1870 Randal Cremer
formed the Workmen's National Peace Association with a group
of former associates from the Reform League.[59] Numerous
conferences were held: for instance one in Glasgow in 1873 which
delegates attended from the Trades Councils of Edinburgh,
Glasgow, Dundee and Greenock, together with some from
individual trade unions.[60] As a result a Scottish department of the
Workmen's Peace Association was formed to agitate in support
of Richard's motion and to make the issue a test question for
parliamentary candidates. A number of unionists attended the

'Peace Conference' in Paris in 1875, among them Cremer, Arch and a delegate from the Glasgow Trades Council.

Though actively involved in these radical associations, the main concern of trade unionists from 1868 onwards was labour legislation: firstly, to get protection for trade-union funds; then, to secure implementation of the minority report of the Royal Commission; and thirdly, after 1871, to get the Criminal Law Amendment Act repealed. The *rationale* of the policy of 1868 had been that a Liberal government was likely to be more sympathetic to the demands of the working class on labour legislation, and that political allies among the radical middle class were likely to prove useful in working-class campaigns for social legislation. The analysis proved, between 1869 and 1871, to be largely mistaken. Neither the Liberal government, nor all the radicals proved sympathetic to trade-union demands. In 1867 and 1868 bills to give protection to union funds got nowhere, giving place to other priorities. With the reports of the Royal Commission, however, a new and more comprehensive bill, drafted by Frederic Harrison, was introduced by Thomas Hughes and A. J. Mundella. It had the support of a large number of radical members, thirty of whom joined the unionists in a deputation to the Home Secretary, H. A. Bruce.[61] In the debate on the second reading Hughes repeated most of his arguments in favour of unionism. They 'had improved the condition of the men'; they contained 'the very best workmen in the country'; their executives were 'for the most part very averse to strikes'.[62] He was seconded by Thomas Brassey, son of the great railway builder, though Brassey's speech had in it an element of 'damning with faint praise': "So far as their action had been brought to bear upon trade he regarded it, he must confess, as essentially illiberal, anti-social and not conducive to the general advantage of society.'[63] Unions could not affect the level of wages, which were bound by the law of supply and demand. Nonetheless he supported the bill, as repressive legislation merely drove the unions underground. John Platt of Oldham also supported the bill, not because he favoured unions but 'because he wished to do away with class legislation'. Mundella spoke of the spread of conciliation boards and the need for masters and workmen 'to be equally free by law to combine'.[64] Only the irreconcilable Edmund Potter openly spoke against the bill, which, like the trade unions, was 'antagonistic to free trade' and it was free trade, not unions, that had brought increased prosperity to the working class.[65] The debate was largely a formality since there was no hope of the bill's getting further that session, but it was important in pinpointing for many Liberals the stumbling block in labour legislation. Their liberalism made them accept the right of unions to combine, but it also made them believe in the importance of protecting the rights of the non-unionist and the non-striker. Brassey believed 'that legislation on the subject would be altogether incomplete unless steps were taken concurrently to extend the law respecting threats'.[66] Platt demanded 'a clause in the Bill to protect those who were not Trades Unionists and who were willing to work at lower wages or on other conditions; there must be no system of picketing or practical intimidation'.[67] Intervention by the Home Secretary promising government legislation in the following session allowed the bill to be withdrawn without the embarrassment of a division, and a temporary bill to protect trade-union funds was rushed through.[68]

Not until February 1871 was a government measure introduced. It certainly gave the unions the legal recognition that they wished but the reservations of Brassey and Platt had been heeded, and attached to the bill were criminal clauses with penalties for the notoriously imprecise crimes of 'molestation', 'obstruction', 'intimidation' and 'threat' during strikes. Pressure on the Government by the TUC persuaded Bruce to divide the measure and the criminal clauses were contained in the Criminal Law Amendment Act. The union leaders were appalled at the Liberal Government's passing such a hostile piece of 'class legislation'; they were even more appalled at the sight of erstwhile radical allies not only voting for the measure, but supporting the harsher House of Lords' amendments, against the advice of the Government. Edward Baines, Alfred Illingworth, Wilfred Lawson, Duncan McLaren, Lyon Playfair, all of whom had been actively associated with the unionists in their political activities, voted in favour of the harsher measure. Expected allies such as the Bass brothers, Thomas Brassey, Joseph Cowen, George Dixon, Auberon Herbert, Edward Miall, T. B. Potter, Henry Richard, and Bernard Samuelson were, as the Parliamentary Committee of the TUC pointed out, 'conspicuous by their absence'.[69]

It brought a massive – if temporary – disillusionment with the policy of alliance with middle-class radicalism. The Labour Representation League began to think in terms of a third party[70] and even George Howell talked of forming a working-class party 'for Whig, Tory, and Middle Class Radicals ignore our wants and requirements'.[71] How far they were willing to go emerged when the mysterious 'new social movement' was exposed in October 1871.

The new social movement was the brainchild of the architect and marine engineer, J. Scott Russell and of an obscure Bradford journalist P. Barry,[72] and it is still not altogether clear how much reality there was in the movement. The story broke at the beginning of October when the mass circulation Sunday paper, *Lloyd's Weekly Newspaper*, hinted at contacts between working men and peers 'to devise great social and domestic reforms for the good of the multitudes, and therefore for the abdication of the Tyrant Capital'. The following week more details were given of a social programme that was reputed to have been agreed upon by representatives of the working class and a number of prominent peers and politicians. The programme consisted of seven resolutions: for the building of homesteads for the working class 'where in the middle of a garden . . . in wholesome air and sunshine they may live and grow up strong, healthy and pure'; for local councils in counties, towns and villages 'with powers for the acquisition and disposal of land for the common good'; for an eight-hour working day; for an expansion of technical education; for the public provision of 'places of public recreation, knowledge and refinement'; for public markets for the sale of goods at wholesale prices; and for the extension of public ownership 'on the model of the Post Office for the common good'.[73] The story was picked up from *Lloyd's* by the *Scotsman* and the *Manchester Guardian* and soon was making headlines in the London press. Gradually details emerged of a 'Council of Skilled Workmen' consisting of most of the leading politically active unionists in London, Applegarth, Guile, Howell, Potter, Broadhurst, Lloyd Jones, and a number of others, together with Latham of the Labour Representation League, and a 'Council of Legislation', consisting of the Earl of Lichfield, the Earl of Carnarvon, the Marquis of Salisbury, the Marquis of Lorne, Lord Henry Lennox, Lord John Manners, Sir John Pakington, Sir Stafford Northcote, and Mr Gathorne Hardy.[74] The Conservative Party leaders, the Duke of Richmond, Lord Derby and Disraeli were reputed to have been privy to the negotiations and the Tory press seems at first to have seen it as another skilful manoeuvre by Disraeli to 'dish the Whigs'.[75] The Liberal press, led by the *Daily News* first treated it as a monstrous Tory plot and then tried to scoff it out of existence.

The truth of the matter remains obscure. Scott Russell had contacts with Applegarth and other working-class leaders who had

F

worked with him in advocating technical education. He had links
with some leading political figures dating back to his membership
of the Prince Consort's committee on the Great Exhibition of
1851. The mounting social discontent in France which he observed
during a visit there in the months before the outbreak of the
Franco-Prussian War had made him once again aware of social
conditions at home and he 'came to the conviction that the social
relations between the different classes of society in England are
too intolerable to last long; they must either be speedily and timely
cured or they will suddenly cure themselves'.[76] He therefore
devised his seven-point social programme. At the beginning of
1871 he approached William Allan of the A.S.E. with it, but seems
to have been met with considerable suspicion. He made more
progress, however, with Applegarth and Potter and a committee
was formed meeting from time to time in the spring of 1871.
Having got the unionists' agreement to his programme he then
turned to the politicians. Approaches to Liberals brought little
response and he came to the Conservatives. There his overtures
were greeted with some sympathy and he had a meeting with
Gathorne Hardy, Viscount Sandon, Lord John Manners, Lord
Carnarvon and other leading Conservatives. He claimed that a
group of ten had formed a 'Council of Legislation' to press the
seven points. Not until the end of September were the workmen
given the names of the politicians,[77] and with this the sensation
broke.

While the episode may have revealed a certain naïveté on the
part of the unionists, significantly they did not disavow Russell's
scheme. In some ways it was quite typical of unionists to distinguish between political and social goals. It was like the Glasgow
unionists asking Elcho to push their Master and Servant Act
reform in the midst of the parliamentary reform campaign. Those
involved did not regard the issue of the seven points as a political
one. Both Potter and Howell declared that the movement 'was
never intended to be political'.[78] But the episode also reveals the
extent of the disillusionment with radicalism that existed during
1871. Howell was quite explicit: 'I hold the doctrine to be most
disastrous that we should confer with one party, and not accept
all the aid we can get, without reference to creed or politics, for
the purpose of improving the condition of our industrial poor.'[79]
And he warned Gladstone, who had condemned those involved in
the movement as 'quacks deluded and beguiled by a spurious
philanthropy',[80] that he should keep in mind 'that those named

on our side helped carry him to power at the last general election'.[81]

The most violent working-class opposition to this scheme came from George Odger and the London Republican Clubs. Odger accused the signatories of being 'speculators in schemes';[82] others suggested that they had been well-paid for their services;[83] while the old reformer Benjamin Lucraft pointed out that it was 'not the first time Messrs Potter and Howell had coquetted with the Tory Party: he recollected their proceedings with Lord Robert Montague during the builders' strike.'[84] Support for the actions of Howell and his associates was never tested, but it was claimed that committees had been formed in Manchester, Leeds, Bradford and other industrial centres largely through the missionary efforts of Barry. The committee in Manchester was an influential one that included W. H. Wood, the Conservative secretary of the Trades Council, Richard Harnott, the respected secretary of the Operative Stonemasons, Peter Shorrocks, General Secretary of the Amalgamated Society of Journeyman Tailors, Henry Slatter, General Secretary of the Typographical Printers' Association, and J. D. Prior, soon to be Applegarth's successor as secretary of the Amalgamated Carpenters.[85]

How far the 'Council of Legislation' had committed itself is not at all clear. Almost all of its members hastened to deny that they had signed any resolutions, but Russell continued to claim that they had 'given their adhesion to the new programme and they were still willing to assist the working men to attain the objects they had in view'.[86] What they were denying, claimed Russell, was not their approval of the real resolutions but of the 'garbled versions' that had appeared in the press. The one who was probably most involved and who did not deny it was the old protectionist, Sir John Pakington.[87] Pakington had a history of sympathy with working-class social aspirations: he had given a contribution to the Preston cotton strikers in 1853 and just as the 'new social movement' was bursting on the public he was delivering an address to the Social Science Association in Leeds calling for a massive social programme and citing the ideas of Scott Russell. What must have been particularly troubling to the Liberals was that the movement did fit in with an emerging Conservative policy. Disraeli had always expressed concern at the social conditions of the working class. The spirit of the 'Young England' movement was well represented in the Conservative Party of the 1870s and at least one Conservative candidate in the election of 1868 had declared himself in favour of the legal recognition of unions 'believing that if the law protects the Unions, the Unions will protect the law' and had asked for legislation to 'improve the houses of the labouring classes'.[88] Lord Derby in 1871 was telling temperance reformers that before they could reform lower-class habits 'they must begin by reforming their dwellings'[89] and telling his party that it was idle to debate the question of whether trade unions were desirable: 'They exist; they are a fact; they were never more strongly supported than now; and they are not likely to disappear.'[90] Six months later in his Manchester speech of April 1872 Disraeli was citing pure air, pure water, pure food, healthy homes and public recreation as matters that 'may be legitimately dealt with by the Legislature'.[91] There were other straws in the wind: trade unionists and Conservative M.P.s were meeting on the committees of the Plimsoll agitation which attracted trade-union support during 1873 and at one point, it seems, the *Bee-Hive* was being offered as a platform for the Conservatives.[92]

The Liberal managers had reason to be worried. That a working-men's party failed to emerge, that the ties with Liberalism were not irrevocably broken, was largely due to the fact that enough radicals in parliament went out of their way to retain and rebuild the links with unionists. As so often in the past Samuel Morley's role was crucial. He had the money to buy the allegiance of at least some of the working-class leaders, but, more than that, he worked hard to keep in touch with the working class and to adjust his views to take account of changes in working-class thinking. He supported the agricultural labourers; he chaired meetings of the Workmen's Peace Association; no doubt his money was involved in the Working Men's Committee for promoting the Separation of Church and State; and there were generous donations from him to working-class candidates. In the months after the Scott-Russell movement, when the threat of a break in the working-class–radical alliance seemed highly likely, Morley was arguing that the programme of the Liberal party could be adapted to satisfy unionists. He arranged meetings with trade-union and other working-class leaders which drew up a new set of goals for the Liberal party, 'because the old Liberal programme is well-nigh exhausted'. It included both political and social reforms: abolition of lodgers' rental qualification; reduction of the residential qualification to get on the electoral register; assimilation of the borough and county franchise; election expenses on the rates; payment of

M.P.s; shorter parliaments; abolition of the Commons Enclosures Act; nationalisation of waste land and its letting to co-operative associations of small cultivators; total abolition of the game laws; free, compulsory education; disestablishment and disendowment of state churches; total abolition of the truck system; transfer of licensing power to the people; repeal of the Criminal Law Amendment Act; purchase of the railways by the state; and a nine-hour factory and workshop act.[93] A. J. Mundella shook his head at such extremism and thought that Morley was 'up in the clouds, drinking tea with all the irreconcilables in London, and persuading them they are of some importance'.[94] But such tea-drinking ensured that the working class could retain at least some hope of change through the Liberal Party.

In the Midlands and the North of England the Birmingham radicals lent support to the agricultural labourers, met with unionists, addressed trades councils and attended meetings of the TUC. In the summer of 1873 they offered yet another radical alternative when Chamberlain proposed his 'quadrilateral' of reforms – free church, free land, free schools and free labour. Other Liberal malcontents, like Vernon Harcourt and Auberon Herbert worked for the parliamentary committee of the TUC in parliament against the Criminal Law Amendment Act, persuading them to try for a fairly modest amendment to the Act rather than to insist on total repeal. In the event the proposals got nowhere and unionists had to await the return of a Conservative government. All this radical activity was enough to keep the trade-union leaders from consolidating ideas for a labour party, though it was not enough to prevent a substantial rebellion from the Liberal party at the general election.

After 1874, both dissident radicals and dissident trade unionists came back into the fold of official Liberalism. In opposition radicals could be even more active in pressing for labour legislation, without fear of embarrassing their party. But the Conservatives, too, had learned to appreciate the importance of the working-class vote and in most of the large towns, especially in Lancashire and Yorkshire, Conservative candidates had committed themselves to repeal of the Criminal Law Amendment Act. One of these, the new Home Secretary, R. A. Cross, introduced his Labour Laws in 1875 granting the unionists' demands and they passed through parliament in something of a euphoria of friendly sentiment towards unionism, with even Robert Lowe and Lord Elcho speaking in support of the measures.

Outside parliament, the National Education League and the Liberation Society blended into the new National Liberal Federation. Politically active working men could find a place in the new Chamberlain-inspired Liberal Associations, those 'traps in which to shut up the working men of the country', as Howell warned. From 1876 unionists could unite behind Gladstone once again, to denounce the pro-Turkish sentiments of the government. It was the American Civil War all over again: a moral issue, far removed from the divisive problems of the domestic policy, on which trade unionists and radicals could unite. There was even another St James's Hall meeting. Randal Cremer, associated with the ever-active Morley in the International Arbitration League, organised a petition, of 300 trade union officials, against British intervention in support of the Turks.[95] Henry Broadhurst more or less emerged the fast disintegrating Labour Representation League into the Eastern Question Association.[96]

The old guard, Allan, Dunning, Kane and Odger were gone. Howell was a kind of free-lance political agent and journalist without any base in the trade-union movement. The *Bee-Hive* was no more and Potter was in limbo. Applegarth was selling mining machinery. In their place were the new young men, Broadhurst, Shipton, John Burnett, J. D. Prior. These were the true lib-labs. The older generation had had to struggle for political acceptance and somewhere in their minds there had always persisted a wariness of entirely succumbing to the charms of the radicals. For the new men there were no such reservations: they had come to office once acceptance had been won; they easily found a place in the Liberal camp. There was little need for them to assert working-class independence. It required the experience of another spell of Liberal government in the 1880s to make them question once again the rightness of their policy.

Chapter 7

Versus the Political Economists

'If political economy be against us, we must be against political economy.' Thus one of the speakers at a Hyde Park reform meeting in 1866 summed up the trade unionists' attitude. It was a formidable challenge, for political economy had in the mid-nineteenth century a position such as no other science has ever attained. It is true there were a few critics, but for most it had reached a state of finality. When the centenary of the *Wealth of Nations* was celebrated in 1876, the views of the bulk of educated public were expressed by the ex-chancellor, Robert Lowe, when he declared that there was little further to be discovered about the subject, 'the great work has been done'.[1] Since Adam Smith's day, political economists had discovered a set of scientific laws on the working of the economy that were as 'inexorable', 'irresistible', 'external' and 'immutable' as those of the physical sciences. And the laws of political economy were against trade unions.

The codex of the laws of 'the dismal science' was John Stuart Mill's great *Principles of Political Economy*: first published in 1848, it went through numerous editions in the 1850s and 1860s. For those who found it too heavy or too obtruse there were countless popularisers, mainly concerned with bringing the gospel to the workers. These popularisers ignored the complexity and the careful qualifications made by Mill to his statements. Instead they turned his cautious reasoning into crude slogans, which they called laws. At the heart of political economy was the law of supply and demand: the price of any commodity depended on the relationship between the supply of it and the demand for it. Since labour was no different from any other commodity, it was argued, the price of labour too was fixed by the law of supply and demand, and 'to declare against the law of gravitation was quite as futile as to declare against the law of supply and demand'.[2] The heresy of trade unions was to believe that they could alter the price of labour, the level of wages.

James Stirling, for long one of the most vocal opponents of trade unionism, spelled out the uselessness of any human intervention:

> The price of labour at any given time and place, is not a matter left to the volition of the contracting parties; but it is determined for them by a self-adjusting mechanism of natural forces. . . . All unknown to the capitalist and labourer, the rate of wages is fixed for them, by the natural adjustment of those antagonistic forces [supply and demand]. . . . When, therefore, the capitalist and the labourer come to divide the product of their joint industry, they find the division ready made to their hand. The profits due to the one, and the wages due to the other, have been apportioned, by the unerring agency of natural influences, and no room is left for cavil or coercion.[3]

Should trade unions be successful in forcing up wages above their 'natural level, such success could only be temporary. By impinging on the profits of the capitalist they would drive out capital to a more lucrative field at home – or worse – overseas, and, thus, the demand for labour would fall, and with it wages. If capital, for some reason, were not driven out there was still nothing to be gained for the labourer by putting up wages to an artificial level for then 'the irresistible instinct of population would baffle his design'.[4] Population would rise in response to higher wages, thus increasing the supply of labour, which in turn would bring wages down to their natural level. As Stirling said, 'No human power can permanently raise the rate of wages, above the level determined by these natural causes.' Wages were held by the cleft stick of population and the wage fund.

Although Stirling and other popularisers based their work on Mill's *Principles*, Mill, himself, when writing of wages, had built on the often vague conclusions of Adam Smith and his successors. Smith had been the first to talk of 'the funds which are destined to the payment of wages', which consisted of 'the revenue which is over and above what is necessary for the employment of their masters'. The demand for labour increased with the increase of revenue and stock and *vice versa*, a bottom level to wages being set by subsistence.[5] Malthus, taking up from Smith, rejected the idea that the demand for labour was in direct proportion to the increase in the national wealth and declared that there were 'real funds destined for the maintenance of labour' and it was the growth of these funds that governed demand. The size of the funds depended on the standard of living of the labourers. Increase in wealth did not, of itself, bring about a rise in wages unless it was accompanied by an improvement in the standard of living, the level of subsistence which the labourer was willing to accept. Because of the pressure of population, wages inevitably tended to subsistence level, but this level varied with habit and custom, with 'the amount of those necessaries and conveniences, without which they could not consent to keep up their numbers'.[6] He propounded a two-way relationship: wages affected habits and habits affected wages.

Ricardo went some way with Malthus in accepting the importance of 'custom and habit' in affecting the wage level, but he differentiated between 'the natural price of labour' and 'the market price of labour'. The former was 'that price which is necessary to enable the labourers, one with another, to subsist and to perpetuate their race, without either increase or diminution'.[7] Market wages, however, could differ from natural wages. These depended on the available stock of capital and would rise quickly as capital increased. Nevertheless, the tendency of wages must be towards subsistence level since a rise in wages would bring a growth in population which would push down wages until population stabilised at subsistence level. This 'iron law of wages' was accepted by all the classical economists from Ricardo to John Stuart Mill and was the subject of much vilification by anti-capitalist economists, as a defence of subsistence wages. A great deal of bitterness stemmed from a misunderstanding of subsistence. To the classical economists, subsistence in no sense meant near starvation nor was it a fixed level. Subsistence meant the minimum level of comfort which was acceptable to the worker and the level would rise as the knowledge and habits of the workers improved – hence, the great stress laid by early-Victorian society on improvement in the habits, comfort and aspirations of the working classes. The market rate of wages could not fall beneath the level necessary to maintain a standard of living that was acceptable to the workers.[8]

McCulloch, Torrens and the other political economists who followed Ricardo firmly implanted the concept of a wage or wages' fund in political economy. 'The market or current rate of wages in any country, at any given period,' wrote McCulloch, 'depends on the magnitude of its capital appropriated to the payment of wages,

compared with the number of its labourers'.[9] Yet, in all cases, a
certain vagueness persisted as to what precisely created and
limited the wage fund.[10] This same imprecision exists in Mill's
writing on wages.

> Wages, then, depend mainly upon the demand and supply of
> labour, or, as it is often expressed, on the proportion between
> population and capital. By population is here meant the number
> only of the labouring class, or rather those who work for hire;
> and by capital, only circulating capital, and not even the whole
> of that, but the part which is expended in the direct purchase of
> labour.[11]

Yet, implicit in Mill is a belief that there were fixed limits to the
wage fund, and this was certainly assumed by the popularisers.
Charles Morrison, for example, regarded the wage fund as 'a
definite proportion of the entire active capital', which employers
must pay out in wages, even if they were 'universally misers'.[12]

Since wages were governed by 'the great natural law of Demand
and Supply' which 'mocks at all human interference',[13] there was
clearly no place for trade unions, concerned with raising wages.
Mill did recognise that unions had succeeded in pushing wages
above the market level, but this had only been at the expense of
those workers who were not combined. Real gains for 'the working
classes at large' could only be achieved by raising their 'habitual
requirements': 'wages never fall permanently below the standards
of these requirements, and do not long remain above that
standard'.[14] He did, however, consider that trade unions did have
a role to play in informing the worker of the state of the market
and in ensuring that he received the full rate that the market would
bear. Few of the popularisers allowed even this. In press and
popular pamphlets the futility of striving against natural law was
constantly being thrown at trade unions.

I

Given the very deliberate propagating of these views in school
books[15] and in lectures at mechanics' institutes and other improving bodies, it would be surprising if the working class had not
been influenced by them. There is evidence that they were. Indeed,
Sidney and Beatrice Webb believed that one of the most significant
features of the 'new spirit' which pervaded unionism from the
1840s onwards was the acceptance of the economic axiom that the

wages of labour depended on the relationship between the supply of it and the demand for it. They quote the Ironmoulders' Society in 1847, 'that wages are to be best raised by the demand for labour' and the Flint Glass Makers in 1849, 'it is simply a question of supply and demand, and we all know that if we supply a greater quantity of an article, than what is actually demanded that the cheapening of that article, whether it be labour or any other commodity, is a natural result'.[16]

In 1860, the erudite secretary of the London Bookbinders in a defence of trade unionism sought to justify it in terms of classical political economy. Thomas Dunning, in his *Trades' Unions and Strikes: Their Philosophy and Intention*, which was published in reply to a lecture by Adam Black, M.P. for Edinburgh, who repeated the old arguments on the futility of unions trying to affect alterations in the rate of wages, did not reject the teachings of political economy. The laws of political economy were accepted by everyone, just like 'two and two making four': 'If the supply of labour *permanently* exceeds demand then wages must fall'. But his case was that unions were not concerned with the extreme. They dealt with temporary situations. For instance, if a reduction of wages took place during a slack period then the reduction was likely to remain for some time after trade got busy again, although there might be no over-supply of workers, unless there was a union to ensure that wages returned to their proper level. On another occasion a slackness of trade might not be due to a lack of demand but to 'undue competition among employers, bidding each other under the other'.[18] Once again only trade union organisation could prevent this. Combination allowed workmen 'to put themselves on something like an equality in the bargain for the sale of their labour with the employers'.[19] With a trade society behind him a workman was not compelled 'to take less than the wages which the demand and supply of labour in the trade had previously adjusted'.[20]

Dunning also accepted the concept of a wage fund, but this too, was used by him as justification for unionism: 'Let, then, the men know how their trade really stands, and they will never desire to have more, for the best of all possible reasons, they will know it is impossible for them to get it'.[21]

When other unionists sought a theoretical justification of unionism they generally did so in terms similar to Dunning's. In 1854, the executive of the A.S.E. saw the function of their union as being to ensure that wages really rose to the market level and were not kept down by 'a tacit understanding between employers not to raise wages above a certain level'.[22] In 1869, George Potter, replying in the pages of *The Times* to an attack on unionism by Edmund Ashworth, admitted that 'No Trade's Union ever did, or ever will, raise wages above the regular demand and supply rate', but continued: 'The value and usefulness of Trade's Unions to the working classes lie in their preventing wages falling below this rate, which they would certainly do, but for the existence of combination among workmen.'[23]

Despite such statements it is a moot point whether trade unionists actually allowed such a theoretical stance to affect their actions, since it is rare for unions to base their conduct on *a priori* assumptions. At a glance they might seem to be doing this in the 1850s and 1860s. Most unions attempted to restrict entry into their trades, where possible by insisting on an apprenticeship, and thus cutting down the supply of labour. But it is very doubtful if it was a belief in the laws of political economy that caused them to do this, rather than the experience of decades. Since the eighteenth century most craft unions had been faced with cheap, partly-skilled labour coming into their trade and undercutting wages. They had constantly striven to prevent it. Since 1815 they had before them the terrifying example of the handloom weavers as evidence of what could happen when there was an unrestricted flow of new workers into an industry. Restriction of entry to those with sufficient skill was a well-established aim of most unions from the late eighteenth century onwards. The talk of over-population and over-supply of labour in the 1840s and 1850s merely confirmed unionists in the rightness of their views and encouraged some tightening of restrictions on entry.

The trade union approach to their problems was much more pragmatic than some historians have allowed. The Webbs, for example, saw the adoption of emigration schemes by a number of trade unions in the late forties and fifties as powerful evidence that unions were guided in their actions by the axioms of political economy. If wages were to rise the supply of labour had to be reduced and emigration was a favourite solution propounded by the supporters of orthodox economics for removing 'surplus labour'. The prosperity of the early years of the 1850s was seen by many as due to the emigration of large numbers of the working class. But, in practice, trade-union support for emigration was half-hearted. The amount of money spent to assist emigration was, in fact, minute and the individual sums made available were certainly not large enough actually to encourage surplus labour to leave the country. The Ironfounders' Society, which spent more than most, devoted only £4,700 to emigration in the twenty years between 1854 and 1874 and provided less than £10 to the emigrant.[24] The average amount paid by other societies was £3 to £7 but could be as low as 10s.[25] Unions did concede that unemployed workers would be tempted to accept work at under the standard rate and that if they emigrated then this was well to the good. As a result, unions tended to encourage emigration at periods of industrial conflict, as the A.S.E. did in 1852. They rarely saw it as a long-term solution to the problems of the supply of labour. During times of depression the emigration fund was likely to be abandoned as an unnecessary luxury. Rather, emigration grants were seen as an additional benefit that could be provided if the funds of the society were good. It gave an individual member an opportunity to improve his lot in the new world, but it was rarely seen as likely to improve the conditions of those who remained.

There was a number of ardent propagandists for emigration among the trade-union leaders, but one can question their motives. Alexander Campbell, doyen of the Glasgow unionists and in the 1860s editor of the influential working-class paper, the *Glasgow Sentinel* persuaded the Glasgow Trades Council to take up the issue of emigration and to press for government aid to emigrants, but he was secretary of the Canadian Land and Railway Investment Association and later an emigration agent for the government of Nova Scotia.[26] Alexander McDonald, the miners' leader and another advocate of emigration, acted as a recruiting agent for the Hampshire and Baltimore Coal Co. of Virginia.[27] George Potter from 1870, acted as a paid secretary of the National Emigration League and the extensive emigration of agricultural workers in the late seventies was encouraged by Joseph Arch and other officials of the agricultural workers' unions, who were also emigration agents. As a policy of trade unionism, emigration was insignificant and does not warrant the emphasis placed on it, by the Webbs and others, as a reflection of unionists' views.

Much more representative of trade unionists' attitudes to political economy were the views expressed by Lloyd Jones that 'the working man accepts such of these views as his experience in the world and workshop justify to him. Where his experience does not do so, he rejects them.'[28] This was the attitude that contemporaries observed. They found little evidence that unions were prepared to accept the 'heavenly-ordained laws of Supply and Demand'.[29] There were still strikes; there were still efforts to impose wages minima – all evidence of a rejection of political economy. Confronted by the political economists, trade unions 'calmly kept on their silent way'.[30]

In the 1860s one begins to get a more explicit rejection by the unions of the teachings of the political economists. The *Bricklayers' Trade Circular* in 1861 thought that the law of supply and demand, which treated labour as a commodity, was a 'fiction', deliberately maintained 'by those who rule the markets'.[31] William MacDonald, the Manchester painters' secretary, scoffed at the economists' claims to exactness: 'Astronomers foretell eclipses . . . why should not the social science teacher warn us against the stormy contests between capital and labour?' The economists talked of 'natural rates' and of 'artificial prices' but 'cannot tell exactly what ought to be the weekly wage of a joiner'.

Produce your economic thermometer, and say what rates of remuneration ought to be given to engineers, mechanics, cotton spinners, masons, joiners, tailors, shoemakers, builders, bakers and all the varied handicraftsmen in the realm.

This has never been done by our professors or doctors of political science. They are the mere partisans of the strongest side, on a level with paid agitators or special pleaders, while assuming the functions of impartial judges.[32]

Trade unionists were convinced that their unions had succeeded in raising wages. It was frequently repeated to the Royal Commission that in any area the workers in unions received higher wages than those outside them. 'Let the political economists say what they will', declared George Potter, but wages 'cannot be adjusted either in strict principles in reasoning or by line and rule in practice.'[33] At the same time, the *Flint Glass Makers' Magazine* was commenting, 'its all very well to talk about the law of supply and demand; we happen to know there is enough for all and to spare'.[34] By the 1870s any claims that political economy had relevance to industrial relations were being rejected entirely. George Howell, while accepting that the theory of supply and demand was applicable in terms of perfect competition, rejected it as having any practical value in an imperfect world, and declared that 'if political economy can do nothing better than suggest checks to population as a means of balancing supply and demand in its application to labour, the sooner its professors seek some other occupation the better'.[35] As for the wage-fund, that was 'at best a figure of speech' and 'never has been and never can be a principle capable of being formulated into a "law" '.[36]

II

In their rejection of political economy, by word and deed in the 1860s, trade unionists were joined by a number of thinkers who were beginning to question the 'immutability' of their laws. The questioning was largely as a result of the continuing activities of trade unions. If the workers would not adjust their actions to political economy, then political economy would have to adjust to take account of the action of the workers. As Charles Neate declared, it was fatuous 'to treat the great body of the artisans of England . . . as being childishly ignorant of what most immediately concerns them, and utterly incapable of comprehending the plainest principles on the observance of which their well-being depends'.[37] Neate, a professor of political economy at Oxford, was one of the first to call for some re-thinking. He was in correspondence with William Allan and was for many years to be an important ally of the unions in the House of Commons. In 1861 he delivered two lectures on trade unions in which he called for political economists to find a place for trade unionism in their scheme of things. He railed at those 'who presume too far upon that sort of acquaintance with the truisms of political economy which a clever schoolboy may acquire in a week'.[38] Neate argued that there was 'no certain law' that decreed the division between wages and profit, and, therefore, unions had a part to play in determining that division. He went on to defend many of the other activities of unions, such as restriction of apprenticeships, to which 'many of the better class of masters seem to have readily acquiesced', and the demand for shorter hours.[39] He ended with a plea to the upper classes for acceptance:

Whether they like it or not, they must accept the fact that the feeling amongst working men, whether Unionists or not, is almost unanimous in favour of the Societies; that the men actually enrolled in those bodies are the very flower of every trade; that their leaders are, as a general rule, able and high-minded men; that their demands are generally reasonable, and attended with success; and lastly, that so far from education being an antidote to the spirit of combination, the latter flourishes in proportion as the former is extended.[40]

The second line of attack came from those who resented the sheer inhumanity of the subject. John Ruskin was one of the most influential critics to approach the matter from this direction. He rejected a science 'based on the idea that an advantageous code of social action may be determined irrespectively of the influence of social affection'.[41] The so-called laws denied man's humanity. It treated the worker as if he were a machine, run on steam when in fact he was 'an engine whose motive power is a soul, the force of this very peculiar agent, as an unknown quantity, enters into all the political economist's equations without his knowledge, and falsifies every one of their results'.[42] He defended the demand for equality of wages, since the alternative was the degradation of a 'dutch auction'. Given a fixed rate the good workman would be employed and the bad workman unemployed. He called for a system that did not 'throw both wages and trade into the form of a lottery' but instead provided security and justice.[43] It was the de-humanising aspect of political economy on which Frederic Harrison concentrated when he took up the attack in the *Fortnightly Review* of 1865. He too rejected the claims of political economy to being a science. It was instead 'a collection of warm controversies on social questions'. The 'laws' might hold true at this point in time but they took no account of changes in society. The 'love of gain' of the 'effective desire for accumulation' would not always hold the place in human motives that they had in 1865. When society changed then the 'laws' were no more. Like Ruskin, he rejected the concept of man as an economic being, 'a producing animal exclusively': there were many other factors that motivated man and none of these did the political economists take into account.[44] As it stood, political economy assumed a social state that was not capable of improvement, 'yet all reasonable social inquiry now proceeds on the ground that the social state required much improvement'.[45]

From 1865 the attack on classical political economy gathered momentum, coming from both theorists and humanitarians. In 1866 Francis D. Longe published a reasoned rejection of the wage-fund theory. Longe was acquainted with the workings of trade unions. A barrister by profession, he was an active member of the Social Science Association and had produced a paper on 'The Law of Strikes' for the Association's committee on trades' societies and strikes. His starting point was from the position of social reformer, for, to him, an acceptance of the wage-fund theory excluded 'altogether the influence of liberal principles from that field of social action, where it is for the interest of society that they should be most influential' and prevented 'public opinion coming to the rescue of a depressed class'.[46] By giving the impression that employers somehow had no responsibility for the level of wages of their workers and that the level was arrived at by some independent process, it encouraged 'hard social principles, bad moral principles and pernicious political principles'.[47] Longe denied that there was any fund 'destined for the purchase of labour' and argued that: 'A true science of Political Economy would teach the labourer that the more he gave his employer, the more would be the wages which his employer could afford to pay him.'[48] Since the supply of labour was always greater than the demand, the law of supply and demand could not be applied to labour and it was 'to the interest of both capital and labour that the competition of labourers be controlled'.[49] T. E. Cliffe Leslie took a similar attitude in 1868 when he rejected the wage-fund theory as one that 'discredits political economy with the labouring class, and diverts the attention alike of labourers, employers and economists from the investigation of means by which the wealth of the working classes might be increased and their relations with their employers placed on a more satisfactory footing'.[50] Cliffe Leslie was one of a growing school of economists who were questioning the methodology of classical political economy. He urged that political economy abandon its 'fictitious title to mathematical exactness and certainty' and adopt an inductive rather than a deductive approach.[51]

Since neither Longe nor Leslie were members of the inner circle of economists their work did not make much impact. It was one of that inner circle, W. T. Thornton, who first, in articles in the *Fortnightly Review* and later in his book, *On Labour, Its Wrongful Claims and Rightful Dues*, made the significant breakthrough. Thornton rejected both the idea of a pre-determined wage fund and the belief that wages must 'bear a certain undefined relation both to his wants and to the value of his services'.[52] To Thornton, 'the only true criterion of wages is the agreement between employer and employed'.[53] As a result there was a role for collective action by the workers to strengthen their bargaining position. The importance of Thornton's work was increased by the support he received from the greatest living economist, John Stuart Mill. In reviewing Thornton's book, Mill cast down his own doctrine of the wage fund.

The doctrine hitherto taught by all or most economists (including myself), which denied it to be possible that trade combinations can raise wages, or which limited their operation in that respect to the somewhat earlier attainment of a rise which the competition of the market would have produced without them – this doctrine is deprived of its scientific foundation, and must be thrown aside. The right and wrong of the proceedings of Trades' Unions becomes a common question of prudence and social duty, not one which is peremptorily decided by unbending necessities of political economy.[54]

Mill still accepted that there were higher and lower limits above and below which wages could not pass, but between these limits there was an 'intermediate region' where the 'higgling of the market' came in and here trade unions had a part to play.[55] Indeed, in his review, he proceeded to defend unions, to reject charges that they had infringed the liberty of working men, and even to justify hostility to non-unionists:

As soon as it is acknowledged that there are lawful, and even useful, purposes to be fulfilled by trades unions, it must be admitted that the members of Unions may reasonably feel a genuine moral disapprobation of those who profit by the higher wages or other advantages that the Unions procure for non-Unionists as well as for their own members, but refuse to take their share of payments, and submit to the restrictions by which the advantages are obtained.[56]

Mill's review reflected the new interest in the working class and his involvement with leading trade unionists such as Odger and Applegarth. When he had first embarked on his *Principles* his interest in the working class had been slight and he had only included his chapter on 'the Probable Future of the Labouring Classes' at the prompting of Harriet Taylor.[57] By the 1860s, through his involvement in politics, in particular in the reform agitation, he had abandoned the seclusion of the India Office and come to know and work with many of the leaders of the working class in London. His recantation of the wage fund was of cardinal importance in opening the way to a reappraisal of the role of unions in wage bargaining. Diehards, like James Stirling, attacked the new 'soft school of Political Economy' which tempered 'its doctrines to suit the delicacy of its nerves',[58] but the new approach answered a widely felt need to adjust theory to reality. Others soon followed. Professor Fleeming Jenkin, the Professor of Engineering at Edinburgh, saw the wage fund as 'a fluctuating quantity altered by every circumstance which affects the minds of capitalists'[59] and found a place for trade unions as enabling 'the labourer to set a reserved price on his merchandise'.[60] Jenkin went on to argue that what determined wages – and prices – was 'the conflict between the desire for the commodity and the reluctance to sell it'.[61]

Some attempt was made to defend classical theory by Mill's disciple, J. E. Cairnes, when, in 1874, he restated the wage-fund theory in *Some Leading Principles of Political Economy Newly Expounded*, but, as Marshall declared, he 'explained away so much that was characteristic of the doctrine that there [was] very little left to justify its title'.[62] The death blow came from an American economist, F. A. Walker in *The Wages Question* (1876). Walker's writings 'gained an acceptance and influence probably greater than that of any writings in the English tongue since the days of the younger Mill'.[63] He rejected the idea that wages were paid out of accumulated capital: they were paid from the product resulting from the employment of labour. In addition, Walker rejected the Ricardian belief that profits were the residue after rent, wages and interest had been paid. He, like W. S. Jevons, argued that labour got the residue after rent, interest and profits. In two ways, therefore, the worker could affect his wages: by increased efficiency he could increase the product; and by combination he could alter the proportion of the product going to the capitalist.[64]

By the end of the seventies it was possible to claim that, under the influence of Thornton, Jevons, Walker and others, there was 'a growing tendency in the organs of cultivated opinion to treat the wage-fund theory as exploded'.[65] All the professional economists came to accept that the rate of wages could be altered through bargaining and only through combination could workers strengthen their bargaining position in relation to their employers. There were limits to what could be achieved, but as F. Y. Edgeworth said in 1881, 'the one thing from an abstract point of view visible amidst the jumble of catallactic molecules, the jostle of competitive crowds, is that those who form themselves into compact bodies by combination do not tend to lose, but stand to gain'.[66] It took longer for these changes in theory to percolate through the thinking of laymen and even in the 1880s the shibboleths of supply and demand were thrown against unionism. But

the toppling of political economy from its pinnacle of immutability made it less serious for trade unionism to be against political
economy. Yet as J. A. Schumpeter has pointed out political
economy fell at the first puff of an adverse wind.[67] The attacks on
the wage fund by Longe and Thornton were 'verbose and incomplete' and very small bricks to throw at the intellectual might
of a century of reasoning, from Adam Smith to John Stuart Mill.
Mill surrendered his cause without a fight and 'with a sigh of
relief . . . in the way in which one delivers oneself of a burden
borne reluctantly',[68] and when he had done so the mighty edifice
collapsed. It was political reasoning not economic reasoning that
destroyed this part of the classical system. Neate, Harrison, Longe
and Mill, all sympathetically involved with trade unionism,
desperately sought a way out of the *impasse* of political economy
being against unions; it was socially untenable to them. No tenet
of classical economics was more closely connected with politics
than the wage-fund theory and, when politics altered, the theory
had to be altered. By surviving and succeeding trade unionism had
pushed the question to the forefront of economic problems and
forced the adaptation of the theory to practice.

III

In the place of the classical system which they had so successfully
helped to destroy, trade unionists put no alternative theory of
wages. What one has is an essentially pragmatic approach, dressed
up in eclecticism. When occasion demanded they would defend
their actions in terms of classical economics, or in terms of some
half-remembered labour theory of value, or in terms of social
justice. In practice, however, as William Allan quite openly told
the Royal Commission in 1867, it was a question of keeping what
they could get.[69]

Trade unions never accepted that the competitive system was
the ideal. There was a recurring criticism of a system that
proclaimed 'cheapness . . . to be the one great and desirable
attainment'[70] and with this went a questioning of a system of
free trade that destroyed native industry. Throughout the 1850s
protectionist groups attracted the support of trade unionists.
Every time the free-trade treaty with France came up for renewal
there was a quickening of agitation against it. At meetings in
Birmingham in 1869, one unionist, Allen Dalzell, described free
trade as 'a suicidal policy and murder to the people'.[71] In 1875 an

essay published by the Edinburgh Trades' Council saw it as vital 'to convince British Statesmen that they are involved in a dangerous experiment in regard to universal free trade, which is absurd as universal protection'.[72] By the end of the 1870s, with the depression firmly entrenched, there was substantial trade-union support for the fair-trade movement. Most trade unionists who got involved in it were insistent that they did believe in the value of free trade and did not wish to return to a protectionist policy, but faced with more and more foreign tariffs on British goods they felt that something ought to be done. By the early 1880s the idea of reciprocal tariffs was appealing to a not insignificant number of unionists. George Shipton, the secretary of the London Trades Council, was a paid agent of the fair trade National Anti-Bounty League and, in Birmingham, both the President and secretary of the Amalgamated Brassworkers pressed Chamberlain at the Board of Trade to impose 'countervailing duties'.[74]

Critics of trade unions were right to see them as opponents of free and open competition: they were protective organisations and their thinking on wages and hours was frequently guided by traditional ideas of craft rights and privileges. They viewed the craft as their property 'bought by certain years of servitude' and it was their duty to protect the status and the standards of that craft. The A.S.E.'s declared aim was 'to exercise the same control over that in which we have a vested interest, as the physician who holds his diploma, or the author who is protected by his copyright'.[75] The Glasgow printers intended 'to protect the interests of the operative portion of the profession against all unjust innovations'.[76] Customary standards and traditions were important since once these went the position of the worker was likely to deteriorate rapidly. This doctrine of vested interests, as the Webbs called it, was, by the end of the 1850s, losing ground as a rationale for trade unionism. At any rate it was less frequently used in public statements, though it is evident that the concept still persisted and influenced unionists, who had a very clear idea of what their wage rates ought to be in relation to other crafts if they were to maintain their position, and they fought for these. The efforts of historians in the 1860s to trace a link between guilds and trade unions may well have helped to keep alive the idea that the craftsman's first duty was to protect the standards of his craft.

More important as a guide to trade-union action was the desire for 'a fair day's wage for a fair day's work'. Such a concept as 'a fair wage' was an explicit rejection of the law of supply and demand. It involved ideas of natural justice that were not to be found in the teachings of the economists. As George Potter wrote, 'the law of supply and demand if left to its natural operation would reduce wages to the lowest possible point'. Trade unions existed to prevent this and to ensure that workmen received a 'fair remuneration for their labour'.[77] A fair wage was one that provided the worker with enough 'for decent maintenance of himself and his family, leaving something over for the future'.[78] The Northamptonshire shoemakers in the 1850s were making similar claims:

> It is high time that the employed should have a fair share of the benefits arising from the productive industry of the country, as well as the employer, and not to be obliged in his old age to finish a life of labour in a poor-law Bastile [sic], and a pauper's grave, while those for whom he has toiled hard, are allowed to revel in luxury, through their assumed rights to dictate their own terms to the workmen, and the carrying out of their favourite dogma of unrestricted competition.[79]

As Lloyd Jones put it in the *Bee-Hive*, in 1874, the aim of the trade unions should be for a minimum wage that would 'secure sufficiency of food, and some degree of personal and home comfort to the worker; not a miserable allowance to starve on, but *living wages*'.[80]

Although most unions accepted the need for wage cuts during severe slump there was a minimum below which they believed wages should not fall. Both implicitly and explicitly this concept of 'fair and equable' remuneration for labour was the most import influence on trade union thinking on wages. If higher wages could be gained by reference to the law of supply and demand then this was appealed to, but it was a one-way process. If the 'natural' level was too low it was rejected as unjust.

The concept of a living wage received support from the writings of the Positivists and from Ruskin. Both believed in wages that were more than subsistence level and allowed the worker to share in the gains of rising productivity. Such a belief influenced the trade-union demand for shorter hours, for in this they were denying the right of the employers to gain sole advantage from technical improvements. Thus, the London building employers in 1859 claimed that the nine-hour claim of their workers 'implied that the benefits to be derived from machinery are not the property of society, of its inventors, of those who apply it, but are to be appropriated by those whose labour it is alleged it will displace'.[81] The Newcastle engineers demanded the nine hours in 1871 because: 'By the introduction of improved machinery into the various departments of labour the profits of the employers have been increased, while no corresponding benefits have accrued to the working classes.'[82]

Linked with the concept of a 'fair wage' was that of the 'right to work'. 'All men who are willing to work', declared George Odger, 'should have work provided for them.'[83] The demand for shorter hours was part of this same belief that society, if properly organised, could and should provide work for all. Most depressions in trade were explained in terms of over-production, and shorter hours were 'the only practical method of giving employment to our surplus labour and thereby enabling the workmen to secure a more reasonable share of the wealth which labour produces'.[84] The miners' union, especially, were committed to the idea of shorter hours in order to cut down output. Excessive stocks of coal were 'like a bold monster, to defy us having our just rights'.[85] The demand for an eight-hour day in mining, which remained a part of the miners' programme from the 1860s into the twentieth century was, to reduce stocks of coal and thus keep up wages.

Older anti-capitalist ideas of the right of the workers 'to the whole produce of labour' were not prominent in the justifications put forward for trade-union action. If they did appear they were in half-remembered slogans. 'Labour is the primary source of all wealth,' wrote the general secretary of the London Bricklayers' Society in 1862, 'but there is a class who believe that they have the right to live upon the produce of others, and hence instead of labour being shared by all (as its fruits are), one class is made subservient to the other, and had to do double work, because they provide subsistence for idlers'.[86] Lip-service was paid to the ideal of the co-operative commonwealth, but, by the 1860s and 1870s William Allan's vision of a land studded with co-operative workshops had given way to a view of co-operative workshops as a means of keeping unemployed labour off the market. Unionists rejected the principle of unrestricted competition, of buying in the cheapest market and selling in the dearest, but in the mid-nineteenth century they had really no alternative to offer. Not until the re-emergence of socialism in the 1880s did some find such an alternative. In the meantime they could only fight to get what they could from the system. Thomas Dunning could declare that 'the true state of employer and employed is that of amity, and that they are the truest of friends',[87] but the reality as the unionists well knew was that 'the working classes have to fight for every advantage which they have gained, and for every privilege which they have won'.[88] Under the existing system there would be no real reconciliation between employers and workers: 'It is their interest to get the labour at as low a rate of wages as they possibly can, and it is ours to get as high a rate of wages as possible.'[89] William Harry of the Amalgamated Carpenters was even more decisive: 'so long as wages slavery . . . exists, strikes and lock-outs are inevitable, and will as surely present themselves as night succeeds day, the victors being those possessing the best filled purses'.[90]

In the last analysis unionists accepted a conflict situation in industrial relations and pressed for what they could get, using the most favourable arguments that came to hand. One can illustrate this in the history of wage negotiation in the Durham coalfields. In the 1860s the miners accepted some loose relationship between the demand for labour and its supply, because it was relatively advantageous to do so. By the early 1870s, with prices rising quickly, and the introduction of sliding scales, wages too, rose. By the middle of the decade, with prices plummeting they were being rejected as the sole criterion of wages and the miners' unions were demanding to know, not only average prices, but the average cost of production. The coal owners, at first, rejected this out of hand, but by September 1876 were giving details of labour costs – it was a short step to taking profits into account and looking at these as a guide to wages.[91] The laws of political economy had little place in the practice of unionism.

Chapter 8

Trade Unions and the Law

If one follows Dicey in accepting a relationship between the law and public opinion, in believing that the evolution of the law has been governed by 'the wishes and ideas as to legislation held by the people of England, or, to speak with more precision, by the majority of those citizens who have at a given moment taken an effective part in public life',[1] then changes in the law relating to trade unions must reflect changes in the attitude of the aristocracy and the upper middle classes to working-class combination. It is, however, less helpful when it comes to the question of the timing of such changes in attitude, since there was likely to be a considerable lapse of time before new thinking affected legislation and an even longer lapse before it affected judicial opinion. The fundamental and far-reaching changes in the legal position of trade unions in the third quarter of the nineteenth century do, however, reflect changes as fundamental in the thinking of the politically dominant classes of the period.

The Combination Laws Repeal Act of 1824 – 'the biggest surprise received by a labour movement before 1906', as one legal historian has called it – freed trade unions from statutory illegality and from common law charges of conspiracy which had been used against workmen's combinations since perhaps the fourteenth century. But the explosion of militancy which the repeal occasioned brought a rapid about-turn by the government and an Amendment Act, the Combination of Workmen Act, more narrowly defined the right to combine. Under this Act of 1825, only combinations concerned with determining wages, prices and hours of work were free from criminality in statute law and protection was given only to combinations consisting of workmen actually present at a meeting to deal with these matters. The protection from common law charges, given only in the previous year, was removed, so that all combinations, wider than that of workers actually attending a meeting, or any attempt to deal with matters other than wages, prices and hours, were criminal conspiracies at common law, as being in unlawful restraint of trade.[3] The 1825 Act also deprived workmen of the right, granted by the 1824 Act, to combine to induce other workers to break their contract of service by striking.[4] It was, therefore, in this legally circumscribed situation that trade unionism grew over the next four decades, in many of their activities and in their organisation clearly outside the law. The economist, Nassau Senior, believed in 1831 that there was 'scarcely an act performed by any workman as a member of a trade union which is not an act of conspiracy and a misdemeanour'.[5]

Courts of law, in the years after 1825, seem to have recognised that it was almost impossible to differentiate between combinations on wages and hours and combinations on other conditions of work and judges, in their guidance to jurors, closed their eyes to such breaches of the law. They seem also to have accepted that the right to combine necessarily involved the right to withhold labour.[6] But freedom of action during strikes was very much limited by Section 3 of the 1825 Act which penalised any action by workmen that involved 'violence', 'threats', 'intimidation', 'molestation', or 'obstruction'. All of these terms, but particularly the last two, left unlimited ground for judicial interpretation and over the years the courts held that, under this section, it was punishable to give an employer notice that his workmen would strike unless he dismissed a particular workman; to tell a workman that he would be struck against or considered 'Black'; to shout 'Ba-ba, black sheep' at non-strikers; or to tell a workman that if he went to work 'there will be a row'.[7] There were differences of judicial opinion on whether acts or threats of violence were necessary in order for such actions to be defined as intimidation, etc., or whether the offence lay in 'the intention to coerce the will of another'.[8] In addition, some opinion held that the existence of a combination could make a non-criminal act indictable as a criminal threat, molestation or obstruction. By 1851 courts were holding that even peaceful persuasion to induce others to leave their employment was unlawful.[9] It was to place some limit on the interpretation of the words 'molestation' and 'obstruction' that the Molestation of Workmen Act of 1859, *22 Vic c. 34* was passed, which allowed workmen 'peaceably' and 'in a reasonable manner' to persuade others to strike work.[10] The term 'reasonable manner'

was open to a judge's interpretation and since the Act dealt only
with 'molestation' and 'obstruction', 'threats' and 'intimidation'
were still there to be interpreted as broadly as judges wished. By
1868, it was being held that to publish advertisements telling of
a dispute and asking people not to take employment at some
works, amounted to criminal intimidation, and Baron Bramwell,
trying the leaders of the London Operative Tailors' Society
declared that even watching non-strikers and the giving of 'black
looks' was to intimidate.[11]

By legislation of 1799 and 1817,[12] which had been aimed at
political clubs and corresponding societies, it was illegal for
societies to have branches. Not until 1846 were these measures
amended, which made it possible for the amalgamated societies to
develop.[13] The most important legal aspect for these large societies
was their position in civil law. Having both property and large
funds they were concerned that these should not be vulnerable
either for damages or at the hands of dishonest officials. But, here
too, the trade-union position was uncertain and precarious. Like
any voluntary association, a trade union had no corporate
identity: its property and funds were in the joint ownership of all
its members and, under common law, no member could be guilty
of stealing the joint property. It was for this reason that, in the
early years of trade unionism, a society's funds were usually held
by someone outside the society, for instance the publican at whose
public house meetings were held. With the accumulating of really
substantial funds by the amalgamated societies it was not possible
for the society's funds to be kept in the traditional wooden chest,
and, in 1855, the A.S.E., helped by Lord Goderich and other
Christian Socialists campaigned successfully to be given protection
by the Friendly Societies' Act of that year. Under Section 44 of the
Act, a society 'for any purpose which is not illegal' could deposit a
copy of its printed rules with the Registrar of Friendly Societies.[14]
Unlike a friendly society the rules of a union were not certified
by the Registrar, but in 1855, legal opinion held that trade-union
funds could be protected under the Act and legal action taken
against fraudulent officers or members.[15] Significantly, however,
the Scottish Registrar of Friendly Societies declined to receive the
rules of unions because he believed that they were in most cases
illegal, being 'in restraint of trade', and, when the issue was tested
in England in 1866 this proved to be the case. In the Hornby v.
Close case of 1866, Hornby, the president of the Bradford branch
of the Boilermakers' Society sued Close for the return of some of

the branch funds. The Bradford Justices threw out the case, claiming that the union's funds could not be protected by the Friendly Societies' Act, even though they were deposited, since some of the registered rules – in particular those forbidding piecework – were 'in restraint of trade' and, therefore, illegal at common law. The court of the Queen's Bench, in January 1867, upheld their ruling.[16]

The immediate concern of the amalgamated societies was to restore protection for their funds and in the Conference of Amalgamated Trades they assiduously began to lobby Parliament. In 1867 Charles Neate introduced a bill for this purpose, drafted by Henry Crompton, for the Conference. It was reintroduced, in 1868 by T. F. Buxton, but on both occasions got no further than a first reading. However, some measure of protection was gained in 1868 under an Act usually known as 'the Recorder's Act', after its sponsor, Russell Gurney, the Recorder of London. By this Act, co-partners could sue in cases of larceny or embezzlement. Great care was taken not to mention trade unions in the discussions on the bill, but it was successfully used by unions against dishonest treasurers.[17]

It was with the law on trade societies and on strikes in this confused position that the Royal Commission on Trades Unions met to consider, not only the organisation and rules of unions, but 'to suggest any improvements to be made in the law'. The Commission accepted that most unions had for long acted in defiance of the law of 1825 and generally had rules which put them outside the protection of the Friendly Societies' Act.[18] Members differed, however, as to the remedy. All were agreed that the right to combine should be fully recognised and that it should be enacted 'that no combination of persons for the purpose of determining among themselves, or stipulating for, the terms on which they will consent to employ or be employed, shall be unlawful by reason only that its operation would be in restraint of trade'.[19] But, the majority were not willing to give any further protection from criminal proceedings, nor were they willing to abandon the words 'molestation' and 'intimidation' in Section 3 of the 1825 Act. They were determined to maintain the right of the non-unionist to dispose of his labour as he wished: 'We deem it of the highest moment that the law, so far as it aims at repressing all coercion of the will of others in the disposal of their labour or capital, should be in no degree relaxed.'[20] The majority of the commissioners were willing to grant some protection to the funds of unions through a system of registration of their rules. They were not willing to grant this protection to societies whose rules were 'in defiance of the well-established principles of economical science', which were specified as rules limiting the number of apprentices, preventing the introduction of machinery, preventing sub-contracting or piecework, or allowing the use of funds to support other unions.[21] While they did not wish to make such rules illegal, they found them objectionable because they bound men for the future and forced them 'to give up the right of judging and acting as they think fit on each occasion as it arises'.[22] They suggested also that before registration should be granted a society should separate its trade and benefit funds.

Thomas Hughes and Frederic Harrison, in their minority report, took a more critical look at the existing legal position and suggested more radical amendment. The essence of their case was that there should be no special legislation, such as the Combination Laws, which made acts committed by workmen illegal solely on the ground that they were committed by workmen. It was, they declared, a denial of the principle of equality before the law. They found three grounds on which the existing law was inequitable: it created an offence of spoken threats and molestation which was uniquely an offence of combinations; it punished acts committed by workmen which were not offences if done by anyone else; and the existing laws were not administered impartially, since legal action against employers rarely, if ever, succeeded.[23] The remedy was, therefore, the repeal of the Combination Laws and 'to deal with all offences which may be committed by members of such associations under the general law of crime applying to all citizens alike'.[24] At civil law, they believed, the funds of unions had to be protected and this could best be done through the Friendly Societies' Act and the depositing of rules with the registrar. They rejected the proposal that the registrar should have power to object to rules which he regarded as being 'contrary to public policy'. To allow this was to put limits on the freedom of workers and like the majority of the commissioners they justified their recommendations in terms of the liberal ethos of the mid-century decades. The theme of 'freedom' was a recurring one in the minority report.

So long as he is limited to demand certain terms, and certain other terms are forbidden him, he [the worker] is not free. There is no logical halting place between the old system of compulsion and that of entire freedom. . . . We can understand no freedom of trade in which workmen are not free to stipulate with an employer in concert for their own conditions. . . . Freedom to combine as to their terms of labour, by all ways not commonly recognised as criminal, is the sum of the amendments of the law we suggest in the case of labourers in general.[25]

Within a month of the publication of the final report of the Royal Commission, Harrison, who had drafted the minority report, had a bill ready. It was introduced into the Commons by Hughes and A. J. Mundella. The proposals of the minority report were closely followed: removing statutory restriction on combination; protecting union funds under the Friendly Societies' Act; abolishing special offences in trade disputes.[26] Setting aside their differences, the Conference of Amalgamated Trades, the London Trades Council and George Potter and his supporters organised a strong campaign in support of the bill. Meetings were held and deputations of unionists and sympathetic members of parliament waited on H. A. Bruce, the Home Secretary. The government at first refused to support the measure, but as a result of pressure from William Rathbone[27] and other friendly members Bruce agreed to support the second reading, thus giving approval to the principle. It was passed without a division. A. J. Mundella thought that 'the House of Commons, the Peers and the country, have come round to our views of the right way of legislating for Trades' Unions'.[28] But, Professor Beesly was probably nearer the truth when he suggested that political pressure had merely silenced the very real opposition to the measure. There was strong pressure from Liberal members to get the bill withdrawn and when this failed opponents refrained from committing themselves openly by dividing the House on the second reading.[29] Having had the principle approved, Mundella and Hughes were persuaded to withdraw their measure and await promised government legislation early in the next session.

The government was not to be rushed. A temporary Trades Unions' Funds Protection Act was passed in 1869,[30] but not until February 1871 was a government bill on trade unions in fact introduced. It followed in many aspects the earlier bill of Mundella and Hughes, giving protection to the funds of registered unions, without limiting the content of the rules other than if they had criminal intent, and freeing unions from liability of charges of criminal conspiracy because their purposes were in restraint of trade. In other words, it went a long way to granting the freedom that Harrison and Hughes had demanded. The principle was, as Gladstone noted, 'in all economical matters the law to take no part'.[31] It did not, however, continue with the minority report and abolish special offences for workmen. The criminal offences of 'molestation', 'obstruction', 'intimidation' and 'threat' by workmen during strikes were to be retained. An immediate campaign of protest against these criminal provisions was taken up by the unions and their parliamentary allies. The Trades Union Congress was convened in London to object, but they succeeded only in persuading the government to divide the bill into two parts, with the criminal clauses contained in a distinct Criminal Law Amendment Bill. From the trade unions' point of view the timing of the legislation was unfortunate. In Paris the events of the Commune were taking their bloody course and Mundella detected that 'London Society . . . is leaning to the opinion that all Liberal progress means the confiscation of property and the cutting of throats'.[32] Since there were those who believed that the trade-union bill 'meant Red Republicanism, Communism and Atheism',[33] there was a hardening of attitudes and the House of Lords stiffened the Criminal Law Amendment Bill by adding 'persistently following' and 'watching and besetting' to the list of offences and by making these criminal if done by '*one* or more persons', rather than by '*two* or more' as in the original bill. The government tried to compromise by accepting the Lords' amendment for cases where the 'watching and besetting' was done at the home of a workman, but suggesting that if it were done at the doors of a factory then more than one would need to be involved if it were to be criminal. The Commons, however, rejected this and by 149 to 97 upheld the Lords' amendments in their entirety with Liberals such as Potter, Baines, Illingworth, Ackroyd, McLaren and Sir Wilfred Lawson joining with the Conservatives.[34]

By the Criminal Law Amendment Act of 1871 the hopes of those unionists who had placed faith in working through the Liberal party were seriously disappointed. Much had been achieved. The Trade Union Act gave the necessary protection to funds by allowing unions to register their rules but without allowing the registrar to reject them other than on the grounds that they had criminal intent. In addition it removed unions from the liability of being in restraint of trade. Trade unions as such were no longer unlawful. To this extent acceptance had been granted. But the Criminal Law Amendment Act retained the grievance of special legislation for working men, to some extent in even vaguer terms than the 1825 Combination Act which it repealed. It was still an offence to use violence, threats, intimidation, molestation or obstruction during a trade dispute if it were done 'with a view to coerce' an employer or a workman to do certain specified acts, such as joining a trade union or quitting work. The word 'coerce' was undefined and imprecise enough to allow for the widest interpretation. Greater precision was attempted with words like 'threats' and 'molestation'. By limiting the definition of 'threats' to action involving a breach of the peace, and by defining 'molestation and obstruction' as persistently following a person, hiding his tools or other property, 'watching and besetting' him or his house or following him through the streets in a disorderly manner, it was thought that the last possibilities of action for conspiracy against trade unions had been removed.[35]

Such a view was quickly shown to be mistaken by Mr Justice Brett when, in December 1872, he delivered judgement against five leaders of the London gas stokers who had gone on strike and caused a black-out of part of London. Brett interpreted 'molestation', not just as it was set out in the Act, but as 'anything done with an improper intent which the jury would think as an unjustifiable annoyance and interference with the masters in the conduct of their business . . . and which would be likely to have a deterring effect upon masters of ordinary nerve'.[36] He justified going beyond the statute by returning to the common law of conspiracy. A strike might no longer be a conspiracy in restraint of trade, but it could be a conspiracy to coerce. (An element in this case was that breach of contract was still criminal under the Master and Servant Act of 1867.) The gas stokers were sentenced to a year's hard labour. There was an immediate outcry against both the judge's interpretation of the law and against the harsh sentence, which was four times the maximum permitted under the Criminal Law Amendment Act. A memorial by the men to the Home Secretary was organised by Thomas Hughes, and Bruce commuted the sentence to four months. There were numerous cases under the Criminal Law Amendment Act with magistrates interpreting 'coercion' very widely. Men and women were imprisoned for distributing handbills, shouting and catcalling and during the nine-hour strikes the Tyneside employers used the Act with some effect against the engineers.

A number of lawyers were seriously disturbed by some of the decisions under the Act and became useful allies in the trade unionists' campaign. Henry James, R. S. Wright, C. H. Hopwood,[37] all future judges, took up the unionists' cause along with more familiar allies like Crompton, Hughes, Mundella and Morley. W. V. Harcourt, who had taken on the role of principal spokesman against the Act in the House of Commons, advised that there was no chance of getting a repeal and suggested that unionists go for an amendment to remove the Lords' amendments. The Parliamentary Committee approved of a bill to this effect drafted by R. S. Wright, only to find itself violently attacked by Harrison and Beesly, in the pages of the *Bee-Hive*, for supporting a measure that came nowhere near removing the worst aspects of the penal legislation.[38] The lack of agreement in the trade-union movement gave many Liberals the necessary excuse for not supporting the measure and in July 1872 Harcourt's bill was effectively buried by Lord Elcho in moving an adjournment of the debate, which had the effect of shelving the bill for the session.

The result was a return to the determination on the part of the unionists to have the Act repealed, and no less. It encouraged them also to broaden their protests and to reject all discriminatory legislation against the working class – for instance the Master and Servant Act, and the property qualification for jury services. The Master and Servant legislation had been a particular source of grievance for some time. Under a series of Acts dating from the eighteenth century, breach of contract by a worker was a criminal offence. What was particularly objected to was its application. A complaint under the Acts in England could bring a summons; in Scotland, however, the only method was by warrant which meant the arrest of the accused before the case. It was, therefore, the Scottish unions led by the Glasgow Trades Council who had organised the agitation against the Acts in the 1860s. Some success had been achieved in 1867 when Lord Elcho's Master and Servant Act took away the right of arrest on warrant, made it necessary for a case to be heard by more than one magistrate, and allowed the alternative of a fine to the compulsory imprisonment of the previous Acts. Decisions in the early 1870s, like that of Mr Justice Brett, had the effect of complicating the law of contract and the law of conspiracy so that the Master and Servant Act now joined the conspiracy law and the Criminal Law Amendment Act at the forefront of Labour's grievances.

During 1873 pressure for an alteration of the laws gathered momentum. There were numerous trade-union demonstrations against the Acts, culminating on 2 June, in a massive one in Hyde

G

Park. Four days later Harcourt introduced a motion on the law of conspiracy and the law of contract. There were signs of a mellowing of parliamentary opinion. The gas stokers' case had caused some members to reconsider their attitude and a few months later there was the further notorious case of sixteen farm labourers' wives at Chipping Norton who were sentenced under the Criminal Law Amendment Act for hooting at and, therefore, 'intimidating', blacklegs. The government attitudes, as expressed by Bruce, was, that despite the judgements in the gas stokers' case and in the Chipping Norton case of which they did not approve, the existing legislation ought to be given a 'further trial'.[39] Harcourt, however, pressed ahead with a Conspiracy Law Amendment Bill only to have it so amended by the government in committee and by the House of Lords as to make it ineffective. By the general election of January 1874, public opinion, as reflected in the press and in parliament, was coming round to accepting the need for action. While Harrison and Beesly and others dithered on whether or not to join with nonconformist dissentients in forming a third party, the unionists used the test questions on labour laws, issued by the parliamentary committee of the TUC to sound out the opinions of candidates. A number of Conservative candidates, including the future Home Secretary, R. A. Cross, assented to them. In the first general election by secret ballot, with a Liberal party tearing itself asunder on the issue of the Education Act, one can only guess that the 'unionists revolt' as much as the 'nonconformist revolt' contributed to Disraeli's victory.

It is a measure of the manner in which the issue had come to the forefront of politics that one of the first acts of the new government was the setting up of a Royal Commission of the Labour Laws. True, it was a stalling measure and, as such, boycotted by almost all the trade-union leaders. But, Cross, the Home Secretary, had no experience of major office, and in a government new to power, from a party that had spent nearly twenty years in the political wilderness, emerging for only brief periods of minority rule on the sufferance of the Liberals, such stalling was probably understandable. In addition the decisions of the early 1870s had made the whole issue unbelievably complicated. In view of the subsequent legislation there is little reason to doubt the assurance of Cross and of Disraeli himself that the Royal Commission was intended to facilitate rather than delay legislation. In the event the majority report offered little positive guidance, recommending only minor modifications of the Master and Servant Act, of the

Criminal Law Amendment Act and of the law of conspiracy.[40]
Only Alexander McDonald, the one trade unionist on the committee, proposed more radical amendment and repeal of the
Criminal Law Amendment Act. The government had to do its own
thinking.

After a year of useful social legislation which had, as Frederic
Harrison admitted, 'done more to meet misery and helplessness
than the Economic Government had in five years',[41] Cross felt
confident enough to undertake sweeping reform. In June 1875 he
introduced his Labour Laws. The Conspiracy and Protection of
Property Act combated Mr Justice Brett's ruling in the gas stokers'
case and removed the application of the doctrine of criminal
conspiracy from acts done 'in contemplation or furtherance of a
trade dispute' unless the acts themselves would be punishable as a
criminal offence. In dealing with picketing, the controversial terms,
'threats', 'molestation' and 'obstruction' were dropped and it was
made clear that to be at a place 'in order merely to obtain or
communicate information' was not the equivalent of 'watching
and besetting'. The other measure, the Employers and Workmen
Act, by its very title, indicated a new attitude. It replaced the
Master and Servant Act of 1867 and made employer and employed
equal before the law in cases of breach of contract. The penal
provisions of previous master and servant legislation were
abolished and breach of contract became a purely civil cause, with
civil procedures, remedies and penalties.

There was a remarkably unanimity of approval in press and
parliament on the Labour Laws, with only *Capital and Labour*
striking a discordant note. The trade-union campaign of eight
years had been wholly successful. The proposals put forward in
the minority report of the Royal Commission of 1869 were put
into practice. The fundamental demand that there should be no
special offences for workers and that all should have equality at
law was allowed. An action done by workers in union was (it was
believed) no longer indictable if such an action done by an
individual was quite lawful. Harrison found that the legislation
'virtually exhausted all the points for which workmen have long
contended' and the parliamentary committee of the TUC believed
that 'the work of emancipation' was 'full and complete'.[42]
Acceptance had been granted.

There was, in fact, one final measure to tidy up matters, the
Trade Union Act Amendment Act of 1876, which re-defined 'trade
union'. Under the 1871 Trade Union Act, the definition of a trade

union was 'such a combination as would, if this Act had not been passed, have been deemed to have been an unlawful combination, by reason of some one or more of its purposes being in restraint of trade'. For a trade union to obtain registration under the Act it had to have some purpose in restraint of trade sufficient to have made it unlawful but for the Act. One had, therefore, the paradoxical situation that a society, such as the A.S.E., could not register and the Registrar's job was not to see whether the rules were legal, but to see whether they would have been illegal but for the Act. The 1876 Amendment Act made the term 'trade union' applicable to 'any combination, whether temporary or permanent, for regulating the relations between workmen and masters, or between workmen and workmen, or between masters and masters whether it was in restraint of trade or not.

The feeling that there was 'little more to be done' quickly passed, and guided by Henry Crompton, the Trades Union Congress pressed ahead with further proposals to improve the position of workers. The Chipping Norton case had brought to the fore the powers of unpaid and untrained magistrates to deal summarily with cases and to mete out heavy sentences without giving the option of trial by jury. From 1873 the parliamentary committee, with all the skills of lobbying that they had now learned, campaigned for the appointment of more trained and paid magistrates. In 1879 the Summary Jurisdiction Act went a long way to meeting the unions' demands. The unions, through the parliamentary committee, also pressed their case for employers' liability in the event of injuries at work. Since 1863 the miners had been seeking a compensation act and it was quickly taken up by other unions. The question was bedevilled by the doctrine of common employment, which since 1837, as applied to workmen, meant that a workman had no claim for compensation against his employer if the injury had been caused by the actions of a fellow workman. It meant that an employer was not responsible for the negligence of his managers and superintendents since they were fellow servants with the ordinary labourers.

Alexander McDonald had campaigned for employers' liability during the 1868 election and on his return to parliament introduced, in 1876, a bill that would have abolished the defence of common employment. The bill was withdrawn and the government appointed a select committee under Robert Lowe to enquire into the doctrine and it recommended that the defence of common employment should be abolished in cases of supervisory staff.

A Royal Commission on the Railways in 1877 recommended a similar change. An Employers' Liability Act was passed by the new Liberal government in 1880. It was hardly a satisfactory measure from the point of view of workmen since it contained many loopholes and litigation under it was deterringly expensive and risky. But, at a number of points it did breach the doctrine of common employment.

From 1867 trade unionists had learned to use parliament and public opinion to create a more favourable legal framework for their activities, and not until the 1890s did they once more face harassment from a hostile judiciary and again take up the struggle against new found doctrines of common law.

Chapter 9

Trade Unions and the Press

The progress made by trade unionism towards acceptance can be most clearly documented in the pages of the weekly and daily press. Here one can see attitudes perceptibly changing from unremitting and violent hostility in the early 1850s, through rather grudging approval of some of their activities and the feeling that there was, perhaps, much to be said on both sides of any dispute, to a guarded acceptance that unions were not unvaluable institutions.

I

In the early 1850s, as the engineers found to their cost, there were few newspapers aimed at a specifically working-class readership from which unions could expect to receive support. In London there was the Sunday publication, *Reynolds' Newspaper*, which had its roots in the chartist years, but was now more interested in the spicier aspects of the courts than in trade-union activity. It did, however, give occasional reports on major trade-union events, as did its rival, *Lloyd's Weekly*. In Glasgow, from 1850 to 1877, there was the *Glasgow Sentinel*, edited in the 1850s and 1860s by the Owenites, Robert Buchanan and Alexander Campbell. From the 1860s it was partly under the control of Alexander McDonald and throughout its existence gave very full reports on trade-union activity in and around Glasgow, particularly among the miners. For a number of years Alexander Campbell attended meetings of the Glasgow Trades Council as a reporter for the *Sentinel* and was a kind of honorary member of the Council until he quarrelled with the leading members. In Staffordshire there was the *Potteries Examiner*, edited for many years by William Owen, who was active in trade-union circles. It was deeply involved in the activities of the potters' unions and an advocate of emigration schemes for the working class. From time to time other working-class papers made a short-lived appearance, for instance, William Newtons' *Operative*, to usher in the A.S.E. and Ernest Jones's *The People's Paper*, which tried to keep alive the spark of chartism. Lloyd Jones and Robert Buchanan launched the *Leeds Express* in 1858, but its existence was brief and financially disastrous for Buchanan.

Not until the 1860s, with the appearance of the *Bee-Hive* did London get a working-class press of any significance. It was backed by the trade unions – eighty-two of whom held shares in the company in 1866[1] – and devoted a great deal of space to trade-union affairs, not just in London, but throughout the country. Most trades councils sent in reports of their activities and even Scottish strikes were reported on. It faithfully followed the twists and turns of George Potter's policies and throughout 1865 and 1866 engaged in bitter polemics with Robert Applegarth and the London Trades Council. As a result, the group around the Trades Council leadership launched a rival paper, the *Commonwealth*, taking over the *Workman's Advocate*, which had been edited by J. Towers, McDonald's rival for the leadership of the miners.[2] The *Commonwealth* was the paper of the Reform League, financed by nonconformist businessmen like Samuel Kell and Edward Miall and by Thomas Hughes. There was great difficulty in finding a suitable editor. Odger tried for a time in 1866, but he was notorious for his lethargy, and he gave way to Howell and Randal Cremer. Even Applegarth tried his hand.[3] It hardly held out the promise of success and, in fact, the paper collapsed in the summer of 1867. Although it was the organ of the London Trades Council, the *Commonwealth* never really succeeded in competing with the *Bee-Hive* in its coverage of trade-union affairs and concentrated mainly on the reform agitation.

After 1867 the *Bee-Hive* had the field to itself. Backed by radical money, its policies and attitudes mellowed, but until the middle of the 1870s it remained the most important public platform for the trade unions. It was also of great significance as the place where the Positivists, Harrison, Beesly and Crompton put forward their views on specific issues and tried to mould the policies of the trade-union movement.

The working-class press had one thing in common, its small circulation. At its peak the *Bee-Hive* was selling about 8,000 a week and the *Commonwealth* half of that. Trade unions were, therefore, still dependent on their own publications to keep their members informed. Since 1850 the Flint Glass Makers' Society had published their *Flint Glass Makers' Magazine*[4] from Birmingham and the London Bookbinders their *Trade Circular*. In 1852 the Provincial Typographical Association began publishing the *Typographical Societies' Monthly Circular*[5] and from the 1860s such publications proliferated. The A.S.E., the Amalgamated Carpenters and the Boilermakers had their *Monthly Reports* and the Stonemasons their *Fortnightly* and *Quarterly*. In 1861 George Howell started the *Operative Bricklayers' Trade Circular*, which was soon taken over as the society's organ. In 1868 the Ironworkers started issuing the monthly *Ironworkers' Journal*, with John Kane as its editor. These trade union journals were mainly concerned with their own union's affairs – the state of trade in particular areas, lists of members who were in arrears or whose activities had brought the union into disrepute – but they also contained more general articles. For instance, while editing the *Operative Bricklayers' Trade Circular*, Howell used it to press his views on political action by trade unions. Thomas Dunning in the *Bookbinders' Trade Circular* published his articles on trade unions and political economy and it was mainly through the *Ironworkers' Journal* that John Kane convinced his members of the value of conciliation and arbitration.

II

These papers were, however, for the converted. If trade unions were to get their place in society they had to convince the newspapers that catered for the ever expanding middle-class readership. At the head of these was *The Times*, which in these years was at the peak of its influence in shaping public opinion, but, at the same time, was a fairly accurate barometer of what the educated gentleman was thinking.

The attitude of middle-class opinion towards the trade unions in the early 1850s was clearly revealed in the comments on the lock-out of the engineers in 1852. Not one middle-class paper gave any sympathy to the union. Despite the efforts of the A.S.E. to concentrate attention on piecework and systematic overtime, the press insisted on focusing on the attempt to prevent semi-skilled workers from manning the new machines. The union was condemned as 'a heartless and vulgar tyranny' and a 'self-created despotism', that sought to bring 'the destinies of the trade under the control of Mr Newton and his colleagues'.[6]

The view of unions as the creation of mouthpiece of a few 'paid agitators' was throughout the decade, a favourite with the press. It was these 'paid agitators' who had most to gain from keeping industrial relations in turmoil. Behind every strike, according to *The Times*, were 'one or two professional agitators'[7] and there seemed to be a belief that if only the working classes kept clear of these agitators industrial peace would reign. It was, therefore, something of a shock for the special correspondents, whom the London press sent to investigate the Preston cotton strike of 1853, to discover that the employers had had a combination, fixing wages and prices, since 1836. It was in the Preston strike that the view that in any dispute the employer must inevitably be right began to be questioned and it was in this strike that the lessons of the value of favourable publicity for trade unions were brought home. The special correspondents who visited Preston sent back favourable reports – hitherto unprecedented – on the conduct of the strikers, surprised that they appeared to be 'endowed with good sense, and capable of such self-control' and that they were showing such an 'improvement over former days'.[8]

The image-building tactics of the union leaders were to some extent already paying dividends. There was no acceptance of the value of trade unions, as such, but there were the first glimmerings of a recognition that the case in any dispute was not a one-sided one and that the only lasting solutions to the problems of industrial relations were compromise ones. It was the unwillingness of employers to compromise that most often antagonised London editors. One sees this in the building workers' strike and lock-out of 1859. The use of the 'document' and of the lock-out were from the uncompromising methods of another age. There was no real support for the unions' demands, but the refusal of the employers' to talk about the issues was generally condemned, and *The Times*, in what must have been a moment of aberration, was willing to go so far as to admit that 'except through combination, the cause of labour against capital cannot be audibly and effectively pleaded'.[9]

The publication of the Social Science Association report of 1860 was important in demolishing the myth of the 'paid agitator'. It still appeared occasionally, but as a significant explanation of strikes it was largely abandoned by the early 1860s. Unions were still regarded as of little value and an unfortunate foible of the working classes, but they were less often 'the dangerous tyrannies' of former years. Nor were the editorials as ready to claim that unions could not alter the rate of wages. Few disputed that, in the short term, well-organised unions were materially improving the conditions of their members. Instead, in the mid-sixties one gets a subtle change of tack. Unions were now criticised less for the harm they did to the workers and more for the irreparable damage they were doing to the country. The workers were gaining at the expense of industry and of the nation's future. By the actions of trade unions 'during the last twenty years hundreds of respectable solvent firms have been reduced to bankruptcy', declared The Times;[10] by the action of unions prosperity had been interrupted and foreign competitors given a distinct commercial advantage.[11] Capital was moving to other countries where it was more productive, making Britain 'second instead of first in the race of competition'.[12] One sign of a new attitude was in the reviews The Times gave to the annual reports of the Amalgamated Carpenters' Society in 1866 and 1868. The success of the union could hardly be denied, 'though it might probably indicate nothing more than a fair readjustment of trade balance in their favour'. But the advances were made 'without regard to any claims on the other side'.[13] Unions were no longer written off as useless, but as 'selfish', making their demands, and reinforcing them, without reference to the state of trade or to estimates of profit.[14]

The outrages at Sheffield in 1866, followed soon afterwards by the arrest and trial for illegal picketing and intimidation, of the leaders of the London Tailors' Society altered the focus of the press yet again to the plight of the non-unionist. The need for the firmest action against violence and intimidation and against coercion of non-strikers through picketing was frequently reiterated, and support was given to the formation of 'Anti-Trade Union Associations', such as the company union of Staveley Colliery in Derbyshire. These associations would 'secure freedom and independence of labour' and were essential 'if the Unions are anywhere to be effectively resisted'.[15]

Yet, surprisingly, the actual outrages were treated, at first, with some equanimity. The Times admitted that unions did 'not connive at such criminal violence as the Sheffield Outrages',[16] and even when the Inquiry exposed Broadhead's and the Saw-Grinders' Society's part in them, The Times still believed that 'the great body of Unionists remain free from complicity'.[17] Only the further revelations of 'rattening' among the brickmakers of Manchester stirred 'strong misgivings' that such violence might extend over a wider area.[18]

The Times views are an important reflection of changes in public attitude, because they were made in a paper that opposed the working classes' political aspirations. Radical papers, like the *Daily News* and the *Daily Telegraph* also modified their views on unionism, but they allowed their opinions to be shaped by their political hopes of winning the newly-enfranchised working-class voters to the Liberal Party. As proprietor of the *Daily News* Samuel Morley ensured that it dropped its old hostile attitudes and, while not always enthusiastic, it adopted an approving tone towards trade-union activities. *The Times* was in a different category and its careful phrases are evidence of just how successful had been the leading unions in persuading even conservative opinion that they had nothing in common with the Sheffield men.

Not all papers were as restrained in their comment. The *Saturday Review*, the most violently anti-unionist weekly, thought that the outrages were 'not such very unnatural or outstanding results of Trades' Union principle',[19] and this was the tone adopted by much of the provincial press. Leader writers outside London were much slower to show a change of attitude towards unions. They were more ready to see the 'thugee' of Sheffield, as the *North British Daily Mail* called it, as something that was very much part and parcel of all unionism. The saw grinders had 'only followed out to barbarous extremity the line of conduct sanctioned by all Trade Unions since they came into existence'.[20] One notable exception to such a tone was the *Newcastle Daily Chronicle*. Owned by Joseph Cowen, the *Chronicle* had, since the 1850s, been an advocate of the most progressive liberal policies and had been among the first to take up Bright's demands for an extension of the franchise. By the 1860s it was one of the most influential and widely read of provincial newspapers. Its attitude to trade unionism was consistently one of support. For instance, it was about the only paper, with the exception of the *Bee-Hive*, to support the North Staffordshire ironworkers in 1865 when they refused arbitration,[21] though its more common advice was to pursue a policy of moderation so as not to lose public sympathy. Unlike any other paper it actively encouraged the formation of unions: as early as 1866 it was suggesting that only through combination were the agricultural labourers likely to improve their conditions of life.[22] Naturally the *Chronicle* regarded the Sheffield exposures as a terrible blow to the unions' cause. It would be better, declared an editorial, if trade unions were suppressed than be allowed 'to carry out the vile machinations of BROAD-HEAD'.[23] However, it quickly recovered its composure and welcomed the denunciations of Sheffield that came from other unions as evidence of the correctness of its previous judgements.

With the Royal Commission steadily gathering its evidence throughout 1868, the main concern of the press turned to the issue of legislation. When the Hornby v. Close decision was given *The Times* did not anticipate that any legislation would be necessary to reverse the court's decision[24] and, when the demands for legal recognition and protection of union funds grew throughout 1867 they were treated coolly. It seemed, thought *The Times* that unions were asking 'to have their "rattening" and shooting done for them by the police and hangman'.[25] The success of the Royal Commission in altering such views becomes clear in the comments on the bill introduced by Hughes and Mundella in 1869. *The Times* believed 'public opinion to be with the promoters of the bill'[26] and a few days later made a momentous pronouncement: 'Trade Unions will continue to exist, and to number half a million members, whether they are protected by Act of Parliament or not. True statesmanship will seek neither to augment nor to reduce their influence, but, accepting it as a fact, will give it free scope for legitimate development.'[27] The 'Thunderer' of Printing House Square, as ever, was sailing before the prevailing winds.

Not everyone realised the change. Sir William Armstrong of Newcastle seems to have been genuinely shocked at the critical reception which *The Times* gave to the engineering employers of Tyneside who refused the nine-hour day. He could only assume that Delane, the editor, was away from home![28] But *The Times* gave the lead to other journals. The *Saturday Review* still inclined to see a 'junta of socialist agitators' behind it, but even it accused the employers of 'short-sightedness and stupidity'.[29] Claims by the employers of their right to do what they wished with their own and 'to see the strike as of the nature of mutiny',[30] which had been greeted with such approval in 1852, were now regarded as totally out-dated. As the *Spectator* commented, 'Masters who reply cavalierly by lawyers' letters to the demands of their men, refuse personal discussion, and act as nearly as they can like despotic governments against revolutionary bodies can hardly expect their moral claim on the sympathy of the public to be conceded.'[31] It was a significant measure of the success of twenty years of union strategy.

There was a great deal of press sympathy, in the early years of the 1870s, for the new unions of agricultural workers and railway workers. The *Daily News* sent its distinguished war correspondent,

Archibald Forbes, to report on the Warwickshire labourers' strike of 1872 and his vivid accounts did much to capture the public's imagination. In the main, the attitude of the press was that the labourers' 'revolt' was inevitable.[32] There were few sympathisers with the landed class and most editors agreed with *The Spectator* that 'education and feudalism are irreconcilable'.[33]

By the middle of the 1870s it was very rare for newspapers to devote editorials to the subject of trade unionism. The activities of the unionists and their leaders had been before the public for the last ten or fifteen years and both press and public were 'a little tired of the question'.[34] The lack of interest in the topic was evidence that unions were now fully accepted. Cross's labour laws were approved of by all the leading papers and only the employers' own *Capital and Labour* introduced a note of doubt into the unanimity. There was no love for unions. Major strikes would still produce a sad shaking of heads at the damage they were doing to the country. But the days of demanding repression were gone and instead many columns of print were devoted to the staid proceedings of the meetings and conferences of trade unions and trade councils. The annual meetings of the Trade Union Congress took their place alongside those of the Social Science Association as one of those vaguely radical, but nevertheless, highly respectable, institutions of Victorian England.

III

Next to the daily newspapers and the weeklies and, indeed, perhaps even more important the shaping opinion, were the monthly and quarterly journals. In the mid-nineteenth century these were flourishing and increasing in number and devoted considerable space to the problems of industrial relations.

The older journals, *Blackwood's Magazine*, the *Edinburgh Review* and the *Quarterly Review* were all hostile to trade unionism and they attacked the unions in the same terms as they had used in the 1830s. Their contributors, shrouded in anonymity, showed remarkable ignorance of the reality of mid-century unionism and clung to long out-dated attitudes. It was little wonder, for their main contributors of unionism had had their views formed in earlier decades. Harriet Martineau and W. R. Greg, both of whom wrote in the *Edinburgh Review*, had studied the working class in the 1830s and 1840s and associated unionism with the shootings, maimings and riotings of the Lancashire and Glasgow cotton workers of these years. They altered neither their opinions nor their information to suit the changed circumstances of latter decades. Stranger still are some of the other contributors who chose to lambast the unions. *Blackwood's Magazine* had a former chaplain-general to the forces, G. R. Gleig, writing on 'Strikes and Trade Unions' in 1867, as well as on the Reform bill, both of which he treated from the point of view of the strong Conservative.[36] There was also the Scottish poet and journalist, Charles Mackay, who produced a blood-curdling article in *Blackwood's Magazine*, on 'Work and Murder', at the time of the Broadhead revelations.[37] The *Quarterly Review*, got Robert Lowe to use his vitriolic prose against the unions in 1867[38] and the *Edinburgh Review*, had a former Drummond professor of political economy, G. K. Rickards, to teach the unionists their economic laws.[39]

The friends of trade unions, in contrast, used the new journals which made a virtue of the signed article: Ludlow and the Christian Socialists wrote on unions in *Macmillan's Magazine* and in *Fraser's Magazine*, both published by Christian Socialist sympathisers.[40] The most important journal from the point of view of trade unions was, however, the *Fortnightly Review*. It began publication in 1865 with G. H. Lewes as editor, but made a fresh start in 1867 when John Morley took over and deliberately made the journal the platform of the intellectual liberal radicals. It was here that the Positivists made their most significant literary contributions for the cause of trade unionism. Morley's aim was to give intellectual and cultural leadership to society, and acceptance of the trade unionism of the large amalgamated societies was part of this. Frederic Harrison's attack on political economy, W. T. Thornton's on the wage fund and John Stuart Mill's review of it were all in the *Fortnightly Review*.[41] Beesly wrote on the Amalgamated Carpenters' Society in the first issue under Morley's editorship and in it published his lecture to trade unionists on 'The Social Future of the Working Class'.[42] Harrison and Henry Crompton both contributed articles on labour legislation and the latter continued to do so throughout the 1870s.[43] The support of the *Fortnightly Review* was important because it was influential: it very deliberately set out to be an opinion shaper and helped rebuff the misrepresentations of the older journals.

The *Fortnightly Review* was very much for the intellectual contributor; working men with journalistic ambitions used the *Contemporary Review*. In the latter in 1870 and 1871, George Potter published five articles on trade unionism and industrial relations[44] and George Odger, in one of his few excursions into print, wrote on 'The Working Man in Parliament'.[45] In the mid-seventies, George Howell published a number of articles in the *Contemporary Review* that were to form the basis of his book, *Conflicts of Capital and Labour*.[46] *Fraser's Magazine* also remained an important outlet: George Howell published two articles in 1879, and it was in *Fraser's Magazine* and in the *Contemporary Review* that 'the Journeyman Engineer', Thomas Wright first published his perceptive studies of the condition of the working class.[47]

The employers' journal, *Capital and Labour* was rightly concerned at the large array of literary talent at the service of the unions. This talent made an important contribution to their acceptance by society. Unions had learned that publicity could only help them, and the interest in unionism, which is clear from the amount of space given over to it in newspapers and journals, particularly at the end of the 1860s and early 1870s, was, in the long run, all to their advantage. Uninformed opinion was based on long-remembered violent incidents in the past; informed opinion, by concentrating mainly on the large societies, could only make a favourable contrast.

Chapter 10

Trade Unions and the Working Class

Although trade unions claimed to speak for the working class as a whole, only a fraction – perhaps about a tenth – of the workers were organised in unions in the mid-nineteenth century. Unions were the creation of the skilled workers, but not even all of these were organised. There were many skilled workers who were prepared to act as strike breakers, though by the 1860s and 1870s there seems to have been an increasing tendency for employers to look to the continent for blacklegs, as, for example, Sir William Armstrong and the Tyneside engineering employers had to do in 1871. This may have been some measure of the increased strength of trade unionism, but it may also indicate a tacit acceptance by skilled workers who were not members of a union, of what the union was doing. W. E. Forster, for one, believed that although only a minority of workers were in trade unions they had the sympathy of a very large number of artisans.[1] The relationship of unions to all grades of labour – above all the unskilled – is complex and calls initially for some examination of the hierarchy of the industrial labour force.

G. D. H. Cole, using Dudley Baxter's figures of 1867, has calculated that 14·4 per cent of the wage earners could be regarded as highly skilled, earning on average, 28s to 35s per week. Some groups were earning much more: for example, a newspaper compositor could get as much as 70s per week, some bookbinders 50s to 60s, a flint glassmaker, 48s, and an iron forge roller as much as 90s. The lower skilled, 33·3 per cent according to Cole, would earn on average, 21s to 25s per week, as machine minders, boot-closers or in the finishing trades in textile factories. The largest group of all were the unskilled workers, 52·3 per cent of the wage earners, with earnings ranging from the carter's 22s per week, the railway porter's 17s 6d, the shipwright's helper's 16s to the 13s of the agricultural labourer and the 12s of the general labourer around a calico printing works.[2] Such wide variations in earnings – which had always existed – inevitably created different social habits and attitudes. Even within the skilled section there were subtle divisions. The printer looked down on the building-trade worker and the builder on the shoemaker. In the building trade itself, the bricklayer regarded the plasterer as his inferior.[3]

The big division was, however, between the skilled and the unskilled. As the editor of the *Bee-Hive* wrote in 1864: 'The working classes . . . by which I mean those who labour a certain number of hours per day for a certain weekly wage, are divided into two large sections, one comprising the skilled artisan and mechanic and the other the labourer, the costermonger, the men who find their daily living by means which they themselves would find difficult to describe, although yet honest withal, and the "roughs" of all description.'[4] And as Thomas Wright, 'the Journeyman Engineer', put it, 'between the artisan and the unskilled labourer a gulf is fixed'.[5]

It was not just earnings that differentiated the skilled from the unskilled, but a whole variety of factors that perpetuated the division. There was the pride of the craftsman in 'having a trade', which he regarded as his 'property' and was in contrast to the propertyless labourer. In many cases it was the skilled man who paid the wages of his labourer or helper. Thus the cotton spinner paid his piecer or the shipwright his helper. In other cases the skilled man might be paid by the piece, while the labourer was paid on time rates. In the building trades in 1861 one of the objections to the introduction of payment by the hour was that it put the craftsman on the same footing as the labourer.[6] Finally, the skilled man had his union while the unskilled labourer had not.

There was nothing new in such divisions within the working class and trade unions had always sharpened them. In the first instance, a trade union was a defensive organisation, concerned with protecting the earnings, the privileges, the status and the standards of one particular group of workers. Therefore unions first appeared among the better-off workers who had something to defend and something that was threatened. Artisans and craftsmen formed unions to defend their position, threatened by the changes caused by the widening of the market and the development of new processes, which brought an influx of 'dishonourable' workers into their crafts. They were followed by factory workers, some of whom transferred the restrictive and exclusive tactics of pre-factory collective organisation to the factory situation, while others, through trade-union action, carved out a special area which they made the exclusive preserve of union members. Thus unions did not only defend 'skill', but often created a task which they labelled their 'skill'. They made a craft where it had not existed before.[6a]

The main threat to any group of workers came from outside the group. There was some danger from those who had the necessary skills, but were willing to forego some of the privileges and some of the earnings in order to obtain work. But, the greatest threat came from the 'mates' and 'helpers' and the 'holders-up', who assisted the craftsmen. Over the years they could pick up the rudiments of the craft and, if allowed, take over some of the craftsman's work. It was from this group that there were likely to come the workers of the new machines that with the speed of technological development were constantly threatening the craftsman's position. Then there was the more general threat from the mass of the unskilled. These were the casual labourers, the porters, the dockers, the farm workers and navvies, who provided an untapped pool of labour, who, in a rather vague way, were seen as a potential threat to the craftsman.

Traditionally, the skilled man had displayed hostility to those unskilled workers who could potentially undermine his position. Apprenticeship restrictions were partly for keeping up the standards of the craft, but mainly they were to keep down numbers entering it. Even where there had been no traditional apprenticeship or no special skill involved, trade unions, as they had done in cotton spinning for example, could create a system of restriction of entry. Schemes for a general union of all workers or for a united working class behind the Charter had broken down because workers did not always subordinate group interests to class interests. It was the constant complaint of the Owenite enthusiasts of the early 1830s that unions persistently pursued sectional interests and ignored the calls for delay until the general strike was called to liberate the whole working class. The *Northern Star* frequently lamented the failure of the better-off workers in their trade unions to support the chartist movement. There was, then, nothing new in division of interest within the working class.

It seems possible (one can hardly put it more strongly than this) that there was some sharpening of the division between skilled and unskilled between 1850 and 1880. According to Professor Royden Harrison there was a distinct widening of the earnings differential between skilled and unskilled in the building trades.[7] In many crafts, with improved union organisation, there were attempts at tightening entry restrictions. Yet, in many ways, the skilled craftsman was even more threatened than in the past. Most industries were expanding rapidly, and, despite technological – and often labour-saving – advances, this expansion could be achieved only by the intake of fresh labour. Hence, there was a constant movement into the towns, bringing country-trained workers to compete with the urban carpenter or mason or cabinetmaker. Farm workers' sons were leaving the land and seeking employment in industry. The engineers at the great railway works at Swindon and Crewe, for instance, were complaining that their own sons were having difficulty getting one of the limited number of apprenticeships because of competition from the sons of agricultural labourers and farmers. In many other crafts there were similar complaints that 'skilled men were finding difficulty in placing their children in a trade'.[8] Most unions, also, had to accept that it was no longer possible to maintain a comprehensive apprenticeship system – try as they might – and had to accept receipt of the standard rate as an alternative measure of a man's skill. With increasing pressure on their position, the craftsmen's response was to try to strengthen their union and, where possible, to restrict employment to union men. They also greeted with approval the attempts of the unskilled to organise their own unions and many craft union leaders gave help to the new unions of unskilled workers. They welcomed them into their councils. Societies of general labourers were affiliated to the Glasgow Trades Council at its formation in 1858, and a few months later, a society of harbour labourers joined. In London, one of the founder members of the Trades Council, William Burn, a shoemaker, represented the Brickmakers' Society, of which he acted as secretary, 'they having no man who could read or write sufficiently to keep the minutes and books'.[9] At the end of the 1860s the Edinburgh Trades Council took upon itself the task of 'assisting to organise trade societies' and its organising and agitating committee helped form a Labourers' Association, which joined the Trades Council in 1868, after being invited to do so. With the explosion of unionism among the unskilled at the beginning of the 1870s many of the leading unionists were involved. George Potter and Henry Broadhurst attended the inaugural meeting of the Amalgamated Gas Stokers' Union and Applegarth played an important part in assisting Patrick Kenny to organise the General

Labourers' Union.[10] Once these unions were established they had no difficulty in getting affiliation to the London Trades Council. The dockers, organised in the General Labourers' Protection League, sent delegates in May 1872 to the general delegate meeting and Venner of the League was elected to the Council. At a meeting in October 1872, Patrick Kenny attended as delegate from the General Labourers' Union and a seamen's union sent a representative in April 1873.[11]

To actually organise trade societies was not seen as part of the function of the London Trades Council. As George Shipton pointed out, the Council 'was solely supported by organised trades for their defence'.[12] But the new unions found no hostility. In the election to the Council of 1874, Patrick Kenny received the second highest number of votes and other members elected included a representative from the Postal and Telegraph Workers' Union and one from the Carmen's Association, both newly formed unions.[13] This pattern was repeated elsewhere. A causewaylayers' society affiliated to the Glasgow Trades Council in 1874 and, the following year, a marine stokers' society joined.

The agricultural labourers received support from unions everywhere, as soon as they began to organise. The Webbs printed the appeal on their behalf, issued by the Birmingham Trades Council, as typical. It stressed the unity of labour:

The cause of the agricultural labourer is our own; the interests of labour in all its forms are closely bound up together, and the simple question for each one is, How much can I do and how soon can I do it? . . . The conflict may be a severe one. It is for freedom and liberty to unite as we have done. We have reaped some advantages of our unions; we must assist them to establish theirs.[14]

There was, of course, much to be gained by the skilled workers from organising the general labourers. If organisation succeeded in improving the labourers' position it would keep them from drifting into the building sites and into the factories in search of work. Also agricultural workers and general labourers were relatively easy to assist since they threatened no vested interests within the trade-union movement. There was much less enthusiasm for organising the craftsmen's helpers, for it was from them that the most immediate threat to the craftsman's position always came. No craftsman ever came out on strike in support of the wage demands of his labourers and there were complaints that strikes by labourers had failed 'in consequence of the aristocracy of mechanics and artisans ignoring the underpaid labourers'.[15] The monthly reports of the Boilermakers' Society contain many critical comments of the attempts being made in 1875 to organise their helpers in the Amalgamated Labour League.[16] Only occasionally was any financial help given by a union to labourers thrown out of work by the skilled men going on strike and usually only when it seemed they might do some blacklegging. More commonly, the labourer was ignored or treated with indifference. It was a frequent complaint that skilled men, paid by the piece, took time off when they felt they had earned enough, with no regard for the effect of this on the hourly-paid labourer.

A very clear gap existed, therefore, in industry between the skilled man and the unskilled and the effect of trade unionism was to perpetuate and widen this division. But there was also a wide social gap between the skilled and the unskilled and the activities of trade unions in the 1850s, 1860s and 1870s did a great deal to widen this gap.

I

It was from the 1850s that the middle class began to see significance in the divisions within the working class. When writers in the 1830s and 1840s looked to the working-class movements of these years they tended to see an undifferentiated mass of workers acting from class motives and threatening order and property. Only a few, looking particularly at Birmingham, with its large class of artisans in small workshops, detected a class with whom the middle classes might find common ground.[17] By the 1850s, however, contemporaries were much more aware of the working-class divisions. Thus, W. R. Greg, who never abandoned the hope of teaching the working class to take a realistic view of their situation, always spoke of 'the working *classes*' because he believed that there was 'less of sympathy, of sense of common interest, or even mutual respect, between the upper and lower strata of the working classes – between, say a skilled and intelligent artisan and an ignorant and half-pauper labourer – than there is between several of the higher strata of those who are spoken of as one class and some of the strata of those spoken of as another and dissimilar class'.[18] Trade unions were often attacked for perpetuating such a division, as by Samuel Smiles, who saw them as 'an exclusive body, whose principal object is to keep as many as possible out of their particular trades, and especially to shut out the poor and unskilled from participating in their peculiar advantages'.[19]

Social commentators of the 1850s and 1860s were also concerned with another division which they saw in the working class, between those who were taking advantage of the free, competitive society to 'improve' and 'elevate' themselves and the 'sunken people', 'those vast, miserable, unmanageable masses' who, if something was not done, threatened to overwhelm society, through their 'want of industry, thrift or self-reliance' and the 'spreading decay of the spirit of independence'.[20] From the 1860s onwards there was a considerable amount of concern at the growth of pauperism and the failure of a large section of the working class to fit in with the image that society had of itself. There was a belief that the possibility of upward mobility was unlimited and that any worker, given intelligence, prudence, thrift and industry could rise up the social scale. It was the *credo* of the self-made men who were coming to the fore, that individual qualities of character had brought them success and it was propagated in the writings of Smiles and others. The converse of the belief was that poverty was a product, not of environment and of economic circumstances, but of a fundamental weakness in character, a lack of those qualities of intelligence, prudence, thrift and industry. The personification of such an attitude was the Charity Organisation Society, who believed that pauperism was on the increase because of indiscriminate alms-giving which encouraged weaknesses in character and failed to bring out the latent spirit of self-help.

This view of a divided working class, which the Charity Organisation Society adopted in 1869 as its fundamental premise, was well-established over the previous decade. In 1858 the Bradford printer, Malcolm Ross, saw the mass of the population divided into 'the sober and the dissipated classes'. Three years later, the *Bradford Observer* remarked on the 'schism 'in the working class,

a schism which, although inarticulate is beyond hope of immediate reconciliation. The hewers of wood and drawers of water are widely separated in sentiment and interest from the educated, intelligent and not infrequently refined fellow-labourer, who is certain of bettering his condition as the ignorant and immoral are for ever of floundering in the mire, although men and gods decreed that they should rise.[21]

On the same theme, Robert Baker, the factory inspector, in his report for 1865 quoted a study of the village of Longton in the Potteries. Here there was found a very distinct division within a group of workmen with similar earnings. On the one hand there were those who invested in savings banks, insurance societies, sick and friendly clubs and building societies. Through such organisations they were able to live in security and comfort in their own houses. Alongside these, however, 'in the same locality, employed at the same work, earning the same wages, and without any extraordinary drawback' was a large number of others 'who possess no such properties, live on from day to day, regardless of every enjoyment which is not sensual; exhibiting no desire for an elevation of character amongst their fellow men, wasting their money in profitless pursuits, or in degrading pastimes, and being for ever unprepared for the commonest vicissitudes, which bring such misery in their train'.[22] What was true of Longton was true elsewhere and the division of the working class into a 'respectable' element and a 'rough' element was as familiar to the social commentator of the 1860s as it was to the sociologist of the 1960s.

From the point of view of trade unions, the real significance of all this was that in the mid-nineteenth century 'respectability' came to be identified first with skill and then with trade unionism, while 'roughness' was seen as the accompaniment of the lack of skill and the lack of a trade union. The first stage was a fairly obvious one. It was the skilled workman who had the money to lay aside in savings clubs and building societies. He had exhibited the qualities of intelligence, industry and self-reliance in undertaking the learning of a craft. The second step of linking this with trade unionism was less easily accomplished. The link with friendly societies helped and all were agreed that the friendly society was an important sign of self-help. By laying such stress on their benefit side, societies like the A.S.E. and the Amalgamated Carpenters certainly helped to convince people that unions could be vehicles for improvement. But it needed more than that, for there were aspects of unionism which the middle class found less appealing and which many believed ought to be separated from the friendly society role. It was the achievement, partly of the unionists themselves, but mainly of their middle-class allies, to identify all aspects of unionism with 'respectability'.

It was people like Ludlow, Hughes and Harrison who associated unionism with the 'superior' skilled workman. It was Ludlow who first wrote of the members of the A.S.E. in 1852 as 'the aristocracy of the trades'[23] and he continued to represent unionists as that respectable elite. Quoting a Yorkshire friend in 1867, he commented on Barnsley, notorious for its 'roughs', and contrasted the unorganised districts with those in union:

In the one, the men get the same pay as the unionists, but waste it uncontrolled. In the union districts, with better pay and shorter hours of work than before, the men are turning their attention to garden plots, to pig-feeding, joining Co-operative and Building Societies. They are saving in Penny Banks and the Post Office has many hundreds of pounds of their money. It is found that though the men work shorter hours daily they do more work and earn more money, because they work more regularly, do not break time, and have no 'Saint Mondays' or 'play days'. There is a very decided improvement, both physical, moral, economic, and social in the whole Yorkshire district where union prevails. But when there is no union discipline, we have dogfights and manfights, riots and manslaughters at every stage.[24]

This was the message of the Social Science Association report and of the union spokesmen at the Royal Commission. It was the message of the pamphlets and of the union reports and of the numerous articles which union leaders and their friends produced for *Fortnightly* and the *Contemporary Review*. 'Show us . . . a trade or a district where no unions exist,' wrote George Potter, 'and you will find the labourer robbed of his hire . . . a miserable, puny, half-starved creature, hovering, with all dependent upon him, upon the verge of pauperism.' In contrast, there was the unionist 'with good wages, good clothing, good feeding, good homes and a good deal of intelligence'.[25] It was the unions who taught restraint and self-government and who committed the working class to progress.

II

The Liberal radicals grasped that this division within the working class had a political significance. Thomas Attwood and the Birmingham Political Union had seized on it in 1831 and 1832 and used the artisans of Birmingham as 'the non-commissioned officers for the movements that united the middle and working classes'.[26] It was, significantly, after his move to Birmingham that John Bright began to focus on the respectable working class and to press for an extension of the franchise. Bright and the radicals who followed him sought to bring this section of the working class within the pale of the constitution. They were concerned only with the elite, 'the honest, intelligent, upright and patriotic artisan, to whom the rights of property and conscience are as sacred as these things can be to the highest and noble in the land'.[27] They saw this elite in the trade unions and set out to court them. The policy runs from Bright, through Samuel Morley to Joseph Chamberlain – and it worked. By 1880 a solid lib-lab working-class vote had been established. Conservatives were well aware of what was being done. A contributor to *Blackwood's Magazine* was amused at how disconcerted were the Liberals at Disraeli's 1867 Reform Bill, because it did take into account the 'residuum' – 'the mere drudges – the unthinking, uneducated labouring men'.[28] Some viewed the Bill with equanimity precisely because they believed that by it 'the aristocracy of labour will be entirely swamped, and the power of the Trades' Union . . . dwindle into insignificance',[29] though the perceptive Robert Lowe noted that unionism was spreading to the unskilled.[30]

Many of the large employers were radical in their politics and their desire to get the political support of the labour aristocracy in some cases influenced their industrial policies and persuaded them to recognise the trade unions. Some believed that the elite could be found in the mechanics' institute and in the temperance societies and tried to make contact with it in these, while remaining hostile to trade unions. The shipbuilder, Charles Palmer of Jarrow, was one example of these. He was a keen supporter of mechanics' institutes, frequently addressing meetings at them in the North East, but using the opportunity of these meetings to denounce the 'fever of trade unionism'.[31] However, most realised that by the 1860s mechanics institutes were used more by clerks and shop-keepers than by the skilled working men and that their members did not provide the leadership of the working class. Only the trade unions could do that. On the other hand, it was probably more usual for the employer to come to appreciate the value of trade unionists in industry before turning to them politically. Thus Morley, Mundella, the Kells, Thomas Brassey and others had learned the disciplining power of unions over their membership in industry before they fully realised their political value.

With the passing of the Second Reform Act the link between industrial action and political considerations may have been strengthened. Trade-union leaders were mixing with employers in the Liberal associations and knowledge generally produces tolerance. The employer with political ambitions was not going to risk the hostility of the local unions, if he could help it, by employing blackleg labour.[32] Similarly, the politically ambitious unionist was not going to antagonise the powerful members of the Liberal Association by taking too militant a line.

On the unions' side, the lib-lab alliance was imposed on the working class by a small group of union leaders, guiding a generally apathetic rank and file. There had always been, even in the chartist period, those among the working class who had seen class collaboration as the best policy. These were able to come to the fore in the 1860s because they were getting a response from the liberals. Some were even willing to go so far as to sacrifice industrial demands for the sake of attracting middle-class sympathy. A number of speakers in the Glasgow Trades Council, for example, warned against embarking on an agitation for shorter hours 'because it was their duty to conciliate the middle classes' who were 'willing to lend their assistance in getting a reform bill'.[33] Most of the politically active union leaders were concerned with getting the vote for the 'respectable' working man. There was a great deal of working-class support for the limited, household suffrage demand of the Reform Union, and although the Reform League was committed to residential manhood suffrage and George Potter's Working Men's Association to the 'lodger franchise', one suspects that it was a question of asking a lot in the hope of getting a little. How else does one explain their acceptance of Gladstone's very moderate bill of 1866? The anti-reform *Blackwood's Magazine* certainly interpreted the unionists' tactics in that way. Of George Potter – in the eyes of many hostile commentators either the string puller behind all the machinations of trade unions or 'the Coryphaeus' of the unions–*Blackwood's Magazine* declared: 'Mr Potter desires to keep the working men apart from the "roughs", because his views extend to a seat in Parliament for himself as soon as the pressure of working men and roughs together shall force the legislature to concede what is demanded. He is willing that the trade unions shall co-operate with the roughs, but not that the two classes should be confounded.'[34] If this was true of Potter, how much more true it was of Howell, Applegarth, Odger and the others at the forefront of political agitation.

III

To understand the significance of the years 1850 to 1880 in labour history it is important to remember that trade unions operate at two levels. At one level they are social organisations reflecting the attitudes and speaking for sections of the working class; at another level they are industrial organisations concerned with the rights and privileges of one particular group within that class. The activities at both levels are inter-related and one reinforces the other. A policy of moderation in industry can hardly succeed unless it is accompanied by moderation in social and political attitudes and *vice versa*. Between 1850 and 1880 the main policy adopted by trade unions, both socially and industrially was a conciliatory one.

There had always been those leaders of the working class who argued for the acceptance of the prevailing values of society and who believed that the best policy for the working class was to seek acceptance and approval by other classes. They were the 'respectable' men who attended the mechanics' institutes, the temperance societies and who read the improving tracts of the Society for the Promotion of Useful Knowledge. These were men thoroughly imbued with the individualist ethic which was propagated by all the channels of communication. There were also those who had a more highly-developed class consciousness and who were concerned with the political and social advancement of the working class as a whole. These were men who had often supported the chartists and still believed in the rightness of the chartist demands. But they recognised 1848 as the end of the road for an *ouvrièriste* policy and now sought advancement in co-operation with other classes. The policy of extracting concessions by force had failed and the alternative was to obtain concessions through reason. Both types were to be found in the leadership of the trade unions in the mid-century, preaching responsibility and respectability within their own organisations and 'selling' their unions to the middle-class public as moderate, reputable and useful bodies.

Related to this was a policy of moderation in industry. Again the roots of this policy can be found in earlier decades. It involved an acceptance of industrialisation and a learning of what Professor Hobsbawm has called 'the rules of the game'.[35] Those who were doing well out of the changes brought about by industrialisation had quickly learned the rules. The protests which had dominated the early years of industrialisation came from those who were being threatened by change, not from those who were moving up in earnings and status. There had never been many strikes of engineers and ironfounders and such workers were not to be found in the ranks of machine smashers, utopian socialists or even chartists. By the 1850s industrialisation was spreading its bounty: not evenly, but to enough workers to create a significant new spirit. Others were learning to play the game and were abandoning the attempt to halt change and were seeking rather to make the most of what the system had to offer. In most industries the traumatic experience of transformation to an industrialised system had taken place. The factory system was here to stay; wood had given way to iron in ships and machines; building had become concentrated in the hands of large contractors; time was burying the problem of the handloom weavers. Once the immediate trauma of industrial impact had passed more workers learned to live with changed circumstances, compensated by higher earnings and an improved standard of living.

Just as social moderation resulted from a recognition of the failure of chartism, so industrial moderation resulted from a recognition of the failure of a policy of confrontation. There was plenty of evidence that continual confrontation of the employers with strike action was disastrous. Many a time in the past a failed strike had destroyed a nascent union. Strikes were always a means of letting into a trade a flood of new workers from other towns, or from the rural hinterland or from Ireland – for there were always plenty willing to act as strike breakers. Frequently it was strikes that had encouraged employers to seek new labour-saving machines, like the self-acting mule in the 1830s, to eliminate the bargaining power of small groups of key workers. The most successful unions, in the long term, had always been those whose rules and regulations, whose standards and whose right to exert some control over entry to a trade, had been accepted by their employers. By the 1850s and 1860s more and more unions had come to accept this and to seek recognition from the employers. To achieve it they had to be willing to bargain and to accept compromises. But, if the reward was survival of the union and slow but steady advance, they were ready for compromise.

The policy of seeking acceptance did not emerge fully-armed from the brain of William Allan or of William Newton in 1850. It was rather the outcome of decades of experience and of favourable economic circumstances. Yet, the A.S.E. came to symbolise the policy; therein indeed lies the true importance of that union. Historians dislike discontinuity and there has been in recent years something of a reaction against the claims of Sidney and Beatrice Webb that the late forties and early fifties brought a sharp change in direction to the trade-union movement with a 'new spirit' accompanying the emergence of a 'new model'. Perhaps, as in all revisions, the reaction has been excessive.

The Webbs do exaggerate the importance of the A.S.E. as a model and its newness. The new amalgamation was built on foundations long- and well-laid by its predecessors like the Journeymen Steam Engine Makers' Society. In organisation and attitude there was not so very much to differentiate the 'Old Mechanics' from the A.S.E.: only in its scale was the A.S.E. new. A few societies, like the Amalgamated Carpenters used the A.S.E. rule book as a model for their own. But many others took bits and pieces of it and adapted them to suit their own needs. The real significance of the A.S.E., which cannot be over-emphasised, was as a *symbol*. Its size, its ability to survive, its steady growth, its large funds, its success in getting recognition from employers, all of these made it different and something to be emulated. There were many who disliked its calm self assurance and the slightly superior air of its leaders. Some felt it placed altogether too much emphasis on benefits, but few denied that, within the limits it set itself, it was a success. It was especially attractive to the union leaders, who sought growth and stability for their societies and who looked enviously at the power which was concentrated in the hands of William Allan and his executive. These were features that other unions sought to copy.

The pressure for imitation came from the leadership. They saw the advantage of benefits for attracting and holding members and, often against considerable rank and file opposition, pressed for an extension of the range of benefits. It was from the leadership that the moves for centralisation and amalgamation came. They inevitably sought to pull more power into their own hands. The trend was resisted: local loyalties were important; to many, democratic processes were more important than efficiency; despite new roads and new railways, the Mancunian's suspicion of the Londoner or the Aberdonian's suspicion of the Glaswegian did not disappear. But, success and efficiency which they saw in the A.S.E., brought by national organisation and central control was attractive and gradually other amalgamations were achieved or strengthened. Executives ceased to perambulate around the country and settled in London or in Manchester or Newcastle. The appointment of full-time officials began and bureaucracy moved in.

The A.S.E. was also important as a symbol to outsiders. To some it stood for all that was dangerous in trade unions, a great nation-wide power that could dictate to the employers and perhaps even threaten the very fabric of society. They saw it only as a bigger and dangerously more efficient version of all that had gone before, which could be effectively dealt with only by a judicious use of special constables and educative texts. To others, however, it was rather a symbol of hope, for it showed that at least among one section of the working class there was the potential for ordered progress, for self-reliance and for self-government. The formation of the A.S.E. (1851), immediately brought to public notice by the national lock-out of engineers, was the first major working-class movement after the chartist demonstrations of 1848 to strike the public consciousness. It gave hope that the working class need not remain alienated from the mainstream of society and that there was the possibility of averting a class war which had often seemed imminent during the preceding two or three decades.

The struggle for acceptance by the unions succeeded because there was a response from the middle and upper classes. Moderate policies required concessions on both sides and without a responsive middle class there would have been a fairly rapid return to confrontation. The first to stretch out a hand to the unionists were those who, influenced by the writings of Arnold and Carlyle saw an urgency in settling 'the condition of England' question – the Christian Socialists, the Positivists. They focused on the progressive features of unionism and sought to convince others to make a response. They also worked closely with union leaders to strengthen the trend towards moderate policies. The careful educating of public opinion, partly by the unionists themselves, but mainly by the Christian Socialists and Positivists, began to have its effect. Other groups within the middle class began to accept that there was an element within the working class with which they could communicate and from which they could get support. Thus radicals like Stansfield and Cowen looked to the trade-union leaders for support in their pro-Italy and pro-Poland agitations; Bright and Beales looked to them as allies in a reform campaign intended to lead finally to the ousting of the aristocracy from their position of political domination; Morley, Kell and the nonconformists saw in them useful backing for the campaign against church establishment; Dixon and Chamberlain used them as allies in their struggle for non-denominational education.

Once begun, the process was a self-generating one. Respectability spread as acceptance spread. When the working-class leaders found they could be accepted by the middle class if they were respectable, then it encouraged them to intensify their efforts to exude respectability. Nothing must be done to disturb the new harmony and there were even those who argued that industrial policies had to be modified if they were not to offend the middle-class allies.

Employers also altered their attitudes to unions. They too were less keen on a policy of confrontation, when trade was expanding and much had been invested in expensive capital equipment. They had learned to live with unionism and by the 1850s and 1860s were coming to appreciate its value. It presented them with the possibility of compromise. They found that they could negotiate with the union leaders and that they were likely to prove more reasonable and open to argument than was a mass meeting of workers. Unions introduced a discipline into industrial relations which the employers welcomed. The larger industrial units which were coming into being made it impossible to deal with each individual workman; some structured system was necessary and this the unions provided. Changing social attitudes had their effect on industrial relations. There was pressure on employers to adopt methods that would bring industrial peace. Strikes in industry were seen by many people as an indictment of a civilisation that strove after peace and freedom and in international affairs seemed to be having some success. If armed conflict could be avoided at the conference table, then so too could industrial conflict. In addition, many leading employers were radical in their politics and it was hardly possible to court the union leaders at a political meeting and then refuse to see them in the factory. In a favourable economic environment, mutual knowledge could only help remove suspicions and smooth the way to union acceptance.

There was then a two-way process: a working class wishing to be accepted socially, having abandoned the hope of altering the system by force, and a middle class ready to grant acceptance and to incorporate the working class into the body politic. There were trade unions learning to adopt new policies of moderate advancement and there were employers ready to grant concessions in return for order and discipline in industrial relations. One can find isolated examples of this process in operation before 1850, but it was not until the end of the 1840s, beginning of the 1850s, that one can detect a distinct national trend, a new spirit.

A policy of social and industrial compromise was adopted by both sides in these years because it worked. When it broke down other tactics were used. Thus, when the Liberal government of 1868 to 1874 failed to live up to expectations the working-class leaders were quite prepared to use the politicians of other parties or to adopt threatening postures of independent action. If the local Liberal association ceased to be responsive to the aspirations of local working-class leaders then they would organise against it. Similarly in industry, moderate industrial policies were only used if they worked and if concessions were being granted without strike. When more militant tactics were necessary they were ready to use them. There *was* continuity in the aims of the working class and of the trade unions: the protection of the rights of their members and the advancement of their interests, their earnings and their standard of living. Times were right for trying new methods, but the old ones were not abandoned entirely nor forgotten. The strike weapon continued to be used, but as a weapon of last resort, not the only weapon. If employers refused conciliation then unions fought. If employers were not giving the concessions the workers believed they had a right to then the unions fought. But neither side now envisaged a struggle to the last ditch. Most unions regarded survival as their first priority: most employers were prepared to sacrifice some of the prerogatives of management in the interests of industrial peace and of maintaining production.

Finally, if one caveat is necessary to the above analysis it is that any expectation of consistency in the trade-union movement of these years – or indeed at any time – is a mistake. The working class in the mid-nineteenth century was a complex organism shaped by many different experiences and many different forces and philosophies. History, myth, tradition could all shape responses to a particular situation just as much as rational policy. The Owenite and the chartist struggles took on a heroic quality with the passing of years and working-class leaders in their unions could still, at times, see themselves in the vanguard of a great working-class struggle for a new world. One can find the same men pursuing moderate, cautious policies, affirming time and again their responsibility and respectability, while, in the next breath, adopting the language of the class war and reminding their members that they were engaged in a vicious struggle with avaricious capitalism. The same speech of a union secretary could contain a reminder that there was little that could be done in the face of a falling market and the inexorable law of supply and demand, and an insistence that workers get a just share in the increasing rewards of industry. On the platforms the union leaders could picture themselves as speaking for the working class as a whole, while in the workshop they were engaging in bitter demarcation disputes with fellow workers in other unions. They could sympathise with the unskilled, while using every restrictive practice to hold them out of their particular craft. They could preach freedom of labour, while adopting protection and laud self-help, while pressing for state regulation.

It is perhaps ironic that in a period laden with new social and political philosophy – the period of Marx and Engels – there was no theoretical dogma to which the trade unions felt themselves bound to conform. Their approach, as it had always been and as it was to remain, was pragmatic. It was a pragmatism that made the dominant strategy of the 1850s, 1860s and 1870s a policy of conciliation, a struggle for acceptance.

H

Biographical Notes on Trade Unionists

ALLAN, WILLIAM (1813–1874), engineer; born in Ulster, worked in Liverpool and Crewe; secretary of the Journeymen Steam Engine Makers' Society 1847–50; with William Newton, the moving spirit in the formation of the A.S.E.; general secretary of the A.S.E. 1851–74; treasurer of the parliamentary committee of the TUC 1871–4.

APPLEGARTH, ROBERT (1834–1924), joiner; born in Hull, worked in Sheffield; general secretary of the Amalgamated Society of Carpenters and Joiners 1861–71; on general council of International Working Men's Association 1865, 1868–72; on committee of Reform League; William Owen described him as 'a keen little lawyer – born to intrigue, and manipulate and pull strings'; member of the Royal Commission on Contagious Diseases 1871–3; resigned the secretaryship of the Carpenters because of criticism of his appointment to the Commission; acted as secretary to Edward Jenkins of the National Education League; later agent for mining equipment company. See A. W. Humphrey, *Robert Applegarth: Trade Unionist, Educationist, Reformer* (1913).

ARCH, JOSEPH (1826–1919), agricultural labourer from Barford; chairman of the National Agricultural Labourers' Union; member of the parliamentary committee of the TUC 1874, 1876; Liberal M.P. for West Norfolk 1855–6, 1892–1900; member of Warwickshire County Council 1888–1900. See *Joseph Arch, The Story of His Life, Told by Himself* (1898).

BATESON, ROGER, Birmingham joiner; treasurer of the General Union of Carpenters and Joiners; first secretary of the Birmingham Trades Council 1866–7; secretary of the Birmingham branch of the Reform League 1866–8; became full-time secretary of the Queen's Hospital Extension Committee.

BIRTWISTLE, THOMAS, secretary of Accrington Weavers' Association; secretary of East Lancashire Power Loom Weavers' Amalgamation 1858–84; secretary of the North-East Lancashire Weavers' Amalgamation 1884–92; member of the parliamentary committee of the TUC 1877–89, 1891; appointed factory inspector in 1892 'as the only person who could be found competent to understand and interpret the intricacies of the method of remuneration in the weaving trade' [Webb, *History*, p. 309].

BROADHURST, HENRY (1840–1911), stonemason; member of the Operative Stonemasons' Society in London; member of the London Working Men's Association and of the Reform League; secretary of the Labour Representation League 1873–8; secretary of the parliamentary committee of the TUC 1875–86, 1886–90; Liberal M.P. for Stoke on Trent 1880–5, for Bordesley Division of Birmingham 1885–6, for West Nottingham 1886–92, for Leicester 1894–1906; under-Secretary of State at the Home Office 1886. See *Henry Broadhurst M.P., The Story of His Life, Told by Himself* (1901).

BURNETT, JOHN (1842–1914), engineer; leader of the Newcastle nine-hour movement 1871; general secretary of the A.S.E. 1874–86; first labour correspondent of the Board of Trade 1886–93; chief labour correspondent under the Commissioner for Labour 1893–1907; William Owen wrote of him that he 'was never any force in Trades Unionism at all – he was not a man of ideas, and was very reactionary' [Webb Trade Union Collection E. A/I/414].

BURT, THOMAS (1837–1922), miner; general secretary of Northumberland Miners' Mutual Confident Association 1865–1913; Liberal M.P. for Morpeth 1874–1918; Parliamentary Secretary to Board of Trade 1892–5; T. P. O'Connor wrote of him: '. . . a small, delicate little man, with a long brownish red beard, a very gentle manner, a very soft voice, a very sweet character. Everyone loved him; and though his opinions were considered extreme at the time, he expressed them with such sweet reasonableness that he was always heard with respect.' See Thomas Burt, *An Autobiography* (1924).

CAMPBELL, ALEXANDER (1796–1871), joiner; for forty years the leading Scottish Owenite; member of the Orbiston community; founder member of the Glasgow Trades' Committee of the 1830s and involved in numerous subsequent attempts to bring about a general union of trades in the West of Scotland; Owenite social missionary in the late 1830s and 1840s; reporter and later editor of the *Glasgow Sentinel* 1857–69. See W. H. Marwick, *Life of Alexander Campbell* (Glasgow, 1964).

COULSON, EDWIN (d. 1893), bricklayer; secretary of the London Order of the Operative Bricklayers' Society 1860–90; associated with Applegarth on the London Trades' Council in the 1860s; re-organised the administration of the Bricklayers' Society.

CREMER, WILLIAM RANDAL (1838–1908), carpenter; member of the

Progressive Society of Carpenters, but joined the Amalgamated Carpenters at its formation; secretary of the workmen's committee that organised the St James's Hall meeting 1863; member of the general council of the International Working Men's Association 1864–6; leading member of the anti-Applegarth group within the Amalgamated Carpenters 1870–1; active in peace movements; Liberal M.P. for Haggerston 1885–1908; Nobel Peace Prize Winner 1902; knighted 1906.

DAVIS, WILLIAM JOHN (1848–1934), Birmingham brassworker; general secretary of the Amalgamated Brassworkers' Society 1872–83, 1889–1920; factory inspector 1883–9; first trade-union secretary to be a member of a school board; elected to Birmingham City Council 1879; later J.P.; very active in establishing conciliation boards. See W. A. Dalley, *The Life Story of W. J. Davis* (1914).

DRONFIELD, WILLIAM (1826–1914), printer; secretary of the Sheffield branch of Typographical Association 1855–90; secretary of the Sheffield Association of Organised Trades 1859–71; secretary of the United Kingdom Association of Organised Trades 1866–9; member of the Reform League; secretary of the committee that nominated A. J. Mundella as candidate for Sheffield in the election of 1868; appointed sanitary inspector 1871.

DUNNING, THOMAS JOSEPH (1799–1873), bookbinder; secretary of the London Consolidated Lodge of Journeymen Bookbinders 1843–73; editor of the *Bookbinders' Trade Circular* 1850–71; member of the executive committee of the Labour Representation League; author of *Trades Unions and Strikes: Their Philosophy and Intention* (1860).

GILLIVER, WILLIAM (d. 1898), cordwainer; first president of the Birmingham Trades Council 1866–8; secretary of the Trades Council 1869–78; active in temperance work; secretary of the Birmingham branch of the Workmen's Peace and International Arbitration League.

GUILE, DANIEL (1814–1883), iron founder; born near Liverpool; joined the Friendly Society of Iron Moulders 1834; secretary of the Friendly Society of Iron Founders 1863–81; member of the London Trades Council 1864–7; member of the parliamentary committee of the TUC 1875–6.

HALLIDAY, THOMAS (b. 1835), miner; secretary of the Lancashire Miners' Association; secretary of the Amalgamated Association of Miners 1869–75; candidate for Merthyr Tydvil in general election of 1874; member of the parliamentary committee of the TUC 1875–6.

HARNOTT, RICHARD (1807–1872), general secretary of the Operative

Stonemasons' Society 1847–72; responsible for the re-organisation of the Society.

HOWELL, GEORGE (1833–1910), bricklayer; secretary of the London Trades Council 1860–2; secretary of the Reform League 1865–9; secretary of the parliamentary committee of the TUC 1871–5; secretary of the Plimsoll and Seamen's Fund Committee 1873–5; Liberal M.P. for North-East Bethnal Green 1885–95; author of a number of books and articles on trade unionism. William Soutter wrote of him: 'Mr George Howell has never worked or been connected with any movement where money was scarce and hard work the only reward' [F. W. Soutter, *Recollections of a Labour Pioneer* (1923), p. 120]. See F. M. Leventhal, *Respectable Radical: George Howell and Victorian Working Class Politics* (1971).

JONES, LLOYD (1811–1886), fustian cutter; Owenite missionary; Christian Socialist; journalist; frequent contributor to the *Bee-Hive*; candidate at Chester-le-Street in election of 1885.

KANE, JOHN (1819–1876), born at Alnwick; ironworker with Hawks, Crawshay & Sons, Gateshead 1836–64; established short-lived iron-workers' union at Gateshead 1840; president of the Association of Malleable Ironworkers 1862–8; general secretary of the National Association of Ironworkers 1868–76; member of the parliamentary committee of the TUC 1872–3, 1875; member of the Land and Labour League; member of the Workmen's International Peace Association; member of the Darlington School Board and of Council of Darlington Ratepayers' Association.

KENNY, PATRICK, Irish labourer; founder and secretary of the General Amalgamated Labourers' Union 1872–9; active in the fair trade movement in 1880s.

KNIGHT, ROBERT (1833–1911), general secretary of the United Society of Boilermakers and Iron and Steel Shipbuilders 1871–1900; member of the parliamentary committee of the TUC 1875–83, 1896–1901.

MCDONALD, ALEXANDER (1821–1881), Lanarkshire miner; attended Glasgow University; miners' agent; leader of the Scottish Miners' Association from 1852; president of the National Association of Coal, Lime and Ironstone Miners of Great Britain 1863–81; member of the parliamentary committee of the TUC 1871–4; M.P. for Stafford 1874–81; Applegarth told the Webbs that McDonald 'lived in good style, liked to give champagne, speculated and made money'. Thomas Burt wrote of him: 'The means of Alexander McDonald were, in fact, rather considerable. He was a workmen's representative in a quite genuine sense, but much water had flown under the bridges since he had been a workman. He was really a capitalist and an employer of labour.'

MACDONALD, WILLIAM, secretary of the Manchester Alliance of House-painters 1855–67; secretary of the Manchester Trades' Political Association 1867–8.

MATKIN, WILLIAM, general secretary of the General Union of Carpenters and Joiners 1883–1920.

MURRAY, CHARLES, London West-End shoemaker; O'Brienite chartist; founder member of the London Trades Council; founder member of the Social Democratic Federation.

NEWTON, GEORGE (1831–1867), Glasgow potter; secretary of local potters' society; secretary of the Glasgow Trades Council 1862–6; secretary of the Master and Servant Act Reform Committee 1864–7; secretary of the Glasgow Reform Union 1864–6.

NEWTON, WILLIAM (1822–1876), born Congleton; member of the Hanley branch of Journeymen Steam Engine Makers' Society 1842; moved to London, but lost his job as a result of his trade-union activities; became a public-house keeper; largely responsible for amalgamation of engineering societies in 1851; stood as working men's candidate in elections of 1852 and 1868 at Tower Hamlets; member of Stepney Vestry and of Metropolitan Board of Works 1862–76.

NORMANSELL, JOHN (1830–1875), miner; checkweighman in South Yorkshire 1859–64; secretary of South Yorkshire Miners' Association 1864–75; vice-president of the National Association of Miners 1870–5; member of Barnsley Town Council 1872–5. An obituary note said of him: 'His firmness in dealing with and his remarkable influence over the men are deserving of remark now that he has gone for they have been favourably spoken of even by Coal Owners' [F. Machin, *The Yorkshire Miners: A History* (Barnsley, 1958), pp. 411–13].

NICHOLSON, SAMUEL CALDWELL, treasurer of the Manchester Typographical Society; president of the Manchester and Salford Trades Council 1866–70; suggested the calling of first TUC 1868.

ODGER, GEORGE (1813–1877), born near Plymouth; chartist; London West-End ladies' shoemaker; secretary of the London Trades Council 1862–72; member of the general council of the International Working Men's Association 1864–71; stood unsuccessfully for parliament on many occasions between 1868 and 1874; active republican; William Owen said of him – 'Odger with all his brilliancy had no force – no big society behind him. He had not the industry to achieve this. Had he been industrious he might have organised the old shoemakers and prepared them for the change to the factory system in their industry, but he was indolent.'

PICKARD, BENJAMIN (1842–1904), miner; secretary of the West Yorkshire Miners' Association 1876–1881; general secretary of the Yorkshire Miners' Association 1889–1904; M.P. for Normanton 1885–1904.

PICKARD, WILLIAM (1821–1887), miners' agent in Wigan; vice-president of the National Association of Miners 1863; stood for Wigan in the election of 1874; J.P. 1886.

POTTER, GEORGE (1832–1895), joiner; born at Kenilworth; secretary of the committee of London building trades' workers 1859–61; manager, editor and proprietor of the *Bee-Hive* at various times between 1861 and 1877; founder of the London Working Men's Association in rivalry with the London Trades Council and the Reform League; member of the Labour Representation League; member of the London School Board 1873–82; unsuccessfully stood for Peterborough in the election of 1868 and for Preston in 1886; author of a number of articles on trade unionism.

PRIOR, JOHN D. (b. 1840), joiner; general secretary of the Amalgamated Society of Carpenters and Joiners 1872–81; appointed factory inspector 1881.

SHIPTON, GEORGE (1839–1911), painter; general secretary of London Amalgamated Housepainters' Society 1866–89; secretary of the London Trades Council 1872–96; editor of the *Labour Standard* 1881–2. Mrs Webb wrote acidly of him in 1889: 'Shipton is not an attractive man. Small, with a weasel-like body and uncertain manner, and an uneasy contorted expression; grey eyes without candour or freshness and with that curious film over them which usually denotes an "irregular" life; deep furrows under the eyes and round the mouth; bald headed with a black beard neatly trimmed; a general attempt at middle-class smartness completes the outward man' [B. Webb, *Our Partnership* (1948), p. 21].

WILLIAMS, CHARLES OWEN, Liverpool plasterer; general secretary of the National Association of Operative Plasterers 1862–85; secretary of the Liverpool United Trades' Protection Association 1861–7.

WOOD, WILLIAM HENRY, printer; secretary of Manchester Typographical Society; secretary of the Manchester and Salford Trades Council 1866–70.

Notes

1   TRADE-UNION GROWTH, STRUCTURE AND POLICY

  1   F. Harrison, 'The Good and Evil of Trade Unionism', *Fortnightly Review*, III (1865), p. 33; G. Howell, 'Are the Working Classes Improvident?', *Contemporary Review*, XXXII (1978), p. 517; W. Trant, *Trade Unions: Their Origin and Objects, Influence and Efficiency* (1884), p. 106.

  2   S. and B. Webb, *The History of Trade Unionism* (1920 ed.), Appendix VI.

  3   H. Mayhew, *London Labour and the London Poor* (1861), III, p. 231.

  4   Royal Commission on Trades Unions and Other Associations 1867–9 (henceforth R.C. on Trades Unions, etc.), *First Report*, Q. 2968.

  5   G. Howell, 'Trade Unions: Their Nature, Character and Work', *Fraser's Magazine*, N.S. XIX (1879), p. 24.

  6   Ibid.

  7   R.C. on Trades Unions, etc., *First Report*, Q. 626.

  8   Ibid., *Fifth Report*, Q. 8650.

  9   Ibid., *Eleventh and Final Repport*, Appendix D.

 10   Biographical details of trade unionists mentioned in the text are to be found on pp. 226–31

 11   G. Howell, *Conflicts of Capital and Labour* (2nd ed., 1890), pp. 152–3.

 12   R. Postgate, *The Builders' History* (1923), pp. 219–27.

 13   Ibid., pp. 308–9.

 14   R.C. on Trades Unions etc., *First Report*, Q. 334.

 15   Postgate, op. cit., p. 231.

 16   Ibid., p. 299; W. MacDonald, *The True Story of Trades' Unions* (1867), p. 23.

 17   R.C. on Trades Unions, etc., *Eleventh and Final Report*, Appendix J.

 18   J. B. Jefferys, *The Story of the Engineers* (1945), pp. 104–5.

 19   R.C. on Trades Unions, etc., *Fifth Report*. See the evidence of John Kane, Wm. Hobson, John Millington and John Jones.

 20   R. Page Arnot, *A History of the Scottish Miners* (1955); F. Machin, *The Yorkshire Miners: A History* (Barnsley, 1958); E. Welbourne, *The Miners' Unions of Northumberland and Durham* (Cambridge, 1923).

21 G. D. H. Cole, 'Some Notes on British Trade Unionism in the Third Quarter of the Nineteenth Century' in *Essays in Economic History* (1962), E. M. Carus-Wilson (ed.), III, pp. 208–12.

22 H. A. Turner, *Trade Union Growth, Structure and Policy: A Comparative Study of the Cotton Unions* (1962); E. Hopwood, *A History of the Lancashire Cotton Industry and the Amalgamated Weavers' Association* (Manchester, 1969).

23 R. Church, *Economic and Social Change in a Midland Town: Victorian Nottingham, 1815–1900* (1966), pp. 271–7.

24 Ibid., pp. 296–8.

25 *Bee-Hive*, 3, 10, 17 January 1863.

26 A. Fox, *A History of the National Union of Boot and Shoe Operatives, 1874–1957* (Oxford, 1958), pp. 1–9.

27 A. E. Musson, *The Typographical Association: Origins and History up to 1949* (Oxford, 1954); S. C. Gillespie, *A Hundred Years of Progress: The Record of the Scottish Typographical Association, 1853–1952* (Glasgow, 1953).

28 C. J. Bundock, *The Story of the National Union of Printing Bookbinding and Paper Workers* (Oxford, 1959); E. Howe and J. Child, *The Society of London Bookbinders, 1780–1951* (1952).

29 Webb, *History*, pp. 120–1

30 *Glasgow Sentinel*, 22 May 1858.

31 R.C. on Trades Unions, etc., *First Report*, Qs. 3120–26; Postgate, op. cit., p. 175.

32 R. Groves, *Sharpen the Sickle! The History of the Farm Workers' Union* (1949), pp. 39–92.

33 P. Bagwell, *The Railwaymen: A History of the National Union of Railwaymen* (1963), pp. 19–69.

34 J. Lovell, *Stevedores and Dockers: A Study of Trade Unionism in the Port of London, 1870–1914* (1969), p. 64.

35 *Reformer*, 21 December 1872.

36 10s p.w. for 14 weeks; 7s p.w. for 30 weeks; 6s p.w. thereafter. R.C. on Trades Unions, etc., *Eleventh and Final Report*, Appendix H.

37 R.C. on Trades Unions, etc., *First Report*, Qs. 1400–19.

38 The one possible exception to this that the author has found is the Scottish Operative Plasterers' Society, formed in 1872.

39 R.C. on Trades Unions, etc., *Fourth Report*, Q. 7868.

40 *Minutes of the Second Delegate Meeting of the Amalgamated Society of Engineers* (1854), p. 38.

41 Jefferys, op. cit., p. 73.

42 H. J. Fyrth and H. Collins, *The Foundry Workers* (Manchester, 1959), p. 52.

43 S. and B. Webb, *Industrial Democracy* (1902 ed.), p. 17.

44 Ibid., p. 16.

45 Turner, op. cit., p. 212. Turner argues that it was the needs of a mobile labour force more than any other factor which encouraged the trend towards centralisation.

46 For the early development of this, see E. P. Thompson, *Making of the English Working Class* (1965), Chapter 8.

47 Turner, op. cit., p. 94.

48 National Association for the Promotion of Social Science, *Trades' Societies and Strikes* (1860) (henceforth cited as *Trades' Societies and Strikes*), pp. 175–6; K. Burgess, 'Trade Union Policy and the 1852 Lock-Out in the British Engineering Industry', *International Review of Social History*, XVII (1972), pp. 650–4.

49 G. Howell, 'Trades Unions, Apprentices and Technical Education', *Contemporary Review*, XXX (1877), p. 854.

50 Rules of the A.S.E. in R.C. on Trades Unions, etc., *Eleventh and Final Report*, Appendix H.

51 R.C. on Trades Unions, etc., *First Report*, Qs. 1078–86, 1496–99.

52 Ibid., Qs. 879–84, 1066, 2009, 3493–8.

53 Ibid., *Tenth Report*, Qs. 314–19.

54 Musson, op. cit., pp. 178–81.

55 R.C. on Trades Unions, etc., *First Report*, Q. 881.

56 Ibid., Q. 926.

57 Turner, op. cit., p. 128.

58 Ibid., pp. 150–6.

59 For example, Operative Stonemasons' Society, R.C. on Trades Unions, etc., *First Report*, Qs. 1062–5.

60 See evidence of Wm. Allan, Robert Applegarth, Edwin Coulson, George Potter, Robert Last, Richard Harnott and others to R.C. on Trades Unions, etc.

61 National Association for the Promotion of Social Science, *Transactions 1871* (1872), p. 117.

62 The R.C. on Trades Unions, etc., was able to find examples of one or two societies placing a restriction on earnings.

63 R.C. on Trades Unions, etc., *First Report*, Qs. 669–71.

64 Webb, *Industrial Democracy*, pp. 288–91.

65 Ibid., p. 302.

66 Ibid., p. 300.

67 J. M. Ludlow and L. Jones, *The Progress of the Working Class since 1832* (1867), pp. 30–6; B. L. Hutchins and A. Harrison, *A History of Factory Legislation* (3rd ed., 1926), pp. 96–199; Webb, *History*, pp. 309–13.

68 R.C. on Trades Unions, etc., *Seventh Report*, Q. 15,584; Cole, 'Some Notes on British Trade Unionism . . .', loc. cit., p. 209.

69 Turner, op. cit., p. 204.

70 *Trades' Societies and Strikes*, pp. 542–3.

71 *Labour League*, 11 November 1848.

72 *Bookbinders' Trade Circular*, November 1853.
73 Postgate, op. cit., p. 252.
74 *Trades Sentinel and Workman's Guide Post* (Sheffield), 9 April 1847.
75 *Operative*, 27 March 1852.
76 *People's Paper*, 26 November 1853.
77 *Reynolds' Newspaper*, 23 January 1859.
78 Glasgow Trades Council, Minutes, 23 July 1858.
79 J. Mendelson et al., *Sheffield Trades and Labour Council 1858 to 1958* (Sheffield, n.d.).
80 *Reynolds' Newspaper*, 23, 30 January, 6, 13 February 1859.
81 Ibid., 28 August 1859.
82 London Trades Council, Minutes, 14 May 1861.
83 The minute books are extant from 1 March 1859.
84 *Glasgow Sentinel*, 29 October 1859.
85 S. Maddocks, 'Liverpool Trades Council and Politics 1878–1918', unpublished M.A. thesis, University of Liverpool (1959), p. 21.
86 *Miner and Workman's Advocate*, 16 September 1865.
87 *Bee-Hive*, 26 May 1866.
88 Amalgamated Society of Carpenters and Joiners, *Monthly Report*, November 1867.
89 Birmingham Trades Council, Minutes, 2, 5, 7, December 1874, 6 October 1875.
90 Webb, *History*, p. 245.
91 *Bee-Hive*, 19 August 1865.
92 *Report of Conference on Law of Masters and Workmen under their contract of service, held in London on May 30th and 31st and 1st and 2nd June 1864* (Glasgow, 1864).
93 London Trades Council, Minutes, 29 May 1866.
94 *Bee-Hive*, 21 July 1866.
95 Howell, *Conflicts of Capital and Labour*, pp. 295–6.
96 Minutes of the Conference of Amalgamated Trades, Webb Trade Union Collection E. B/X/viii, British Library of Political and Economic Science.
97 *Bee-Hive*, 9 March 1867.
98 There was, in the mid-nineteenth century, no consistency in the use of the terms 'trade union', 'trades unions', 'trades' union' or even 'trade's union'. Each was used by unionists and middle-class commentators alike seemingly as the fancy took them. It is sometimes suggested that the *Trades* Union Congress was so-called because it was intended originally that it would consist of representatives of trades councils and trades federations. I suspect it was rather another example of the loose use of the terms.
99 Edinburgh unionists complained of similar treatment in 1862: 'We, as a Trades Council, feel ourselves much aggrieved, on account of the short space allowed in the book of Social Science

in support of opinion bearing on the good effects of, and necessity for trade unions, while on the opposite side full allowance is given.' *The Minutes of Edinburgh Trades Council* (Edinburgh, 1968), I. MacDougall (ed.), 7 April 1862. [When citing this book dates of the relevant minute rather than page references will be given.]

100 A. E. Musson, *The Congress of 1868: The Origins and Establishment of the Trades Union Congress* (1955).
101 *Bee-Hive*, 14 March 1868.
102 B. C. Roberts, *The Trades Union Congress* (1958), p. 65.

2 TRADE-UNION STRATEGY

1 *The Life of Thomas Cooper, written by himself* (1872), p. 393.
2 Samuel Smiles, *Self-Help* (1866 ed.), p. 13.
3 'Laws of the United Branches of Operative Potters', in G. D. H. Cole and A. W. Filson, *British Working Class Movements: Selected Documents, 1789–1875* (1951), p. 475.
4 *Address of the Executive Council of the Amalgamated Society of Engineers to their fellow-workmen throughout the United Kingdom* (1855), p. 7.
5 Amalgamated Society of Carpenters and Joiners, *Monthly Report*, July 1869.
6 *A Lecture on the Currency delivered in the City Hall, Glasgow, by Sir Archibald Alison, on Tuesday 15 March 1859* (Birmingham), 1859).
7 A. W. Humphrey, *Robert Applegarth: Trade Unionist, Educationist, Reformer* (1913), pp. 193–5.
8 *Bee-Hive*, 10 November, 1 December 1866.
9 B. Harrison, *Drink and the Victorians: The Temperance Question in England, 1815–1872* (1971), p. 336.
10 Humphrey, op. cit., p. 8.
11 R.C. on Trades Unions, etc., *Fifth Report*, Q. 8745.
12 *Operative Bricklayers' Society Trade Circular*, 1 November 1861.
13 *Address of the Executive Council of the Amalgamated Society of Engineers . . .* (1855), p. 4.
14 See, for example, *Ironworkers' Journal*, 1 April 1877, *Potteries Examiner and Workman's Advocate*, 22 June 1844.
15 T. Brassey, *Trade Unions and the Cost of Labour* (1870), p. 59.
16 *Annual Report 1870*, quoted Humphrey, op. cit., p. 23.
17 All from Wm. Allan's evidence to R.C. on Trades Unions, etc., *First Report*, Qs. 657–827.
18 Quoted by A. J. Mundella in National Association for the Promotion of Social Science, *Transactions 1868* (1869), p. 526.
19 National Association of Ironworkers, *Rules 1869* (Darlington, 1870), preface by John Kane.

20   J. Watts, *What are the Social Effects of Trades Unions, Strikes and Lock-outs?* (1878), pp. 7–8.
21   J. F. Clarke, 'Labour Relations in Engineering and Shipbuilding in the North East Coast in the Second Half of the Nineteenth Century', unpublished M.A. (Economic Studies) thesis, University of Newcastle upon Tyne (1966), pp. 205–6.
22   Ibid., p. 207.
23   D. C. Cummings, *An Historical Survey of the Boiler Makers and Iron and Steel Shipbuilders' Society* (1905), p. 86. The lines were spoken at a public dinner of the Society in Hull in September 1872.
24   Amalgamated Society of Carpenters and Joiners, *Monthly Report*, July 1869.
25   *Scottish Typographical Circular*, 1 February 1869.
26   Amalgamated Society of Carpenters and Joiners, *Monthly Report*, October 1866.
27   E. V. Neale, *May I not do what I will with my own?* (1852), p. 5.
28   *Trades' Societies and Strikes*, pp. 207–63.
29   Ibid., p. 230. One doubts if the strikers were all that 'friendly' and the Lancashire press contains plenty of examples of intimidation of blacklegs; but they managed to convince outsiders that things had changed.
30   *The Labour Question: An Address to Capitalists and Employers, of the Building Trades, being a few reasons in behalf of a reduction of the hours of labour etc. Signed on behalf of the Building Trades by George Potter, 30 May 1861*, p. 3.
31   The letters of Burnett and Armstrong are reprinted in E. Allen et al., *The North-East Engineers' Strikes of 1871* (Newcastle upon Tyne, 1971), pp. 151–63.
32   Quoted in S. Coltham, 'The *Bee-Hive* Newspaper: Its Origin and Early Struggles', in *Essays in Labour History* (1967), A. Briggs and J. Saville (eds), p. 180.
33   *The Times*, 26, 27 March 1866, 1 May 1868.
34   *Trades' Societies and Strikes*, p. vii.
35   Amalgamated Society of Carpenters and Joiners, *Monthly Report*, July 1866.
36   R.C. on Trades Unions, etc., *Fifth Report*, Q. 8745.
37   Quoted in S. M. Lipset et al., *Union Democracy* (Glencoe, 1956), p. 4.
38   Amalgamated Society of Carpenters and Joiners, *Monthly Report*, April 1865.
39   Ibid., July 1865.
40   *Bee-Hive*, 21 October 1865.
41   G. Howell, 'Intimidation and Picketing: Two Phases of Trades-Unionism', *Contemporary Review*, XXX (1877), p. 606.
42   *Ironworkers' Journal*, 1 July 1874.

43 L. Bather, 'A History of Manchester and Salford Trades Council', unpublished Ph.D. thesis, University of Manchester (1956), pp. 67–8.
44 R.C. on Trades Unions, etc., *Fourth Report*, Q. 7577.
45 Amalgamated Society of Carpenters and Joiners, *Monthly Report*, July 1864.
46 Ibid., February 1866. Perhaps it was significant that they failed to raise the necessary money.
47 National Association for the Promotion of Social Science, *Transactions 1860* (1862), p. 763.
48 *Bee-Hive*, 10 February 1866.
49 W. MacDonald, op. cit., p. 18.
50 Quoted in S. Higgenbottam, *Our Society's History* (Manchester, 1939), p. 37.
51 *Bee-Hive*, 24 June 1865.
52 London Trades Council, Minutes, 28 August 1865.
53 *Bee-Hive*, 20 May 1865.
54 S. Coltham, 'George Potter, the Junta and the *Bee-Hive*', *International Review of Social History*, IX (1964), p. 416.
55 G. Potter, 'Trades' Unions, Strikes and Lock-outs: A Rejoinder', *Contemporary Review*, XVII (1871), p. 529; *Report of the Conference of Trades Delegates held in the Town Hall, Leeds, on December 2nd 1871* (Leeds, 1872), p. 11.
56 London Trades Council, Minutes, 8 August 1867.
57 R.C. on Trades Unions, etc., *Fourth Report*, Q. 6600.
58 Jefferys, op. cit., p. 75.
59 Ibid., pp. 90, 106–7.
60 *Manchester City News*, 13 October 1866.
61 *Operative*, 27 March 1852.
62 *Glasgow Sentinel*, 23 February 1861.
63 Glasgow Trades Council, *To the Trade Unionists of Scotland* (1872).
64 *Reformer*, 28 June 1873; letter from John Miller ɪGlasgow 30 May 1873, in the correspondence of the Edinburgh Bookbinders' Society, National Library of Scotland.
65 Amalgamated Society of Carpenters and Joiners, *Monthly Report*, January 1875.
66 The Scottish societies were the exception. See review by F. and R. Harrison in *Bulletin of the Society for the Study of Labour History* No. 23 (1971), p. 82.
67 Lecture by William Rathbone of Liverpool, quoted in *Capital and Labour*, 24 January 1877.
68 *Address and Provisional Rules of the Working Men's International Association* (1864).
69 Birmingham Trades Council, Minutes, 2 July 1873.
70 'The Working Classes', *Blackwood's Magazine*, CI (1867), p. 224.

71 Amalgamated Society of Carpenters and Joiners, *Annual Report 1867*, quoted in Humphrey, op. cit., p. 31.
72 *Glasgow Sentinel*, 4 March 1875.

3 ENEMIES AND FRIENDS

1 Greg, William Rathbone (1809–1881), member of great Cheshire mill-owning family; writer and critic on social issues; staunch supporter of undiluted *laissez faire*.
2 W. R. Greg, *Mistaken Aims and Attainable Ideals of the Artizan Class* (1876), p. iv.
3 'Secret Organisation of Trades', *Edinburgh Review*, CX (1859), pp. 526–9.
4 'Trades' Unions', ibid., CXXVI (1867), p. 457.
5 'Trades Unions', *Quarterly Review*, CXXIII (1867), pp. 378–9.
6 *The Times*, 25 August, 2 September 1859.
7 Ibid., 8 November, 6 December 1869, 10 January 1870.
8 *Capital and Labour*, 19 November 1879.
9 P. Brantlinger, 'The Case Against Trade Unions in Early Victorian Fiction', *Victorian Studies*, XIII (1969), pp. 37–52.
10 *Reform: Look Before You Leap* (1859), p. 46, an anonymous pamphlet.
11 W. R. Greg, op. cit., p. 142.
12 'The Working Classes', *Blackwood's Magazine*, CI (1867), p. 224.
13 *Reform: Look Before You Leap*, p. 46.
14 National Association for the Promotion of Social Science, *Transactions 1871* (1872), p. 117, speech by the economist William Newmarch.
15 'Secret Organisation of Trades', loc. cit., p. 529.
16 *The Times*, 8 November 1869.
17 E. Potter, *Some Opinions on Trades' Unions and the Bill of 1869* (1869), pp. 17–18.
18 'Trades' Unions', *Edinburgh Review*, loc. cit., p. 447.
19 J. H. F., 'The Working Man and His Friends', *Fraser's Magazine*, LXXIX (1869), p. 686.
20 Maurice, Frederick Denison (1805–1872), Anglican theologian; chaplain of Lincoln's Inn 1846–60; Professor of Divinity at King's College, London 1846–53; first Principal of London Working Men's College 1854; Knightsbridge Professor of Moral Philosophy at Cambridge 1866–72.
21 Ludlow, John Malcolm (1821–1911), barrister; secretary to the Royal Commission of Friendly Societies 1870–74; Chief Registrar of Friendly Societies 1875–91.
22 Kingsley, Charles (1819–1875), Anglican clergyman and novelist; author of *The Water Babies*, *Alton Locke* et al.; Professor of Modern History at Cambridge 1860–70; Canon of Westminster 1873.

23 Hughes, Thomas (1822–1896), barrister; author of *Tom Brown's Schooldays*; M.P. for Lambeth 1865–74; county court judge.

24 Robinson, George Frederick Samuel, Viscount Goderich (1827–1909), M.P. for Huddersfield 1853–59; succeeded to Earldoms of Ripon and de Grey 1859; created first Marquess of Ripon 1880; secretary for war 1863; secretary for India 1866; lord president of the council 1868–73; viceroy of India 1880–4; colonial secretary 1892–5; lord privy seal 1905–8; converted to Roman Catholicism 1874.

25 C. E. Raven, *Christian Socialism* (1920), pp. 75–93, T. Christensen, *Origin and History of Christian Socialism, 1848–1854* (Aarhus, 1962), pp. 23–34, *The Life of Frederick Denison Maurice, Chiefly Told in His Own Letters* (1884), F. Maurice (ed.).

26 *Charles Kingsley: His Letters and Memories of His Life* (1883), edited by his wife, Vol. I, pp. 117–8.

27 Christensen, op. cit., pp. 51–3.

28 Ibid., pp. 136–7.

29 Raven, op. cit., pp. 182–224.

30 Ibid., p. 234.

31 Ibid., pp. 250–7.

32 Christensen, op. cit., p. 266; Raven, op. cit., p. 256.

33 Jefferys, op. cit., p. 43.

34 Ibid., p. 88.

35 A. W. Humphrey, op. cit., pp. 22, 94.

36 *Representation of the Case of the Executive Committee of the Central Association of Employers of Operative Engineers, etc.* (1852), p. 11, quoted in Christensen, op. cit., p. 253.

37 Maurice, op. cit., Vol. II, pp. 106–7.

38 *Charles Kingsley*, Vol. I, pp. 253–4.

39 L. Wolf, *Life of the First Marquess of Ripon* (1921), Vol. I, p. 28.

40 J. M. Ludlow, *The Master Engineers and Their Workmen* (1852), p. 8.

41 Christensen, op. cit., pp. 364–6.

42 Ibid., p. 365.

43 R.C. on Trades Unions, etc., *Fourth Report*, Qs. 7475–7501.

44 B. Rodgers, 'The Social Science Association, 1857–86', *The Manchester School of Economics and Social Studies*, XX (1952), p. 283.

45 Bennett, Thomas Randle (1821–1885), barrister; son of a Manchester merchant; lectured in law and history at Working Men's College.

46 Raven, op. cit., p. 280. Buxton, Charles (1822–1871), partner in Truman, Hanbury & Co., brewers; M.P. for Newport, I.O.W. 1857–9, for Maidstone 1859–65, for East Surrey 1865–71.

47 Hutton, Richard Holt (1826–1897), Unitarian minister; Professor of Mathematics at Bedford College 1856–65; edited *National*

Review with Bagehot 1855; assistant editor of the *Economist* 1858–60; editor of the *Spectator* 1861–86.

48 Lushington, Godfrey (1832–1907), barrister; fellow of All Souls; Counsel to Home Office 1869; assistant under-secretary of state Home Department 1876.

49 Parker, J. W. (1820–1860), editor of *Fraser's Magazine* 1848–60.

50 Acland, Thomas Dyke (1809–1898), politician who moved with Gladstone from Conservatism to Liberalism; fellow of All Souls; M.P. for West Somerset 1837–47, for North Devon 1864–85, for West Somerset 1885–6.

51 Forster, William Edward (1818–1886), Bradford worsted manufacturer; member of a Quaker family, but left the Society of Friends after his marriage to a daughter of Dr Thomas Arnold; M.P. for Bradford 1861–85; President of the Board of Education 1868–74; Chief Secretary for Ireland 1880.

52 The other members of the committee were: Edward Akroyd, a Halifax worsted manufacturer and M.P. for Huddersfield from 1857 to 1859; John Ball, botanist, alpinist, philosopher and Irish M.P.; T. J. Dunning, elder statesman of the London Bookbinders' Society; J. T. Danson, Liverpool businessman and statistician; Andrew Edgar, a writer of Scottish church affairs; William Farr, the statistician; Henry Fawcett, the recently-blinded economist; G. W. Hastings, a barrister and secretary of the Social Science Association; W. A. Jevons, a writer on legal education; George Shaw Lefevre, later a Liberal M.P., Commissioner of Works and Postmaster General; Horace Mann, who had been responsible for the religious census of 1851; Lord Robert Montague, Conservative member for Huntingdonshire; Lord Radstock, a leading opponent of Maurice on the Council of King's College; J. P. Kay-Shuttleworth, public health reformer, first secretary of the education committee of the Privy Council, who was chairman of the committee; Professor John Wilson, Whyte's Professor of Moral Philosophy at Oxford; J. W. Crompton, H. W. Freeland, C. Hawkins, and Rev. Brooke Herford. [These last four it has not been possible to identify.] P. H. Rathbone of Liverpool, one of the main instigators of the inquiry acted with Thomas Hughes as secretary.

53 *Trades' Societies and Strikes*, p. 599; *Economist*, 26 November 1859.

54 *Trades' Societies and Strikes*, p. vii.

55 Ibid., p. ix.

56 Ibid., p. xiii.

57 Ibid., p. xv.

58 Ibid.

59 Ibid., p. xviii.

60 J. M. Ludlow, 'The West Yorkshire Coal-Strike and Lock-out of 1858', *Trades' Societies and Strikes*, p. 40.

61 T. Hughes, 'Lock-Out of Engineers 1851-2', ibid., p. 187.

62 Ibid., p. 603. Potter, Edmund (1802-1883), calico-printer; M.P. for Carlisle 1861-80; supporter of extension of the franchise and the ballot; active in National Education League.

63 Ibid., pp. 595, 597.

64 Ibid., pp. 601, 606.

65 Harrison, Frederic (1831-1923), barrister; president of English Positivist Committee 1880-1905; Professor of Jurisprudence, Constitutional and International Law for the Council of Legal Education 1877-89; alderman of L.C.C. 1889; stood unsuccessfully as candidate for London University in the general election of 1886. Beesly, Edward Spencer (1831-1915), Professor of History at University College, London 1860-93; Professor of Latin, Bedford College 1860-89; sometime editor of the *Positivist Review*. Crompton, Henry (1836-1923), barrister; Clerk of Assize of Chester and North Wales circuit 1858-1901; author of *Industrial Conciliation* 1876. For a full examination of the relations between the Positivists and the English trade unionists, see R. Harrison, *Before the Socialists: Studies in Labour and Politics, 1861-1881* (1965).

66 H. B. Acton, 'Comte's Positivism and the Science of Society', *Philosophy*, XXVI (1951), pp. 291-310.

67 E. S. Beesly, 'Trades' Unions', *Westminster Review*, N.S. XX (1861), pp. 532-3.

68 E. C. Mack and W. H. G. Armytage, *Thomas Hughes: The Life of the Author of Tom Brown's Schooldays* (1952), p. 123.

69 *The Times*, 15 July 1861; R. Harrison, op. cit., p. 259. Litchfield, Richard Buckley, was an active Christian Socialist and co-operator.

70 Beesly, loc. cit., p. 510.

71 Ibid., p. 542.

72 F. Harrison, 'The Good and Evil of Trade Unionism', *Fortnightly Review*, III (1865), p. 37.

73 E. S. Beesly, 'The Amalgamated Society of Carpenters', *Fortnightly Review*, N.S. I (1867), p. 320.

74 Beesly, 'Trades' Unions', loc. cit., p. 512.

75 F. Harrison, loc. cit., pp. 45, 52.

76 R. Harrison, op. cit., p. 266.

77 Troup, George (1811-1879), journalist; editor of various newspapers in 1830s and 1840s, e.g. *Liverpool Weekly Telegraph* 1837, *Montrose Review*, 1838 *Aberdeen Banner* 1839, *North British Daily Mail* 1847; editor of the *Bee-Hive* 1861-4.

78 Hartwell, Robert, a founder member of the London Working Men's Association 1836; active in chartism and radical politics; closely associated with George Potter and acted as editor of the

Bee-Hive for a short period. The phrases are in various undated letters of Harrison to Beesly from the period 1864 and 1865, in the Harrison papers, British Library of Political and Economic Science.

79 E. S. Beesly, *The Social Future of the Working Class: A lecture delivered to a meeting of trades' unionists, May 7th 1868* (1881), p. 9.

80 E. S. Beesly, 'The Social Future of the Working Class', *Fortnightly Review*, N.S. V (1869), p. 348.

81 J. M. Ludlow and Lloyd Jones, *The Progress of the Working Class, 1832–1867* (1867), p. 228.

82 R.C. on Trades Unions, etc., *First Report*.

83 *Parl. Debs.*, 3S **CLXXXV**, 524.

84 R.C. on Trades' Unions, etc., *Eleventh and Final Report*, Appendix E, pp. 123–4.

85 Erle, Sir William (1793–1880), judge; responsible for the controversial judgement on the Wolverhampton tinplate workers in 1852; Lord Chief Justice of Common Pleas 1859–66.

86 Gooch, Daniel (1816–1889), railway pioneer and inventor; chairman of the Great Western Railway Co. 1865–87; M.P. for Crickdale 1865–85.

87 Mathews, William, a leading Staffordshire ironmaster.

88 Roebuck, John Arthur (1801–1879), M.P. for Sheffield; first elected to Parliament 1832; a leading radical politician in 1830s and 1840s; elected to Sheffield 1849; leading critic of conduct of the Crimean War; by the 1860s he had lost much of his radicalism, but still retained a biting turn of phrase that had earned him, in earlier days, the nickname 'Tear 'Em'.

89 Merivale, Herman (1806–1874), under secretary of state at the India Office in early 1860s; Professor of Political Economy at Oxford 1837; frequent contributor to the *Edinburgh Review*.

90 Booth, James (1796–1880), legal writer; secretary to the Board of Trade 1850–65.

91 Head, Edmund (1805–1868), Poor Law Commissioner 1841; Governor-General of Canada 1854–61.

92 Wemyss-Charteris-Douglas, Francis, Lord Elcho (1818–1914), 10th Earl of Wemyss and March; Conservative M.P. for East-Gloucestershire 1841–6; 'Liberal-Conservative' M.P. for Haddingtonshire 1847–83; founder and chairman of Liberty and Property Defence League 1882; active in volunteer movement. Anson, Thomas Michael, 2nd Earl of Lichfield (1825–92), M.P. for Lichfield 1847–54; chairman of the Society for the Reformation of Juvenile Offenders; brother-in-law of Lord Elcho.

93 See my article, 'Trade Unions, Reform and the Election of 1868 in Scotland', *Scottish Historical Review*, L (1971), pp. 138–57.

94 Harrison to Beesly 15 December 1868, quoted in R. Harrison,

op. cit., p. 286. For Harrison's role on the Commission, see H. W. McCready, 'British Labour and the Royal Commission on Trade Unions, 1867–69', *University of Toronto Quarterly*, **XXIV** (1955), pp. 394–409.

95 R. Harrison, op. cit., p. 286.
96 R.C. on Trades Unions, etc., *Eleventh and Final Report*, pp. xiv–xv.
97 Ibid., p. xxii.
98 Mack and Armytage, op. cit., p. 161.
99 R.C. on Trades Unions, etc., *Eleventh and Final Report*, pp. xxxii–xxxvi.
100 R. Harrison, op. cit., pp. 290–1.
101 Mack and Armytage, op. cit., pp. 147–8.
102 Ibid., p. 213.
103 N. C. Masterman, *John Malcolm Ludlow: The Builder of Christian Socialism* (Cambridge, 1963), pp. 203–5. Manning, Henry (1807–1892), Archdeacon of the Church of England; converted to Roman Catholicism 1851; Archbishop of Westminster 1865; acted as mediator in the London dock strike of 1889.
104 Bass, Michael Thomas (1799–1884), brewer at Burton-on-Trent; M.P. for Derby 1848–83; employed Leone Levi to inquire into the *Wages and Earnings of the Working Classes* 1866; notable philanthropist.
105 Langley, Baxter, editor of the *Newcastle Chronicle* in 1850s; later an officer in the Reform League; parliamentary candidate for Greenwich in by-election of 1873; active in building societies' movement.
106 A full account of the formation of the Amalgamated Society of Railway Servants and of Bass's role can be found in P. Bagwell, op. cit., from which most of the above is taken.
107 For all of these, see below, Chapter six.
108 R. Groves, op. cit., p. 51.
109 Webb, *History*, p. 332.
110 S. H. Mayor, 'The Relations between Organised Religion and English Working-Class Movements, 1850–1914', unpublished Ph.D. thesis, University of Manchester (1960), pp. 192–201. The London dockers also attracted some support from churchmen. The rector of Bethnal Green, Rev. Hansard, was involved with the first efforts at organisation in 1871 and Thomas Hughes approved the dockers' resistance to wage cuts.

4 THE EMPLOYERS

1 R.C. on Trades Unions, etc., *First Report*, Q. 2971.
2 Report of meeting of employers in Leeds, 3 April 1867, quoted in R.C. on Trades Unions, etc., *Third Report*, Q. 4572.

3 *Trades' Societies and Strikes*, p. 178; H. Ashworth, *The Preston Strike, an Enquiry into its Causes and Consequences* (Manchester, 1854), p. 16.
4 *Trades' Societies and Strikes*, pp. 214, 226.
5 O. Ashmore, 'The Diary of James Garnett of Low Moor. Clitheroe, 1858–65: Part I', *Transactions of the Historic Society of Lancashire and Cheshire*, **CXXI** (1969), p. 85.
6 R.C. on Trades Unions, etc., *Sixth Report*, Q. 11,739.
7 E. Allen et al., *The North-East Engineers' Strikes of 1871* (Newcastle upon Tyne, 1971), p. 165.
8 R.C. on Trades Unions, etc., *Ninth Report*, Q. 16,712.
9 Ibid., Q. 17,253.
10 *Trades' Societies and Strikes*, p. 110.
11 R.C. on Trades' Unions, etc., *Eleventh and Final Report*, Appendix D, pp. 56–85.
12 *Trades' Societies and Strikes*, pp. 175–6.
13 Ibid., p. 113; R.C. on Trades Unions, etc., *Tenth Report*, Q. 18,662.
14 Ibid., *Seventh Report*, Q. 14,201.
15 Ibid., *Ninth Report*, Q. 17,406.
16 Ibid., *First Report*, Q. 101.
17 Amalgamated Society of Carpenters and Joiners, *Monthly Report*, January 1867.
18 *Henry Broadhurst M.P. The Story of His Life from a Stonemason's Bench to the Treasury Bench. Told by Himself* (1901), pp. 31–2.
19 Mary Brigg, 'Life in East Lancashire, 1856–60: A Newly Discovered Diary of John O'Neil (John Ward), Weaver, of Clitheroe', *Transactions of the Historic Society of Lancashire and Cheshire*, **CXX** (1968), p. 131.
20 R.C. on Trades Unions, etc., *Seventh Report*, Q. 14,526.
21 *Trades' Societies and Strikes*, p. 175.
22 T. Brassey, Lectures on the Labour Question (1878), p. 72.
23 R.C. on Trades Unions, etc., *Seventh Report*, Q. 14,209.
24 Boilermakers' Society, *Monthly Report*, No. 128, quoted in J. F. Clarke, op. cit., p. 207.
25 Samuel Morley quoted by A. J. Mundella in R.C. on Trades Unions, etc., *Tenth Report*, Q. 19,383.
26 A. Fox, 'Industrial Relations in Nineteenth Century Birmingham', *Oxford Economic Papers*, **VII** (1955), pp. 63–6.
27 T. Brassey, 'Co-operative Production', *Contemporary Review*, **XXIII** (1874), p. 215.
28 R.C. on Trades Unions, etc., *Seventh Report*, Q. 14,209; Broadhurst, op. cit., p. 44.
29 T. Brassey, *On Work and Wages* (3rd ed., 1872), pp. 25–6.
30 Brassey, *Lectures on the Labour Question*, p. 41.
31 R.C. on Trades Unions, etc., *First Report*, Q. 166.

32 Extracts from 'The Diary of John Ward of Clitheroe, Weaver, 1860–64', edited by R. Sharpe Francis were published in the *Transactions of the Historic Society of Lancashire and Cheshire*, CV (1953), pp. 137–85, but Ward has since been identified as John O'Neil. See Mary Brigg, loc. cit., pp. 87–133.

33 Brigg, loc. cit., pp. 129–31; R. Sharpe Francis, loc. cit., pp. 159–61.

34 The above is based largely on H. A. Turner, op. cit., pp. 129–35.

35 Ibid., pp. 135–8.

36 F. Harrison, 'The Iron-Masters 'Trade Unions', *Fortnightly Review*, I (1865), cf. *Bradford Review*, 30 April 1864.

37 National Association for the Promotion of Social Science, *Transactions 1868* (1869), p. 526.

38 For example, J. M. Ludlow, 'Trade Societies and the Social Science Association', *Macmillan's Magazine*, III (1860–61), p. 369.

39 Mundella, Anthony John (1825–1897), Nottingham stocking manufacturer; Liberal M.P. for Sheffield 1868–95; Vice-President of the Committee of the Council on Education 1880–5; President of the Board of Trade 1886, 1892–4.

40 A. J. Mundella and G. Howell, 'Industrial Association' in *The Reign of Queen Victoria*, T. H. Ward (ed.) (1887), Vol. II, p. 80.

41 *Trades' Societies and Strikes*, p. 623.

42 *Report from the Select Committee of Masters and Operatives (Equitable Councils of Conciliation)* (1856), p. 141.

43 R.C. on Trades Unions, etc., *Third Report*, Q. 4170.

44 I. Garbati, 'British Trade Unionism in the Mid-Victorian Era', *University of Toronto Quarterly*, XX (1950), p. 76.

45 J. Stirling, *Trade Unionism: With Remarks on the Report of the Commissioners on Trades' Unions* (Glasgow, 1869), p. 50.

46 *Report from Select Committee of Masters and Operatives* (1856), p. 1.

47 Howell, *Conflicts of Capital and Labour*, pp. 394–5.

48 Mackinnon, W. A. (1789–1870), elected to Parliament in 1830 and 1831 as a Tory; 1835–52 Liberal M.P. for Lymington; for Rye 1853–65. Sugden, Edward, First Baron St Leonards (1781–1875), barrister; M.P. for Weymouth 1826–30; Solicitor-General 1829–30; Lord Chancellor of Ireland 1835, 1841–6; M.P. for Ripon 1837–41; Lord Chancellor of Great Britain 1852.

49 Webb, *Industrial Democracy*, p. 226. For a fuller examination of the activities of *conseils des prud'hommes*, see the evidence of Viscount Goderich to the Select Committee on Masters and Operatives, 1856, Qs. 2817–30.

50 *Glasgow Sentinel*, 19 February 1859.

51 G. Potter, 'Conciliation and Arbitration', *Contemporary Review*, XV (1870), pp. 544–5.

52 *Bee-Hive*, 2 May 1868.
53 National Association for the Promotion of Social Science, *Transactions 1868* (1869), p. 534.
54 *Reformer*, 31 October 1869.
55 Ibid., 30 April 1870.
56 Webb Trade Union Collection E. A/XLIV/169.
57 J. R. Hicks, 'The Early History of Industrial Conciliation in England', *Economica*, X (1930), p. 26.
58 *Parl. Debs.*, 3 S. CLVI, p. 2018.
59 Clarke, op. cit., p. 101.
60 Mundella's evidence to the R.C. on Trades Unions, etc., *Tenth Report*, Qs. 19,341–480.
61 H. Crompton, *Industrial Conciliation* (1876), pp. 37–9.
62 Potter, 'Conciliation and Arbitration', loc. cit., p. 552.
63 National Association for the Promotion of Social Science, *Transactions 1868*, p. 527.
64 Kettle, Rupert (1817–1894), barrister; appointed judge of Worcestershire County Court 1859; knighted for services to arbitration 1880.
65 R.C. on Trades' Unions, etc., *Eleventh and Final Report*, p. xxvii.
66 National Association for the Promotion of Social Science, *Transactions 1868*, p. 576 – Rupert Kettle during discussion.
67 A. J. Mundella to R. Leader, 11 July, 14 August 1868, Leader Correspondence, University of Sheffield Library.
68 J. H. Porter, 'Industrial Conciliation and Arbitration 1860–1914', unpublished Ph.D. thesis, University of Leeds (1968), p. 102. Dale, David (1829–1906), Quaker; Managing Director of Consett Iron Company; director North Eastern Railway.
69 E. Allen et al., op. cit., pp. 167–71.
70 *Ironworkers' Journal*, 1 May 1869.
71 L. L. Price, *Industrial Peace, Its Advantages, Methods and Difficulties* (1887), p. 74.
72 Ibid., p. 66.
73 Quoted by V. L. Allen in 'The Origins of Industrial Conciliation and Arbitration' in *The Sociology of Industrial Relations* (1971), p. 81.
74 Price, op. cit., p. 66.
75 Webb, *History*, p. 340.
76 Porter, op. cit., pp. 517–18.
77 *Northern Echo*, 17 September 1870.
78 *The Paper Making Trade: Arbitration on the Question of an Advance in Wages at Cannon Street Hotel, London 10 July 1874*, Webb Trade Union Collection E. B/LXXIII/22.
79 Porter, op. cit., p. 93.
80 V. L. Allen, op. cit., p. 81.
81 R. A. Church, op. cit., p. 273.

82   Mundella to Leader 24 February 1876, Leader Correspondence.
83   Brassey, *Lectures on the Labour Question*, pp. 210, 242.
84   *Capital and Labour*, 31 December 1873.
85   Ibid.
86   The quotations are taken from the Federation's statement of objectives published in the preliminary number of *Capital and Labour*, 31 December 1873.
87   One surprising name in the list of the Council of the Federation was David Dale. By the spring of 1874, he had dropped out.
88   There is no full list of members in *Capital and Labour* and these names are taken from lists of supporters that were published in the early months and from reports of the federation's deputations to ministers.
89   Bazley, Thomas (1797–1885), cotton spinner and politician; founder member of the Anti-Corn Law League; M.P. for Manchester 1858–80; president of Manchester Chamber of Commerce; created baronet 1869.
90   *Capital and Labour*, 31 December 1873.
91   Ibid.
92   Ibid., 4 April 1877.
93   Ibid., 18 March 1874.
94   Ibid., 16 June, 27 October 1875.

5   TRADE UNIONS AND POLITICS

1   Ms. Autobiography in Howell Collection, Bishopsgate Institute.
2   J. B. Leno, *The Aftermath, with Autobiography of the Author* (1892), p. 55.
3   S. Shipley, *Club Life and Socialism in Mid-Victorian London* (History Workshop Pamphlet, No. 5), pp. 1–20.
4   *Operative*, 9 August 1851.
5   Ibid., 19 July 1851.
6   F. E. Gillespie, *Labour and Politics in England, 1850–1867* (1966 ed.), pp. 48–9.
7   *Glasgow Sentinel*, 19 November 1859.
8   Ibid., 20 November 1858, 15 January 1859, cf. *Recollections* by T. Frost, quoted in Gillespie, op. cit., pp. 163–4.
9   *Glasgow Sentinel*, 2 November 1861.
10   Reform League Letter Book, 24 September 1867, in Howell Collection.
11   Howell wrote to Matthew Laurence, the secretary of the Glasgow Trades Council – 'I received your letter of the 12th inst. [containing news of the Address] and read the same to the Council on Tuesday last, 15th inst; it was received with applause by the members. I may inform you that we have been making some arrangements already to commence an agitation for an extension

of political rights.' There had, in fact, been no official discussions within the Trades Council on political action and these 'arrangements' of which Howell writes were probably the work of only a small group.

12 *Bricklayers' Trade Circular*, December 1861.
13 Stansfield, James (1820–1898), M.P. for Halifax 1859–95; under-secretary for India 1866; Lord of the Treasury 1868–9; President of the Poor Law Board 1871; campaigned against C.D. Acts and for women's suffrage.
14 London Trades Council, Minutes, 17 December 1861.
15 Ibid., 17 February 1862.
16 Ibid., *Second Yearly Report*, March 1862.
17 Ibid.
18 Ibid.
19 *Bee-Hive*, 25 October 1862. A slightly longer version was issued two years later – see *Miner and Workman's Advocate*, 22 October 1864.
20 London Trades Council, Minutes, 21 October 1862.
21 *Bee-Hive*, 25 October 1862.
22 T. Rothstein, *From Chartism to Labourism* (1929), p. 185.
23 *Bee-Hive*, 22 November 1862.
24 *Miner and Workman's Advocate*, 15 October 1864.
25 The Address is in Howell's Ms. Autobiography in Bishopsgate Institute.
26 Gillespie, op. cit., pp. 214–20. Beales, Edmund (1803–1881), barrister; President of the National League for the Independence of Poland 1863; President of the Reform League 1865–9.
27 Masterman, op. cit., p. 191.
28 Gillespie, op. cit., p. 216.
29 *Minutes of Edinburgh Trades Council*, 10 February 1863. A dissenting note was struck by an amendment which suggested that Lincoln's Emancipation Proclamation 'did not emanate from a desire to give freedom to the slaves, but to attain political supremacy', but this was heavily defeated.
30 *Bee-Hive*, 5 December 1863. It was also published in full in the *Bricklayers' Trade Circular*, 1 January 1864.
31 *Bee-Hive*, 23 January 1874.
32 London Trades Council, *Annual Report*, April 1864. Odger later admitted that during the three years of the Civil War he spent a third of his time working 'to avert so sad a calamity as the recognition by England of a slavish government'. *St Crispin's Journal*, 12 June 1869.
33 *Bookbinders' Trade Circular*, 2 March 1864.
34 *Glasgow Sentinel*, 15 January 1859, 30 November 1861.
35 Ibid., 21 January 1860.

36 Dalglish, Robert (1770–1880), merchant; M.P. for Glasgow 1857–74; independent radical; favoured extension of the franchise, vote by ballot, more equal distribution of electoral districts and extended education.

37 Webb Trade Union Collection E. A/III/79.

38 *Report of Conference on the Law of Masters and Workmen under their contract of service, held in London on May 30th and 31st and 1st and 2nd June 1864* (Glasgow, 1864).

39 D. Simon, 'Master and Servant' in *Democracy and the Labour Movement* (1954), J. Saville (ed.), p. 181.

40 *Bee-Hive*, 5 May 1866.

41 See my 'Trade Unions, Reform and the Election of 1868 in Scotland', loc. cit., pp. 138–57.

42 T. J. Dunning, 'The Application of Trades Union Organisations to the Political Enfranchisement of the People', *Newcastle Weekly Chronicle*, 26 November 1864.

43 F. B. Smith, *The Making of the Second Reform Bill* (Cambridge, 1966), p. 55.

44 Gillespie, op. cit., p. 256.

45 Ibid., pp. 253–9.

46 London Trades Council, Minutes, 19 December 1866.

47 *Birmingham Daily Post*, 27 March 1865.

48 *Birmingham Journal*, 7 July 1866.

49 *Bee-Hive*, 20 October 1866.

50 *Glasgow Reform Union, 6 June 1865*, a single sheet in the lists of departments and branches of the Reform League in Howell Collection.

51 Howell to Newton, 27 November 1865 in Reform League Letterbooks.

52 *Scottish National Reform League. Great Reform Demonstration in Glasgow, Tuesday 16 October 1866*, pamphlet in Mitchell Library, Glasgow.

53 *Report of Speeches delivered at the great meeting of the working classes held in the Music Hall, Edinburgh, 27 June 1865* (Edinburgh, 1865).

54 *Scotsman*, 15 October 1866.

55 *Reform Demonstration, Statement of Executive Committee* (Edinburgh, 1866).

56 Gillespie, op. cit., p. 275.

57 Ibid.

58 Ibid., p. 276.

59 London Trades Council, Minutes, 19 December 1866.

60 *Manchester City News*, 12 January 1867.

61 M. Dunsmore, 'The Working Classes, the Reform League and the Reform Movement in Lancashire and Yorkshire', unpublished M.A. thesis, University of Sheffield (1961), p. 120.

62 Birmingham Trades Council, Minutes, 20 February 1868.

63 Dunsmore, op. cit., p. 120.

64 Quoted by R. Harrison, 'The British Working Class and the General Election of 1868', *International Review of Social History*, V (1960), p. 446.

65 *Bolton Evening News*, 29 May 1868.

66 Ibid., 18 June 1868.

67 Ibid.

68 Ibid., 14, 18 November 1868; R. Harrison, op. cit., p. 162.

69 M. Higginbotham, 'A. J. Mundella and the Sheffield Election of 1868', *Transactions of the Hunter Archaeological Society*, V (1943), pp. 286–9.

70 Dunsmore, op. cit., p. 280.

71 *Bee-Hive*, 16 May 1868.

72 Dunsmore, op. cit., p. 280; H. J. Hanham, *Elections and Party Management: Politics at the time of Gladstone and Disraeli* (1959), pp. 95–6. Simon, John (1818–1897), Serjeant-at-Law; Jewish barrister; M.P. for Dewsbury 1868–88; opposed by Liberal Association in 1874 and 1880; active in Jewish causes; knighted 1886.

73 Dunsmore, op. cit., p. 30.

74 Ibid., Miall, Edward (1809–1881), editor of the *Nonconformist*; secretary of the Liberation Society; M.P. for Bradford 1868–74.

75 *North British Daily Mail*, 8 July 1868.

76 *Glasgow Sentinel*, 7 November 1868.

77 *Kilmarnock Advertiser*, 10 October 1868.

78 *Scotsman*, 18 September 1868.

79 Ibid.

80 *Kilmarnock Advertiser*, 12 September 1868.

81 For Beesly's views, see R. Harrison, op. cit., *passim*.

82 *Edinburgh Evening Courant*, 30 January 1868.

83 *Scotsman*, 27 April 1868.

84 McLaren, Duncan (1800–1886), Lord Provost of Edinburgh 1851–4; M.P. for Edinburgh 1865–80; independent radical; known as 'the Member for Scotland'.

85 *Bee-Hive*, 19 September 1868.

86 *Reformer*, 26 December 1868.

87 *The Daily Telegraph*, 20 November 1868, cit. D. R. Moberg, 'George Odger and the English Working-Class Movement 1860–1877', unpublished Ph.D. thesis, University of London (1954), p. 246.

88 G. Odger, 'The Working Man in Parliament', *Contemporary Review*, XVI (1870), p. 122.

89 G. D. H. Cole, *British Working Class Politics, 1832–1914* (1941), p. 49.

90 Ibid., p. 51.

91 Moberg, op. cit., p. 270.
92 *Aris's Birmingham Gazette*, 6 November 1869.
93 *Bee-Hive*, 19 March 1870.
94 F. M. Leventhal, *Respectable Radical: George Howell and Victorian Working Class Politics* (1971), p. 129; Cole, op. cit., p. 56.
95 D. C. Cummings, op. cit., p. 98.
96 *Bee-Hive*, 2 September 1871.
97 *Reformer*, 2 September 1871.
98 H. J. Hanham, 'Liberal Organisations for Working Men, 1860–1914', *Bulletin of the Society for the Study of Labour History*, No. 7 (1963), p. 5.
99 *Bookbinders' Trade Circular*, 25 November 1872.
100 *Bee-Hive*, 7 June 1873.
101 *Reformer*, 11 October 1873.
102 *Birmingham Daily Gazette*, 3 July 1873.
103 *Edinburgh Evening Courant*, 11 February 1870.
104 Birmingham Trades Council, Minutes, 5 March 1873.
105 *Birmingham Daily Gazette*, 14 August 1873.
106 *Birmingham Daily Post*, 14 August 1873.
107 *Birmingham Daily Gazette*, 2 October 1873.
108 *Birmingham Daily Post*, 29, 30 January 1874.
109 *Birmingham Daily Gazette*, 3 November 1873.
110 Webb Trade Union Collection E. A/III/180.
111 W. J. Davis to H. M. Cashmore, 1932, in Birmingham Reference Library.
112 A. Briggs, *History of Birmingham* (1952), Vol. II, p. 193.
113 W. W. Bean, *The Parliamentary Representation of the Six Northern Counties of England* (Hull, 1890), pp. 1200–1.
114 *Glasgow Sentinel*, 6 December 1873.
115 *Reformer*, 4 October 1873.
116 Ibid., 18 November 1871.
117 *Bolton Chronicle*, 31 January 1874.
118 These were Alexander McDonald (Stafford), Thomas Burt (Morpeth), George Howell (Aylesbury), James Hardaker (Bradford), Henry Broadhurst (Chipping Wycombe), Thomas Halliday (Merthyr Tydvil), John Kane (Middlesbrough), George Potter (Peterborough), Thomas Mottershead (Preston), George Odger (Southwark), Randal Cremer (Warwick), Benjamin Pickard (Wigan).
119 Surprisingly, McDonald's election was in a borough where there were no miners. Cole, op. cit., p. 69.
120 W. K. Lamb, 'British Labour and Parliament, 1865–1893', unpublished Ph.D. (Econ.) thesis, University of London (1933), pp. 297–8.
121 *Reformer*, 14 March 1874, cf. editorial in *Bee-Hive*, 26 December 1874.

122 H. W. McCready, 'The British General Election of 1874', *Canadian Journal of Economic and Political Science*, **XX** (1954), p. 169.
123 R. Harrison, op. cit., p. 301.
124 Ibid.
125 Beesly in *Bee-Hive*, 28 February 1874.
126 London Trades Council, Minutes, 17 June 1879.
127 W. A. Dalley, *The Life Story of W. J. Davis* (Birmingham, 1914), pp. 46–54.
128 Bather, op. cit., pp. 123–4.
129 Aberdeen Trades Council, Minutes, 25 October 1879.
130 Ibid., 5 November 1879; K. D. Buckley, *Trade Unionism in Aberdeen 1878 to 1900* (Edinburgh, 1955), pp. 117–18.

6   POLITICIANS AND PRESSURE GROUPS

 1 *The Times*, 1 May 1848, cit. T. R. Tholfsen, 'The Transition to Democracy in Victorian England', *International Review of Social History*, **VI** (1961), p. 238.
 2 T. R. Tholfsen, 'The Artisan and the Culture of Early Victorian Birmingham', *Birmingham University Historical Journal*, **IV** (1953–4), p. 146.
 3 Bright, John (1811–1889), Quaker cotton spinner of Rochdale; with Richard Cobden the leading spokesman of the Anti-Corn Law League; M.P. for Durham 1843–7, for Manchester 1847–57, for Birmingham 1857–86; President of the Board of Trade 1868–70; Chancellor of the Duchy of Lancaster 1873–4, 1880–1.
 4 G. M. Trevelyan, *Life of John Bright* (1913), pp. 267–8.
 5 J. Vincent, *The Formation of the Liberal Party, 1857–1868* (1966), pp. 185–6.
 6 Ibid., p. 187.
 7 *Scotsman*, 20 November 1861.
 8 Vincent, op. cit., p. 190.
 9 M. L. Ellison, 'The Reaction of Lancashire to the American Civil War', unpublished Ph.D. thesis, University of London (1968), pp. 181–2.
10 *The Times*, 23 June 1864.
11 *Newcastle Weekly Chronicle*, 26 November 1864.
12 Quoted by Lord Elcho during the reform debate of 1865, *Parl. Debs.* 3 S., **CLXXVII**, p. 1407.
13 *Glasgow Sentinel*, 2 February 1867.
14 G. Howell, *Labour Legislation, Labour Movements and Labour Leaders* (1902), p. 390. Howell was exaggerating Bright's influence on affairs. Bright was not in the government from the end of 1870 until August 1873 and, indeed, because of illness, was out of public life completely during that time.

15   Vincent, op. cit., p. 182.
16   Ibid., p. 190.
17   Ibid., p. 182.
18   Gillespie, op. cit., pp. 23–4.
19   Ibid., p. 99.
20   Morley, Samuel (1809–1886), head of the hosiery firm of I. and R. Morley with mills in Nottinghamshire, Leicestershire and Derbyshire; a leading Congregationalist; elected M.P. for Nottingham 1865, but unseated; M.P. for Bristol 1868–85; member of the London School Board 1870–6; proprietor of the *Daily News*. Salt, Titus (1803–1876), alpaca cloth manufacturer of Bradford; Mayor of Bradford 1848; builder of Saltaire in 1850s; M.P. for Bradford 1859–61; created baronet 1869; active Congregationalist. Rylands, Peter (1820–1887), partner of Rylands Bros., manufacturers of steel and iron wire at Warrington; active member of the Anti-Corn Law League; M.P. for Warrington 1868–74; M.P. for Burnley 1876–87. Taylor, Peter Alfred (1819–1891), silk mercer married into the Courtauld family; friend of Mazzini; chairman of the Society of Friends of Italy; M.P. for Leicester 1862–84; treasurer of London Emancipation Society 1863; active in peace movements and in many other radical causes. Kell, Samuel C. (1812–1869), Bradford merchant; unitarian; active in local Liberal politics. Kell, Robert (1808–1894), merchant in partnership with his brother; treasurer Bradford Liberal Association; J.P. and Alderman.
21   S. C. Kell, *The Political Attitude of our Law-Making Classes Towards the Unenfranchised and the Duties incumbent upon those in Consequence* (Bradford, 1861), p. 13.
22   Robert Kell, cit. D. G. Wright, 'Politics and Opinions in Nineteenth Century Bradford 1832–1880', unpublished Ph.D. thesis, University of Leeds (1966), Vol. II, p. 547.
23   *Bee-Hive*, 17 February 1866.
24   Charles Reed was a son-in-law of Edward Baines, the proprietor and editor of the *Leeds Mercury* and important member of the Liberation Society. Among other contributors to the *Bee-Hive's* finances were A. S. Ayrton and Charles Butler, Radical M.P.s for Tower Hamlets; Thomas Chambers, M.P. for Marylebone; and John Locke and A. H. Layard, M.P.s for Southwark. See leaflet entitled 'The General Election and Working Men' bound inside the *Bee-Hive* 1870 in John Burns' Library, Congress House.
25   E. Hodder, *Life of Samuel Morley* (1887), pp. 268–9.
26   R. Harrison, op. cit., p. 147.
27   Cowen, Joseph (1831–1900), proprietor of the *Newcastle Chronicle*; friend of Mazzini, Kossuth and Louis Blanc; Radical M.P. for Newcastle upon Tyne 1873–1885.
28   R. Harrison, op. cit., pp. 146–9.

29 T. Wemyss Reid, *Life of Rt. Hon. W. E. Forster* (1970 ed.), Vol. I, pp. 281–3.
30 *Sheffield and Rotherham Independent*, 19 November 1861.
31 *Parl. Debs.*, 3 S., **CLXXVIII**, p. 1644.
32 Mill, John Stuart (1806–1873), philosopher and political economist; official in the East India Co. office 1823–58; M.P. for Westminster 1865–8; active in the Italian and American causes. Smith, Goldwin (1823–1910), Regius Professor of Modern History at Oxford 1858–66; active in Emancipation Society, Jamaica Committee, Reform League; first Professor of English and Constitutional History at Cornell 1868–81; anti-imperialist.
33 *Autobiography of John Stuart Mill* (New American Library, 1964), pp. 190–1.
34 Ibid., p. 203.
35 *Essays on Reform* (1867), pp. 22–3.
36 Ibid., p. 36.
37 Ibid., p. 121.
38 *Parl. Debs.*, 3 S., **CLXXV**, p. 325.
39 Ibid., p. 322.
40 *Bee-Hive*, 12 March 1864.
41 *Parl. Debs.*, 3 S., **CLXXIII**, p. 1577.
42 *Bee-Hive*, 19 March 1864; J. Morley, *Life of Gladstone* (1903), Vol. II, p. 125.
43 *Parl. Debs.*, 3 S., **CLXXV**, p. 322.
44 *Ironworkers' Journal*, 1 July 1874.
45 A. Patchett Martin, *Life and Letters of the Rt. Hon. Robert Lowe, Viscount Sherbrooke, G.C.B., D.C.L.* (1893), Vol. II, pp. 130, 158. Lowe, Robert (1811–1892), barrister; member of the Legislative Council of New South Wales in 1840s; a leader writer of *The Times* in 1850s; M.P. for Kidderminster 1852–9; M.P. for Calne 1859–68; M.P. for University of London 1868–80; Vice-President of Committee of Council on Education 1859–64; Chancellor of the Exchequer 1868–73; Home Secretary 1873–4.
46 *Parl. Debs.*, 3 S., **CLXXXII**, p. 161.
47 'Trades' Unions', *Quarterly Review*, **CXXIII** (1867), pp. 351–9.
48 *Parl. Debs.*, 3 S., **CLXXXII**, p. 232.
49 Ibid., p. 1217.
50 Ibid., p. 1287.
51 Speech by Viscount Sandon, 1867, quoted in P. Smith, *Disraelian Conservatism and Social Reform* (1967), p. 97.
52 Quoted in D. A. Hamer, *John Morley: Liberal Intellectual in Politics* (Oxford, 1968), p. 92.
53 A. W. Humphrey, op. cit., p. 204. Dixon, George (1820–1898), merchant; Mayor of Birmingham 1866; M.P. for Birmingham 1867–76; chairman of Birmingham School Board 1876–97; Liberal Unionist M.P. for Edgbaston 1885–98; brother-in-law

of James Stansfield. Chamberlain, Joseph (1836–1914), Birmingham screw manufacturer; Mayor of Birmingham 1873–6; M.P.
for Birmingham 1876–85; M.P. for West Birmingham 1885–1914;
President of the Board of Trade 1880–5; President of the Local
Government Board 1886; Secretary of State for Colonies
1895–1903. Collings, Jesse (1831–1920), Mayor of Birmingham
1878–9; M.P. for Ipswich 1880–6; M.P. for Bordesley 1886–1918;
Under-Secretary of State for Home Office 1895–1902.

54 *North British Daily Mail*, 5, 13, 28 March 1873; *Reformer*, 22
March, 5 April 1873.

55 R. Harrison, op. cit., pp. 215–50.

56 Dilke, Charles (1843–1911), Radical M.P. for Chelsea 1868–86;
leading republican in early 1870s; President of the Local Government Board 1882–5; M.P. for Forest of Dean 1892–1911; active
with his wife in assisting women's trade unions and in combating
'sweating'; spoke for most trade-union legislative demands after
his return to House of Commons in 1892.

57 *Reformer*, 21 October 1871; Leventhal, op. cit., pp. 138–9.

58 *Birmingham Daily Gazette*, 6 May 1872; *Aberdeen Daily Free
Press*, 3 July 1873; *North British Daily Mail*, 22 May 1873;
Souvenir of Bolton Trades Council (1916).

59 H. Evans, *Sir Randal Cremer: His Life and Work* (1909).

60 *Scotsman*, 20 May 1873.

61 McCready, 'British Labour's Lobby', loc. cit., p. 143.

62 *Parl. Debs.*, 3 S., CXCVII, pp. 1344–57.

63 Ibid., p. 1358.

64 Ibid., pp. 1373–8.

65 Ibid., pp. 1370–3.

66 Ibid., p. 1363.

67 Ibid., p. 1366.

68 W. H. G. Armytage, *A. J. Mundella, 1825–1897: The Liberal
Background to the Labour Movement* (1951), p. 71.

69 *Bee-Hive*, 15 July 1871.

70 Ibid., 9 September 1871.

71 Leventhal, op. cit., p. 153.

72 Barry, the author of *Workmen's Wrongs and Workmen's Rights*
(1871), is not to be confused with Michael Maltman Barry, though
in the mystery surrounding them and in their politics they seem
not dissimilar.

73 *Lloyd's Weekly Newspaper*, 8 October 1871.

74 *Scotsman, Manchester Guardian*, 11 October 1871.

75 There is evidence that Disraeli knew what was going on and did
not disapprove. See P. Smith, op. cit., p. 152.

76 *Reformer*, 18 November 1871.

77 *The Times*, 26 October 1871.

78 *The Times*, 8 November 1871; *Manchester Guardian*, 2 November 1871.
79 *Manchester Guardian*, 2 November 1871.
80 *The Times*, 14 November 1871.
81 *Manchester Guardian*, 2 November 1871.
82 *Reynolds's Newspaper*, 29 October 1871.
83 *The Times*, 7 November 1871.
84 *Reynolds's Newspaper*, 12 November 1871. Montague had been invited by Potter to address a meeting of the building workers during the nine-hours strike and lock-out of 1859. See S. Coltham, 'The *Bee-Hive* Newspaper', loc. cit., p. 179.
85 *Lloyd's Weekly Newspaper*, 29 October 1871.
86 *Reynolds's Newspaper*, 3 December 1871.
87 Pakington, John (1799–1880), Conservative M.P. for Droitwich 1837–74; Secretary for War and the Colonies 1852; Secretary for War 1867–8.
88 This was in Birmingham: see A. Briggs, *The Age of Improvement* (1959), pp. 519–20.
89 B. Harrison, op. cit., p. 271.
90 *Parl. Debs.*, 3 S., CCV, p. 1914.
91 *Tory Democrat: Two Famous Disraeli Speeches*, Sir Edward Boyle (ed.) (1950), p. 30.
92 P. Smith, op. cit., pp. 153–4.
93 *Reformer*, 3 August 1872.
94 Armytage, op. cit., p. 117.
95 Evans, op. cit., p. 98.
96 *Henry Broadhurst M.P.*, pp. 79–81.

7 VERSUS THE POLITICAL ECONOMISTS

1 Political Economy Club, *Revised Report of the Proceedings at the Dinner of 31 May, 1876, held in celebration of the Hundredth Year of the publication of the 'Wealth of Nations'* (1876), pp. 20–1.
2 S. Smiles, *Workmen's Earnings, Strikes and Savings* (1861), p. 149.
3 J. Stirling, 'Mr Mill on Trades Unions' in *Recess Studies* (Edinburgh, 1870), A. Grant (ed.), pp. 311–2.
4 Ibid., p. 316.
5 Adam Smith, *Wealth of Nations*, Chapter III.
6 T. Malthus, *Principles of Political Economy* (1836), p. 248.
7 David Ricardo, *Works* (1951), p. 50.
8 For a discussion of this, see L. Robbins, *The Theory of Economic Policy in English Classical Political Economy* (1961), pp. 71–82.
9 J. R. McCulloch, *A Treatise on the Circumstances which Determine the Rate of Wages and the Condition of the Labouring Classes* (2nd ed. 1854), pp. 26–7.

I

10 F. W. Taussig, *Wages and Capital: An Examination of the Wages Fund Doctrine* (1896), p. 213.
11 J. S. Mill, *Principles of Political Economy*, Bk. II, Chapter xi.
12 C. Morrison, *An Essay in the Relations between Labour and Capital* (1856), pp. 19–20.
13 G. H. Smith, *Outlines of Political Economy Designed Chiefly for the use of Schools and Junior Students* (1866), p. 44.
14 Mill, *Principles*, in *Collected Works* (1965), Vol. III, p. 931.
15 For an interesting examination of political economy in school textbooks, see J. M. Goldstrom, 'Richard Whatley and Political Economy in School Books, 1833–1880', *Irish Historical Studies*, XV (1966–7), pp. 131–46.
16 Webb, *History*, p. 201.
17 T. J. Dunning, *Trades' Unions and Strikes: Their Philosophy and Intention* (1860), p. 5.
18 Ibid., p. 7.
19 Ibid.
20 Ibid.
21 Letter in the *Engineer*, 4 January 1867.
22 *Address of the Executive Council of the A.S.E., etc.* (1855), p. 7.
23 *The Times*, 10 November 1869.
24 R. V. Clements, 'Trade Unions and Emigration', *Population Studies*, IX (1955), pp. 172–3.
25 Ibid., p. 173.
26 W. H. Marwick, *Life of Alexander Campbell* (Glasgow, 1864), p. 14; *Glasgow Sentinel*, 9 June 1866.
27 *Glasgow Sentinel*, 14 January 1865.
28 R. V. Clements, 'British Trade Unions and Popular Political Economy 1850–1875', *Economic History Review*, 2 S., XIV (1961–2), p. 101.
29 J. Stirling, *Unionism*, p. 55.
30 *Rules and Regulations of the United Operative Masons' Association of Scotland* (1867).
31 *Operative Bricklayers' Trade Circular*, 1 December 1861.
32 W. MacDonald, op. cit., pp. 9–11.
33 *The Times*, 11 December 1869.
34 Clements, 'British Trade Unions and Popular Political Economy', loc. cit., p. 102.
35 G. Howell, *Conflicts of Capital and Labour*, p. 200.
36 Ibid., p. 203.
37 C. Neate, *Two Lectures on Trades Unions, delivered in the University of Oxford, in the year 1861* (Oxford and London, 1862), p. 3.
38 Ibid., p. 10.
39 Ibid., p. 16.
40 Ibid., p. 50.

41 J. Ruskin, *Unto This Last* (1901 ed.), p. 1.
42 Ibid., p. 10.
43 Ibid., pp. 22–37.
44 F. Harrison, 'The Limits of Political Economy', *Fortnightly Review*, I (1865), pp. 361–2.
45 Ibid., pp. 372–3.
46 F. D. Longe, *A Refutation of the Wage-Fund Theory of Modern Political Economy as enunciated by Mr Mill M.P. and Mr Fawcett M.P.* (1866), p. 8.
47 Ibid., p. 76.
48 Ibid., p. 68.
49 Ibid., p. 80.
50 T. E. Cliffe Leslie, 'Political Economy and the Rate of Wages', *Fraser's Magazine*, LXXVIII (1868), p. 82.
51 Ibid., p. 95.
52 W. T. Thornton, *On Labour. Its Wrongful Claims and Rightful Dues. Its Actual Present and Possible Future* (1869), p. 110.
53 Ibid.
54 J. S. Mill, 'Thornton on Labour and its Claims', *Fortnightly Review* N.S., V (1869), p. 517.
55 Ibid., p. 690.
56 Ibid., p. 692.
57 *Autobiography of John Stuart Mill*, p. 176.
58 J. Stirling, 'Mr Mill on Trades Unions', loc. cit., p. 320.
59 F. Jenkin, 'The Graphic Representation of the Laws of Supply and Demand, and their Application to Labour', *Recess Studies*, p. 172.
60 Ibid., p. 173.
61 Quoted in E. Whittaker, *A History of Economic Ideas* (1943), p. 587.
62 A. Marshall, *Principles* (8th ed., 1920), p. 825.
63 Taussig, op. cit., p. 299.
64 Whittaker, op. cit., pp. 590–1.
65 H. Sidgwick, 'The Wages-Fund Theory', *Fortnightly Review*, N.S. XXVI (1879), p. 401.
66 F. Y. Edgeworth, *Mathematical Physics* (1881), p. 44.
67 J. A. Schumpeter, *Economic Doctrine and Method: An Historical Sketch* (1954), pp. 143–4.
68 Ibid.
69 R.C. on Trades Unions, etc., *First Report*, Q. 858.
70 *Address of the Metropolitan Trades' Delegates to their Fellow Countrymen, on the interests and present position of the Labouring Classes of the Empire* (1850).
71 *The Times*, 16 November 1869.
72 R. Pearson, *Combination or Trades'-Unionism absolutely the duty of work people in general* (Edinburgh Trades Council, 1875), p. 13.

I*

73 *Labour Standard*, 22 October 1881.
74 *Birmingham Daily Gazette*, 10 January 1881.
75 Webb, *Industrial Democracy*, pp. 563–4.
76 *Articles of the Glasgow Typographical Society* (1848).
77 *The Times*, 11 December 1869.
78 G. Potter, 'Strikes and Lock-Outs, from the Workman's Point of View', *Contemporary Review*, XV (1870), p. 32.
79 J. Plummer, *Songs of Labour, Northamptonshire Rambles, and other poems* (London and Kettering, 1860), p. xxvii.
80 *Bee-Hive*, 18 July 1869.
81 *Trades' Societies and Strikes*, p. 62.
82 Quoted in E. Allen, et al., op. cit., p. 88.
83 Moberg, op. cit., p. 130.
84 *Bee-Hive*, 20 March 1869.
85 *Articles and Regulations of the Scottish Iron and Coal Miners Association* (Dunfermline, 1856).
86 London Operative Bricklayers' Society, *Report and Balance Sheet* (1861).
87 T. J. Dunning, *Trades' Unions and Strikes*, p. 31.
88 Howell, *Conflicts of Capital and Labour*, p. 351; T. Burt, *An Autobiography* (1924), p. 196.
89 R.C. on Trades' Unions, etc., *First Report*, Q. 924.
90 Amalgamated Society of Carpenters and Joiners, *Monthly Report*, November 1866.
91 *Ironworkers' Journal*, 1 February 1877.

8 TRADE UNIONS AND THE LAW

1 A. V. Dicey, *Lectures on the Relation between Law and Public Opinion in England during the Nineteenth Century* (2nd ed., 1914), pp. 9–10.
2 G. Abrahams, *Trade Unions and the Law* (1968), p. 26.
3 *Citrine's Trade Union Law* (3rd ed., 1927), pp. 6–7; 'Memorandum on the Law relating to Trade Unions' by Sir William Erle, in R.C. on Trades Unions, etc., *Eleventh and Final Report*, lxxx (henceforth referred to as Erle).
4 Erle, p. lxxx.
5 Howell, *Labour Legislation, Labour Movements, Labour Leaders*, p. 84.
6 *Citrine*, p. 7.
7 R.C. on Trades Unions, etc., *Eleventh and Final Report*, p. lv.
8 *Citrine*, p. 8.
9 Ibid.
10 Ibid.
11 Ibid., p. 9; R. v. Druitt, 10 Cox 592.

12 Unlawful Societies Act (39 Geo. III, c. 79), Seditious Meetings Act (57 Geo. III, c. 19).
13 Ludlow and Jones, op. cit., p. 43.
14 Ibid., p. 44.
15 Howell, *Conflicts of Capital and Labour*, p. 123.
16 Hornby *v.* Close, 10 Cox 393–401.
17 Howell, *Labour Legislation, Labour Movements, Labour Leaders*, p. 175.
18 R.C. on Trades Unions, etc., *Eleventh and Final Report*, p. xx.
19 Ibid., p. xxii.
20 Ibid., p. xxiii.
21 Ibid., p. xxiv.
22 Ibid., p. cvii.
23 Ibid., p. lvii.
24 Ibid., p. lxiii.
25 Ibid., pp. lxi–lxii.
26 F. Harrison, 'The Trade Union Bill', *Fortnightly Review*, N.S. VI (1869), p. 33.
27 Rathbone, William (1819–1902), Liverpool merchant and philanthropist; active in organising education of nurses; Liberal M.P. for Liverpool 1868–80, for Carnarvonshire 1880–5, for West Carnarvonshire 1885–95.
28 Mundella to R. Leader, 9 July 1869, Leader Correspondence, University of Sheffield Library.
29 E. S. Beesly, *Letters to Workmen* (1870).
30 Howell, *Labour Legislation, Labour Movements, Labour Leaders*, pp. 176–7.
31 H. W. McCready, 'British Labour's Lobby 1867–75', loc. cit., p. 145.
32 Mundella to R. Leader, 28 May 1871.
33 Ibid., 2 May 1869.
34 *Bee-Hive* 15 July 1871.
35 *Citrine*, p. 12; Abrahams, op. cit., pp. 56–7.
36 Abrahams, op. cit., p. 57.
37 James, Henry (1828–1911), Liberal M.P. for Taunton 1869–85; Liberal-Unionist M.P. for Bury 1886–95; Attorney-General 1873–4, 1880–5; created first Baron James of Hereford 1895. Wright, Robert Samuel (1839–1904), barrister and judge; active in liberal causes; knighted 1891; Hopwood, C. H. (1829–1904), Recorder of Liverpool 1886; Liberal M.P. for Stockport 1874–85, for Middleton 1892–5.
38 R. Harrison, op. cit., p. 295.
39 Howell, *Labour Legislation, Labour Movements, Labour Leaders*, p. 294.
40 Thomas Hughes, who was steadily moving away from sympathy with trade unionists, signed the majority report.

41 F. Harrison to John Morley, 9 May 1874, quoted in McCready, 'British Labour's Lobby', loc. cit., p. 158.

42 Ibid., p. 160.

9 TRADE UNIONS AND THE PRESS

1 S. Coltham, 'English Working Class Newspapers in 1867', *Victorian Studies*, **XIII** (1969), p. 160. The following paragraphs on the *Bee-Hive* and the *Commonwealth* lean heavily on Dr Coltham's article and on his 'The *Bee-Hive* Newspaper' in *Essays in Labour History*, pp. 174–204 and 'George Potter, the Junta and the *Bee-Hive*', *International Review of Social History*, **IX** (1964) and **X** (1965).

2 Founded in 1862 as the *British Miner and General Newsman*, it successively altered its name to the *Miner*, the *Miner and Workman's Advocate* and, finally, the *Workman's Advocate*. Coltham, 'English Working Class Newspapers', loc. cit., p. 162.

3 Ibid., p. 163.

4 The Webbs describe the *Flint Glass Makers' Magazine* as the best of the trade publications. They were able to see a complete set of it in 1893, but copies do not seem to have survived.

5 In 1875, this became the *Provincial Typographical Circular* and, in 1877, the *Typographical Circular*.

6 *Economist*, 3 January 1852; *Manchester Guardian*, 7 January 1852; *The Times*, 2 January 1852. A very full study of press attitudes to trade unionism is to be found in R. A. Buchanan, 'Trade Unions and Public Opinion 1850–1875', unpublished Ph.D. thesis, University of Cambridge (1957) and a few of the references in this chapter are taken from this source. The general interpretation is, however, my own.

7 *The Times*, 19 October 1853.

8 Ibid., 3 May 1854; *Economist*, 6 May 1854.

9 *The Times*, 8 September 1859.

10 Ibid., 6 December 1866.

11 Ibid., 31 December 1866.

12 *Glasgow Herald*, 30 November 1866.

13 *The Times*, 26, 27 March 1866.

14 Ibid., 27 November 1866.

15 Ibid., 8, 14 December 1866; 10 August, 15 September 1867.

16 Ibid., 20 November 1866.

17 Ibid., 24 June 1867.

18 Ibid., 7 September 1867.

19 *Saturday Review*, 29 June 1867.

20 *Glasgow Herald*, 29 October, 1867.

21 *Newcastle Daily Chronicle*, 13 March 1865.

22 Ibid., 11 January 1866.
23 Ibid., 10 July 1876.
24 *The Times*, 21 January 1867.
25 Ibid., 20 August 1867.
26 Ibid., 25 June 1869.
27 Ibid., 8 July 1869.
28 W. G. Armstrong to Stuart Rendel 13 September 1871, Armstrong papers, Newcastle City Archives.
29 *Saturday Review*, 9 September 1871.
30 *Pall Mall Gazette*, 20 September 1871.
31 *Spectator*, 16 September 1871.
32 *The Times*, 1 April 1872.
33 *Spectator*, 30 March 1872.
34 Howell, *Labour Legislation, Labour Movements, Labour Leaders*, pp. 369–70.
35 'Secret Organisation of Trades', *Edinburgh Review*, CX (1859), pp. 525–63.
36 'Strikes and Trade Unions', *Blackwood's Magazine*, CII (1867), pp. 718–36. 'Who are the Reformers?', ibid., CI (1867), pp. 115–32.
37 *Blackwood's Magazine*, CII (1867), pp. 487–507. See also his 'The Working Classes', ibid., CI (1867), pp. 220–9.
38 'Trades' Unions', *Quarterly Review*, CXXIII (1867), pp. 351–83.
39 'Trades' Unions', *Edinburgh Review*, CXXVI (1867), pp. 415–57.
40 J. M. Ludlow, 'Trade Societies and the Social Science Association', *Macmillan's Magazine*, III (1860–1), pp. 313–25, 362–72.
41 Harrison, 'The Limits of Political Economy', *Fortnightly Review*, I (1865), pp. 356–76; Thornton, 'On Labour', a number of articles in ibid., N.S. II (1867) and III (1868); Mill, 'Thornton on Labour and its Claims', ibid., N.S. V (1869), pp. 505–18, 680–700.
42 Ibid., N.S. I (1867), pp. 319–34; ibid., N.S. V (1869), pp. 344–63.
43 F. Harrison, 'The Trades-Union Bill', ibid., N.S. VI (1869), pp. 30–45; Crompton, 'The Workmen's Victory', ibid., N.S. XVIII (1875), pp. 399–406.
44 'Strikes and Lock-Outs from the Workman's Point of View', *Contemporary Review*, XV (1870), pp. 32–54; 'The Trade Societies of England from the Workman's Point of View', ibid., XIV (1870), pp. 404–28; 'Conciliation and Arbitration', ibid., XV (1870), pp. 543–66; 'The Future of Capital and Labour', ibid., XVI (1871), pp. 437–53; 'Trades' Unions, Strikes and Lock-Outs. A Rejoinder', ibid., XVII (1871), pp. 525–39.
45 Ibid., XVI (1870).
46 'Intimidation and Picketing: Two Phases of Trades-unionism', ibid., XXX (1877), pp. 598–624; 'Trades Unions, Apprentices, and Technical Education', ibid., XXX (1877), pp. 833–57; 'Are the Working Classes Improvident?', ibid., XXXII (1878), pp. 501–19.

47 'The English Working Classes and the Paris Commune', *Fraser's Magazine*, N.S. IV (1871), pp. 62–8; 'On the Condition of the Working Classes', ibid., IV (1871), pp. 426–40; 'Composition of the Working Classes', *Contemporary Review*, XVIII (1871).

10 TRADE UNIONS AND THE WORKING CLASS

1 *Parl. Debs.*, 3 S., CCVIII, pp. 285.
2 G. D. H. Cole, *Studies in Class Structure* (1955), p. 57. The wage rates are taken from Leone Levi, *Wages and Earnings of the Working Classes* (1867).
3 *Bee-Hive*, 25 February 1865; *Standard*, 29 September 1876.
4 *Bee-Hive*, 2 July 1864.
5 T. Wright, *Our New Masters* (1873), p. 5.
6 *The Times*, 15 July 1861.
6a A full discussion of this process in cotton and in other industries can be found in H. A. Turner, op. cit., pp. 139–68.
7 R. Harrison, op. cit., pp. 30–1.
8 R.C. on Trades Unions, etc., *First Report*, Q. 926; T. Wright, 'On the Condition of the Working Classes', *Fraser's Magazine*, N.S. IV (1871), p. 437.
9 Notes in the Howell Collection, Bishopsgate Institute.
10 G. Tate, *London Trades Council – A History 1860–1950* (1950), p. 40.
11 London Trades Council, Minutes, 11 June, 8 October 1872, 29 April 1873.
12 Ibid., 20 May 1873.
13 Ibid., 12 March 1874.
14 Webb, *History*, pp. 330–1.
15 R. Harrison, op. cit., p. 31.
16 J. F. Clarke, op. cit., p. 321.
17 For the significance of the artisan in Birmingham in the years before 1850, see T. R. Tholfsen, 'The Artisan and the Culture of Early Victorian Birmingham', loc. cit., pp. 146–66.
18 W. R. Greg, *Rocks Ahead: or the Warnings of Cassandra* (1874), pp. 6–7.
19 S. Smiles, *Workmen's Earnings, Strikes and Savings* (1861), p. 147.
20 Quoted in Gareth Steadman Jones, *Outcast London: A Study in the Relationship between Classes in Victorian Society* (Oxford, 1971), pp. 241–4.
21 D. G. Wright, op. cit., p. 369.
22 *Report of the Inspectors of Factories to the Home Secretary for the half year ending 30th April 1865*, *P.P.* 1865 [3473] XX, pp. 519–24.
23 J. M. Ludlow, *The Master Engineers and Their Workmen* (1852), p. 86.

24 Ludlow and Jones, op. cit., pp. 221–2.
25 G. Potter, 'The Trade Societies of England: From the Workman's Point of View', *Contemporary Review*, **XIV** (1870), pp. 409–10.
26 Tholfsen, 'The Artisan and the Culture of Early Victorian Birmingham', loc. cit., p. 146.
27 'The Bill as it is', *Blackwood's Magazine*, **CII** (1867), p. 250.
28 Ibid.
29 [Robert Lowe], 'Trades' Unions', loc. cit., p. 351.
30 Ibid.
31 J. F. Clarke, op. cit., pp. 136–7.
32 Ibid., p. 536.
33 *Glasgow Sentinel*, 1 January 1859.
34 'Who are the Reformers, and What do they Want?', *Blackwood's Magazine*, **CI** (1867), p. 126.
35 E. J. Hobsbawm, *Labouring Men: Studies in the History of Labour* (1964), p. 350.

Select Bibliography

1. UNPUBLISHED SOURCES

(A) Trade-Union Records

At Aberdeen University Library
Aberdeen Trades Council, Minute Books from 1876.
At the Birmingham Reference Library
Birmingham Trades Council, Minute Books from 1869.
In the possession of Mr E. P. Thompson
Bradford Trades Council, Minute Books from 1874.
At the Mitchell Library, Glasgow
Glasgow Trades Council, Minute Book 1858-9.
In the possession of Mr Julius Jacob
London Trades Council, Minute Books from 1860.
At the National Library of Scotland
Minutes and correspondence of the Union Society of Journeymen
Bookbinders, Edinburgh (on microfilm).
At the Head Office of the National Union of Furnishing Trade Operatives
Alliance Cabinetmakers, Executive Committee, minute books from
1876.

(B) Other

At the Bishopsgate Institute
George Howell papers: Ms. autobiography and other notes; letters to
Howell; Reform League letters and papers.
At British Library of Political and Economic Science
Webb Trade-Union Collection E.
Frederic Harrison Papers.
Broadhurst Correspondence.
*At Gosford House, by courtesy of His Grace the Earl of Wemyss and
March*
Elcho Muniments.
At Sheffield University Library
Letters of A. J. Mundella to R. Leaders.
At Newcastle City Archives
Armstrong Papers.

(C) Theses

P. Adelman, 'The Social and Political Ideas of Frederic Harrison in
Relation to English Thought and Politics, 1855-1886', London Ph.D.
thesis, 1967.

L. Bather, 'History of the Manchester and Salford Trades Council', Manchester Ph.D. thesis, 1956.

R. A. Buchanan, 'Trade Unions and Public Opinion 1850–1875', Cambridge Ph.D., 1957.

J. F. Clarke, 'Labour Relations in Engineering and Shipbuilding on the North East Coast in the Second Half of the Nineteenth Century', Newcastle M.A. (Economic Studies) thesis, 1966.

M. Dunsmore, 'The Working Classes, the Reform League and the Reform Movement in Lancashire and Yorkshire', Sheffield, M.A. thesis, 1961.

M. E. Ellison, 'The Reaction of Lancashire to the American Civil War', London Ph.D. thesis, 1968.

G. C. Halverson, 'Development of Labour Relations in the British Railways since 1860', London Ph.D. thesis, 1952.

R. J. Harrison, 'The Activity and Influence of the English Positivists upon Labour Movements, 1859–1885', Oxford Ph.D. thesis, 1955.

P. W. Kingsford, 'Railway Labour, 1830–70', London Ph.D. thesis, 1951.

W. K. Lamb, 'British Labour and Parliament', London Ph.D. thesis, 1933.

S. Maddock, 'Liverpool Trades Council and Politics, 1878–1918', Liverpool M.A. thesis, 1959.

S. H. Mayor, 'The Relations between Organized Religion and English Working Class Movements, 1850–1914', Manchester Ph.D. thesis, 1960.

D. R. Moberg, 'George Odger and the English Working Class Movement, 1860–1877', London Ph.D. (Econ.) thesis, 1954.

J. H. Porter, 'Industrial Conciliation and Arbitration 1860–1914', Leeds Ph.D. thesis, 1968.

D. G. Wright, 'Politics and Opinion in Nineteenth Century Bradford, 1832–1880', Leeds Ph.D., 1966.

2. PRINTED SOURCES

(A) Trade-Union Reports

Alliance Cabinetmakers' Association, *Annual Reports*, 1872–80.

Amalgamated Society of Brassworkers, *Annual Reports*, 1872–80.

Amalgamated Society of Carpenters and Joiners, *Monthly Reports*, 1863–80.

Associated Carpenters and Joiners of Scotland, *Annual Reports*, 1863–80.

General Union of Carpenters and Joiners, *Annual Reports*, 1866–80.

General Union of Carpenters and Joiners, *Monthly Reports*, 1864–80.

Operative Stonemasons' Society, *Fortnightly Return*, 1856–80.

Trades Union Congress, *Annual Reports*, 1869–80.

Trades Union Congress, *Reports of the Parliamentary Committee,* 1872–80.
Birmingham Trades Council, *Annual Reports,* 1870–1, 1871–2.
Edinburgh Trades Council, *Annual Reports,* 1871–2, 1879–80.
Glasgow Trades Council, *Annual Report,* 1876–7.
London Trades Council, *Annual Reports,* 1861–2, 1863–4 — 1866–7, 1872–3, 1873–4, 1875 — 1880.
Liverpool Trades Council, *Annual Reports,* 1858 — 1861.
Nottingham Association of Organised Trades, *Annual Reports,* 1866–7, 1872–3 — 1877–8, 1879–80.
Sheffield Association of Organised Trades, *Annual Reports,* 1859–60, 1865–6.

(B) Newspapers and Periodicals

Aberdeen Free Press
Bee-Hive
Aris's Birmingham Gazette, later
Birmingham Daily Gazette
Birmingham Daily Post
Bolton Chronicle
Bolton Evening News
Bookbinders' Trade Circular
Bradford Observer
Builder
Capital and Labour
Commonwealth
Daily News
Daily Telegraph
Economist
Edinburgh Evening Courant
Engineer
Glasgow Herald
Glasgow Sentinel
Industrial Review
Ironworkers' Journal
Kilmarnock Advertiser
Labour League
Lloyd's Weekly Newspaper
Manchester City News
Manchester Examiner
Manchester Guardian
Miner and Workman's Advocate
Newcastle Courant
Newcastle Daily Chronicle
Newcastle Weekly Chronicle
North British Daily Mail (Glasgow)
Northern Echo (Darlington)
Operative
Operative Bricklayers' Society Trade Circular
Pall Mall Gazette
People's Paper
Reformer (Edinburgh)
Reynolds's Newspaper
Saturday Review
Scotsman
Scottish Typographical Circular
Sheffield & Rotherham Independent
Spectator
Standard
The Times
Trades Sentinel and Workman's Guide Post (Sheffield)

(C) Official Reports

(R.C. = Royal Commission, S.C. = Select Committee)

Masters and Operatives (Equitable Councils of Conciliation), S.C. report, minutes of evidence, etc. 1856 (343) xiii.

The Best Means of Settling Disputes between Masters and Operatives, S.C. report, minutes of evidence, etc. 1860 (307) xxii.
Reports of the Inspectors of Factories to the Home Secretary for the half year ending 30th April 1865. 1865 [3473] xx.
The Organization and Rules of Trades Unions, etc., R.C. reports, minutes of evidence, etc. 1st rep. 1867 [3873] xxxii; 2nd rep. 1867 [3893] xxxii; 3rd rep. 1867 [3910] xxxii; 4th rep. 1867 [3952] xxxii; 5th–10th reps. 1867–8 [3890 — I–VI] xxxix; 11th rep. 1868–9 [4123] xxxi.
Working of the Master and Servant Act, 1867, and the Criminal Law Amendment Act, 34 & 35 Vict. Cap. 32, etc. R.C. reports, minutes of evidence, etc. 1st rep. 1874 [1094] xxiv; 2nd rep. 1875 [1157] xxx.

Hansard's Parliamentary Debates, 3rd series.

(D) Address, Pamphlets etc.

(There are a very large number of leaflets and pamphlets in the various collections used, in particular in the Howell Collection and in the British Library of Political and Economic Science. Only the most important of these are given below.)

(H.C. = Howell Collection; B.L. = British Library of Political and Economic Science)

Address of the Executive Council of the Amalgamated Society of Engineers, etc., to their fellow workmen throughout the United Kingdom and Colonies (1855). B.L.
Address of the Metropolitan Trades' Delegates to their fellow countrymen, on the interests and recent position of the labouring classes of the Empire (1850). Goldsmith's Library.
Address of the United Trades Committee appointed in aid of the miners, to the various organised bodies in Scotland and elsewhere, 9 June 1856 (Glasgow, 1856). B.L.
Address to the Working Men of the United Kingdom from the Council of the United Trades of Glasgow (Glasgow, 1861). Bound in London Trades Council Minutes.
Articles and Regulations of the Scottish Iron and Coal Miners' Association (Dunfermline, 1856). B.L.
Extension of the Franchise. Report of the Speeches delivered at the Great Meeting of the Working Classes held in Edinburgh, 27 June 1865 (Edinburgh, 1865). Edinburgh Public Library.
General Trades Council of Birmingham and District, Circular 8 June 1866. B.L.
Glasgow Council of United Trades. Proposed Basis for a Federation of the Various Trades of Scotland, 22 May 1861 (Glasgow). London Trades Council Minutes.
Glasgow Trades Council. To the Trade Unionists of Scotland (Glasgow, 1872). National Library of Scotland.

Glasgow Trades Council. Repeal of the Criminal Law Amendment Act. Address to the Trade Unionists of Scotland, 24 April 1873. H.C.

The Labour Question. An Address to Capitalists, and Employers, of the Building Trades, being a few reasons in behalf of a reduction of the hours of labour, etc., 30 May 1861. British Museum.

A Lecture on the Currency delivered in the City Hall, Glasgow by Sir Archibald Alison, on Tuesday 15 March 1859 (Birmingham, 1859). B.L.

London Trades Council. Mr Potter and the London Trades Council, 29 March 1865. H.C.

London Trades Council. Special Circular to the Trades, April 1872. B.L.

London Trades Council. To the Trade Societies and all organized bodies of workmen. Repeal of the Criminal Law Amendment Act (2 June 1873). National Library of Scotland.

London Trades Council to the Workmen of London, February 1878. Expulsion of Mr Patrick Kenny, Secretary of the General Labourers' Amalgamated Union, from the delegate meeting of the London Trades (1878). H.C.

Lord Elcho and the Miners. Employers and Employed. (1867). British Museum.

Masters and Workmen. Evidence of Sidney Smith and William Newton, given before a select committee of the House of Commons on causes of strikes and the Desirability of Establishing Equitable Councils of Conciliation (1856). B.L.

The Papermaking Trade. Arbitration on the Question of an Advance in Wages 10 July 1874 (Maidstone, 1874). B.L.

Reform Demonstration, Statement of Executive Committee (Edinburgh, 1866). Edinburgh Public Library.

Report of the Conference of Trades Delegates held in the Town Hall, Leeds, on December 2nd 1871, called to consider the statements by Wm. Newmarch, Esq., in his address to the Social Science Congress lately held in Leeds. Leeds City Library.

Report of the Conference on the Law of Masters and Workmen under their contract of service, held in London on 30th and 31st May and 1st and 2nd June 1864 (Glasgow, 1864). B.L.

Report of Meetings between Employers and Employed in the Papermaking Trade to consider the question of an advance in Wages (1873). B.L.

Report of the Trades Conference held in St Martin's Hall on March 5, 6, 7 and 8 1867. Birmingham Reference Library.

Report of the various proceedings taken by the London Trades Council and the Conference of Amalgamated Trades in reference to the Royal Commission on Trade Unions and other subjects in connection therewith. (1867). H.C.

Scottish National Reform League. Great Reform Demonstration in Glasgow, Tuesday 16 October 1866. Mitchell Library, Glasgow.

The Strike of the Bricklayers at Messrs. Doulton's Buildings at Lambeth in September 1876 (1877). B.L.

Trades' Societies and Lock-Outs. Report of the Conference of Trades Delegates of the United Kingdom, held in the Temperance Hall, Townhead Street, Sheffield, on July 17th 1866, and four following days. (Sheffield, 1876). Congress House.

(E) Contemporary Books and Articles

ABRAM, W. A., 'Social Condition and Political Prospects of the Lanca-shire Workmen', *Fortnightly Review*, N.S.IV (1868), pp. 426–41.

ARGYLL, DUKE OF, *The Reign of Law* (1867).

ARMSTRONG, G. F., *Essays and Sketches of Edmund J. Armstrong* (1877).

ASHWORTH, H., *The Preston Strike, an Enquiry into its Causes and Consequences* (Manchester, 1854).

BLACK, A., *On Wages, Trades' Unions and Strikes* (Edinburgh, 1859).

BEESLY, E. S., 'The Amalgamated Society of Carpenters', *Fortnightly Review*, N.S. I (1867), pp. 319–34.

Letters to the Working Classes (1870).

'Positivists and Workmen', *Fortnightly Review*, N.S. XVIII (1875), pp. 64–74.

The Sheffield Outrages and the Meeting at Exeter Hall (1867).

'The Social Future of the Working Class', *Fortnightly Review*, N.S. V (1869), pp. 344–63.

'Trades' Unions', *Westminster Review*, N.S. XX (1861), pp. 510–42.

'The Trades' Union Commission', *Fortnightly Review*, N.S. II (1867), pp. 1–18.

BRASSEY, T., 'Co-operative Production', *Contemporary Review*, XXIV (1874), pp. 212–33.

Lectures on the Labour Question (1878).

On Work and Wages (3rd ed., 1872).

Trades' Unions and the Cost of Labour (1870).

BURNETT, J., *Nine-Hours' Movement: A History of the Engineers' Strike in Newcastle and Gateshead* (Newcastle, 1872).

[CONDER, F. R.], 'Work and Wages', *Edinburgh Review*, CXXXVIII (1873), pp. 334–66.

COOPER, T., *The Life of Thomas Cooper, written by himself* (1872).

CRANBROOK, J., *On Wages, in relation to Trade Unions and Strikes* (Edinburgh, 1868).

CROMPTON, H., 'Arbitration and Conciliation', *Fortnightly Review*, N.S. V (1869), pp. 622–8.

Industrial Conciliation (1876).

Letters on Social and Political Subjects (1870).

'The Workmen's Victory', *Fortnightly Review*, N.S. XVIII (1875), pp. 399–406.

CUNNINGHAM, W., 'The Progress of Socialism in England', *Contemporary Review*, XXXIV (1879), pp. 245–60.

DICEY, A. V., 'Legal Etiquette', *Fortnightly Review*, N.S. **II** (1867), pp. 169–79.

DUNNING, T. J., *Trades' Unions and Strikes: Their Philosophy and Intention* (1860).

ESSAYS ON REFORM (1867).

J.H.F., 'The Working Man and His Friends', *Fraser's Magazine*, **LXXIX** (1869), pp. 685–701.

FINLAY, J. F., *On the Best Means of Improving the Relations between Capital and Labour* (Edinburgh, 1877).

[GLEIG, G. R.], 'The Bill as it is', *Blackwood's Magazine*, **CI** (1867), pp. 245–56.

'Strikes and Trades Unions', *Blackwood's Magazine*, **CII** (1867), pp. 718–36.

'Who are the Reformers, and what do they want?', *Blackwood's Magazine*, **CI** (1867), pp. 115–32.

GOSTICK, J., 'Trade Unions, and the Relations of Capital and Labour', *Cobden Club Essays*, 2 S. (1871–2), pp. 361–402.

GRANT, A. (ed.), *Recess Studies* (Edinburgh, 1870).

GREG, W. R., 'The Echo of the Antipodes', *Contemporary Review*, **XXVI** (1875), pp. 221–33.

Mistaken Aims and Attainable Ideals of the Artizan Class (1876).

Rocks Ahead: or the Warnings of Cassandra (1874).

HARRISON, F., 'The Good and Evil of Trade Unionism', *Fortnightly Review*, **III** (1865), pp. 33–54.

'The Iron-Masters' Trade-Union', *Fortnightly Review*, **I** (1865), pp. 96–116.

'The Limits of Political Economy', *Fortnightly Review*, **I** (1865), pp. 356–76.

The Political Function of the Working Classes: A Lecture delivered at the Cleveland Street Institution, on March 25, 1868 (1868).

'The Trades-Union Bill', *Fortnightly Review*, N.S. **VI** (1869), pp. 30–45.

HONEYMAN, T., *Trades Unionism: The Blight on British Industries and Commerce* (Glasgow, 1877).

HOWELL, G., 'Are the Working Classes Improvident?', *Contemporary Review*, **XXXII** (1878), pp. 501–19.

'Strikes: Their Cost and Results', *Fraser's Magazine*, N.S. **XX** (1879), pp. 767–83.

'Trades Unions, Apprentices and Technical Education', *Contemporary Review*, **XXX** (1877), pp. 833–57.

'Trade-Unions: Their Nature, Character and Work', *Fraser's Magazine*, N.S. **XIX** (1879), pp. 22–31.

IGNOTUS, *The Last Thirty Years in a Mining District or Scotching and the Candle versus Lamp and Trades Unions* (1867).

INGRAM, J. K., *Work and the Workman* (Dublin, 1880).

IRONSIDE, I., *Trades' Unions* (London and Sheffield, 1867).

JEANS, J. S., *Pioneers of the Cleveland Iron Trade* (Middlesbrough, 1875).

JEVONS, W. S., *A Lecture on Trades' Societies: Their Objects and Policy* (Manchester, 1868).

KELL, S. C., *The Political Attitude of Our Law-Making Classes Towards the Unenfranchised, and the Duties incumbent upon those in Consequence* (Bradford, 1861).

LENO, J. B., *An Essay on the Nine Hours' Movement* (1861).

LESLIE, T. E. CLIFFE, 'Political Economy and the Rate of Wages', *Fraser's Magazine*, **LXXVIII** (1868), pp. 81–95.

LEVI, L., *Wages and Earnings of the Working Classes* (1867).

LONGE, F. D., *A Refutation of the Wage-Fund Theory of Modern Political Economy as enunciated by Mr Mill M.P. and Mr Fawcett M.P.* (1866).

[LOWE, R.], 'Trades' Unions', *Quarterly Review*, **CXXIII** (1867), pp. 351–83.

LUDLOW, J. M., *The Master Engineers and Their Workmen* (1852).

'The Social Legislation of 1867', *Contemporary Review*, **VII** (1868), pp. 86–97.

'Trade Societies and the Social Science Association', *Macmillan's Magazine*, **III** (1860–1), pp. 313–25, 362–72.

LUDLOW, J. M. and JONES, L., *Progress of the Working Class, 1832–1867* (1867).

M., 'Trades Unionism in the City and May Fair', *Fraser's Magazine*, **LXXVIII** (1868), pp. 159–74, 443–60.

MACDONALD, A., *Handybook of the Law relative to Masters, Workmen, Servants, and Apprentices, in all Trades and Occupations* (1868).

MACDONALD, W., *The True Story of Trades' Unions* (Manchester, 1867).

[MACKAY, C.], 'The Working Classes', *Blackwood's Magazine*, **CI** (1867), pp. 220–9.

'Work and Murder', *Blackwood's Magazine*, **CII** (1867), pp. 487–507.

MAGNUS, P., *Labourers and Capitalists. How Related. How separated. How united. A Study for Working Men* (1873).

[MARTINEAU, H.], 'Secret Organization of Trades', *Edinburgh Review*, **CX** (1859), pp. 525–63.

MAYHEW, H., *London Labour and London Poor* (1865).

MILL, J. S., *Autobiography* (1873).

'Thornton on Labour and its Claims', *Fortnightly Review*, N.S. **V** (1869), pp. 505–18, 680–700.

MORRISON, C., *An Essay in the Relations between Labour and Capital* (1856).

NATIONAL ASSOCIATION FOR THE PROMOTION OF SOCIAL SCIENCE, *Trades' Societies and Strikes* (1860).

NEALE, E. V., *May I not do what I will with my own?* (1852).

NEATE, C., *Two Lectures on Trades Unions, delivered in the University of Oxford in the year 1861* (Oxford and London, 1862).

ODGER, G., 'The Working Man in Parliament', *Contemporary Review*, **XVI** (1870), pp. 102–23.

PARIS, COMTE DE, *The Trades' Unions of England* (1869).

PEARSON, R., *Combination or Trades' Unionism absolutely the duty of workpeople in general* (Edinburgh, 1875).

PLUMMER, J., *Songs of Labour, Northamptonshire Rambles, and other poems* (Kettering and London, 1860).

Strikes: Their Causes and Their Evils (1859).

POLE, W. (ed.), *The Life of Sir William Fairbairn, Bart* (1877).

POLITICAL ECONOMY CLUB, *Revised Report of the Proceedings at the Dinner of 31 May, 1876, held in celebration of the Hundredth Year of the publication of the 'Wealth of Nations'* (1876).

POTTER, E., *Some Opinions on Trades Unions and the Bill of 1869* (1869).

POTTER, G., 'Conciliation and Arbitration', *Contemporary Review*, XV (1870), pp. 543–66.

'The Future of Capital and Labour', *Contemporary Review*, XVI (1871), pp. 437–53.

'Strikes and Lock-Outs from the Workman's Point of View', *Contemporary Review*, XV (1870), pp. 32–54.

'The Trade Societies of England from the Workman's Point of View', *Contemporary Review*, XIV (1870), pp. 404–28.

'Trades' Unions, Strikes and Lock-Outs. A Rejoinder', *Contemporary Review*, XVII (1871), pp. 525–39.

PRICE, G., *Combinations and Strikes: Their Costs and Results* (1854).

RATHBONE, W., *The Increased Earnings of the Working Classes and their effect on themselves and on the future of England* (1877).

REDIVUS, 'The Strike. To the Builders, Gasmen, and Others on Strike', *Once a Week*, I (1859), pp. 155–7.

Reform: Look before you leap (1859).

'The Representation of Labour', *Bankers' Magazine*, XXXIII (1873), pp. 923–7.

[RICKARDS, G. L.], 'Thornton on Labour', *Edinburgh Review*, CXXX (1869), pp. 390–417.

'Trades Unions', *Edinburgh Review*, CXXVI (1867), pp. 415–57.

ROBINSON, S., *Friendly Letters on the Recent Strikes from a Manufacturer to his own Workpeople* (1854).

ROGERS, J. E. THOROLD, 'Capital – Labour – Profit', *Fraser's Magazine*, N.S. I (1870), pp. 500–12.

ROSS, M., *Address to Trades' Unionists on the Question of Strikes* (London and Bradford, 1860).

RUSKIN, J., *Unto This Last: Four Essays on the First Principles of Political Economy* (1901).

SAMUELSON, J., *Trade Unions and Public Houses* (1871).

Work, Wages and the Profits of Capital: An Essay on the Labour Question (London and Liverpool, 1872).

SAUNDERS, W., *Trades Unionism. Question: Is the Development of Trades Unionism a serious National Danger?* (1878).

SARGANT, W. L., *Economy of the Labouring Classes* (1857).

SIDGWICK, H., 'The Wages-Fund Theory', *Fortnightly Review*, N.S. **XXVI** (1879), pp. 401–13.

SMILES, S., *Self-Help with Illustrations of Conduct and Perseverance* (1866 ed.).

Workmen's Earnings, Strikes and Savings (1861).

SMITH, G., 'The Labour Movement', *Contemporary Review*, **XXI** (1873), pp. 226–51.

SMITH, G. H., *Outlines of Political Economy designed chiefly for the use of schools and of junior students* (1866).

STIRLING, J., *Trade Unionism, with remarks on the Report of the Commissioners on Trades Unions* (Glasgow, 1869).

THORNTON, W. T., *On Labour. Its wrongful claims and rightful dues. Its actual present and possible future* (1869).

WATTS, J., *What are the Social Effects of Trades Unions, Strikes and Lock-Outs* (1878).

WHITE, H. M., *The Principles of Trades Unions* (1867).

WRIGHT, T., 'The English Working Classes and the Paris Commune', *Fraser's Magazine*, N.S. **IV** (1871), pp. 62–8.

'On the Condition of the Working Classes', *Fraser's Magazine* N.S. **IV** (1871), pp. 426–40.

'The Composition of the Working Classes', *Contemporary Review*, **XVIII** (1871), pp. 514–26.

Some Habits and Customs of the Working Classes (1867).

The Great Unwashed (1868).

Our New Masters (1873).

(F) Secondary Sources

1. *Articles:*

ACTON, H. B., 'Comte's Positivism and the Science of Society', *Philosophy*, **XXVI** (1951), pp. 291–310.

ARMYTAGE, W. H. G., 'William Dronfield and the Good Name of the Sheffield Workmen in the 1860s', *Notes and Queries*, 3 April 1948.

ASHMORE, O., 'The Diary of James Garnett of Low Moor, Clitheroe, 1858–65', *Transactions of the Historic Society of Lancashire and Cheshire*, **CXXI** (1969), pp. 77–98.

BELL, A. D., 'Administration and Finance of the Reform League, 1865–67', *International Review of Social History*, **X** (1965), pp. 385–409.

BRAND, C. F., 'The Conversion of British Trade Unions to Political Action', *American Historical Review*, **XXX** (1925), pp. 251–70.

BRANTLINGER, P., 'The Case against Trade Unions in Early Victorian Fiction', *Victorian Studies*, **XIII** (1969), pp. 37–52.

BRIGG, M., 'Life in East Lancashire 1856–60: A Newly Discovered Diary of John O'Neil (John Ward), Weaver, of Clitheroe', *Transactions of the Historic Society of Lancashire and Cheshire*, **CXX** (1868), pp. 87–133.

BROCK, P., 'Polish Democrats and English Radicals, 1832–1862', *Journal of Modern History*, **XXV** (1953), pp. 139–56.

CLEMENTS, R. V., 'British Trade Unions and Popular Political Economy', *Economic History Review*, **XIV** (1961–2), pp. 93–104.

'Trade Unions and Emigration, 1840–80', *Population Studies*, **IX** (1955–56), pp. 167–80.

COLE, G. D. H., 'Some Notes on British Trade Unionism in the Third Quarter of the Nineteenth Century', *Essays in Economic History* (1962), Vol. III, pp. 202–21, E. M. Carus Wilson (ed.).

COLTHAM, S., 'George Potter, the Junta and the *Bee-Hive*', *International Review of Social History*, **IX** (1964), pp. 391–432, **X** (1965), pp. 1–85.

'The *Bee-Hive* Newspaper: Its Origin and Early Struggles', *Essays in Labour History* (1967), A. Briggs and J. Saville (eds), pp. 174–204.

'English Working Class Newspapers in 1867', *Victorian Studies*, **XIII** (1969), pp. 159–80.

FOX, A., 'Industrial Relations in Nineteenth-Century Birmingham', *Oxford Economic Papers*, **VII** (1955), pp. 57–70.

FRANCE, R. SHARPE, 'The Diary of John Ward of Clitheroe, Weaver, 1860–64', *Transactions of the Historic Society of Lancashire and Cheshire*, **CV** (1953), pp. 137–85.

GARBATI, I., 'British Trade Unionism in the Mid-Victorian Era', *University of Toronto Quarterly*, **XX** (1950), pp. 69–83.

GOLDSTROM, J. M., 'Richard Whatley and Political Economy in School Books, 1833–80', *Irish Historical Studies*, **XV** (1966–7), pp. 131–46.

HANHAM, H. J., 'Liberal Organisations for Working Men, 1860–1914', *Bulletin of the Society for the Study of Labour History*, No. 7 (1963), pp. 5–7.

HARRISON, R., 'The British Working Class and the General Election of 1868', *International Review of Social History*, **V** (1960), pp. 424–55, **VI** (1961), pp. 74–109.

'E. S. Beesly and Karl Marx', *International Review of Social History*, **IV** (1959), pp. 22–58, 208–38.

'The 10th April of Spencer Walpole: The Problem of Revolution in Relation to Reform', *International Review of Social History*, **VII** (1962), pp. 351–99.

HERRICK, F. H., 'The Second Reform Movement in Britain, 1850–1865', *Journal of the History of Ideas*, **IX** (1948), pp. 174–92.

HICKS, J. R., 'The Early History of Industrial Conciliation in England', *Economica*, **X** (1930), pp. 25–39.

HIGGINBOTHAM, M., 'A. J. Mundella and the Sheffield Election of 1868', *Transactions of the Hunter Archaeological Society*, **V** (1943), pp. 285–93.

E. R. J., 'Industrial Harmony: How Attained', *Shipping World*, **XXXVIII** (1908), pp. 432–8.

MCCREADY, H. W., 'The British Election of 1874: Frederic Harrison and the Liberal–Labour Dilemma', *Canadian Journal of Economics and Political Science*, XX (1954), pp. 166–75.

'British Labour and the Royal Commission on Trade Unions, 1867–69', *University of Toronto Quarterly*, XXIV (1956), pp. 390–409.

'British Labour's Lobby 1867–75', *Canadian Journal of Economics and Political Science*, XXII (1956), pp. 141–60.

MARWICK, W. H., 'Alexander McDonald', *Scottish Educational Journal*, 4 March 1932.

POLLARD, S., 'The Ethics of the Sheffield Outrages', *Transactions of the Hunter Archaeological Society*, VII (1953–4), pp. 118–39.

PORTER, J. H., 'David Dale and Conciliation in the Northern Manufactured Iron Trade, 1869–1914', *Northern History*, V (1970), pp. 157–70.

RODGERS, B., 'The Social Science Association, 1857–86', *Manchester School of Economics and Social Studies*, XX (1952), pp. 283–310.

THOLFSEN, T. R., 'The Artisan and the Culture of Early Victorian Birmingham', *University of Birmingham Historical Journal*, IV (1953–4), pp. 146–66.

'The Transition to Democracy in Victorian England', *International Review of Social History*, VI (1961), pp. 226–48.

2. Books

ABRAHAMS, G., *Trade Unions and the Law* (1968).

ADAMS, W. E., *Memoirs of a Social Atom* (1903).

ALLEN, E., CLARKE, J. F., MCCORD, N., ROWE, D. J., *The North-East Engineers' Strikes of 1871: The Nine-Hours' League* (Newcastle upon Tyne, 1971).

ALLEN, V. L., *The Sociology of Industrial Relations: Studies in Method* (1971).

ANDREW, S., *Fifty Years' Cotton Trade* (Oldham, 1887).

APPLEMAN, P., MADDEN, W. A., WOLFF, M., *1859: Entering an Age of Crisis* (Indiana, 1959).

ARCH, J., *The Story of His Life, told by Himself* (1898).

ARMYTAGE, W. H. G., *A. J. Mundella 1825–1897: The Liberal Background to the Labour Movement* (1951).

ARNOT, R. PAGE, *A History of the Scottish Miners* (1955).

The Miners, 1889–1945 (1949).

BAGWELL, P. S., *The Railwaymen* (1963).

BARNSBY, G., *The Origin of the Wolverhampton Trades Council: Centenary 1865–1965* (Wolverhampton, 1965).

BEAN, W. W., *The Parliamentary Representation of the Six Northern Counties of England* (Hull, 1890).

BEER, M., *A History of British Socialism* (1919, 1929).

BELL, J. F., *A History of Economic Thought* (New York, 1953).

BLAKE, R., *Disraeli* (1966).

BOYLE, E. (ed.), *Tory Democrat: Two Famous Disraeli Speeches* (1950).

BOYSON, R., *The Ashworth Cotton Enterprise: The Rise and Fall of a Family Firm 1818–1880* (Oxford, 1970).

BOWLEY, A. L., *Wages in the United Kingdom in the Nineteenth Century* (Cambridge, 1900).

BRIGGS, A., *The Age of Improvement, 1783–1867* (1959).

History of Birmingham, Vol. II (1952).

Victorian People: A Reassessment of Persons and Themes, 1851–67 (1965 ed.).

BRIGGS, A. and SAVILLE, J. (eds), *Essays in Labour History: In Memory of G. D. H. Cole* (1960).

BROADHURST, H., *Henry Broadhurst M.P.: The Story of His Life from a Stonemason's Bench to the Treasury Bench* (1901).

BROWN, E. H. PHELPS, *The Growth of British Industrial Relations* (1959).

BRUCE, H. A., *Letters of the Rt. Hon. Henry Austin Bruce G.C.B., Lord Aberdare of Duffryn* (Oxford, 1902, for private circulation).

BUCKLEY, K D., *Trade Unionism in Aberdeen 1878–1900* (Edinburgh, 1955).

BUNDOCK, C. J., *The Story of the National Union of Printing, Bookbinding and Paper Workers* (Oxford, 1959).

BURN, W. L., *The Age of Equipoise* (1964).

BURT, T., *Thomas Burt M.P., D.C.L., Pitman and Privy Councillor: An Autobiography* (1924).

CAIRNES, J. E., *Some Leading Principles of Political Economy* (2nd ed. 1896).

CLEGG, H. A., FOX, A., THOMPSON, A. F., *A History of British Trade Unions since 1889*, I (Oxford, 1964).

CHRISTENSEN, T., *The Origin and History of Christian Socialism, 1848–1854* (Aarhus, 1962).

CHURCH, R. A., *Economic and Social Change in a Midland Town: Victorian Nottingham 1815–1900* (1966).

CLARK, G. KITSON, *The Making of Victorian England* (1962).

COLE, G. D. H., *British Working Class Politics 1832–1914* (1941).

A Short History of the British Working-Class Movement, 1789–1847 (1948 ed.).

Studies in Class Structure (1955).

COLE, G. D. H. and FILSON, A. W., *British Working Class Movements: Select Documents, 1789–1875* (1951).

COLLINS, H. and ABRAMSKY, C., *Karl Marx and the British Labour Movement: Years of the First International* (1965).

CORBETT, J., *The Birmingham Trades Council, 1866–1966* (1966).

CONNELLY, T. J., *The Woodworkers, 1860–1960* (1960).

COWAN, R. M. W., *The Newspaper in Scotland* (Glasgow, 1946).

COWLING, M., *1867. Disraeli, Gladstone and Revolution: the Passing of the Second Reform Bill* (Cambridge, 1967).

CUMMINGS, D. C., *A Historical Survey of the Boilermakers' and Iron and Steel Ship Builders' Society from August 1834 to August 1905* (Newcastle upon Tyne, 1905).

DALE, D., *Thirty Years' Experience of Industrial Conciliation and Arbitration* (1899).

DALLEY, W. A., *The Life Story of W. J. Davis, J.P.* (Birmingham, 1914).

DAVIS, W. J., *The British Trades Union Congress – History and Recollections* (1910).

DICEY, A. V., *Lectures on the Relation Between Law and Public Opinion in England during the Nineteenth Century* (2nd ed., 1914).

Documents of the First International, 5 vols. (Moscow, 1963–6).

EDGEWORTH, F. W., *Mathematical Psychics* (1881).

ENSOR, R. C. K., *England, 1870–1914* (Oxford, 1936).

ESCOTT, T. H. S., *England: Its People, Polity and Pursuits* (1885).

EVANS, H., *Sir Randal Cremer: His Life and Work* (1909).

FLANDERS, A. and CLEGG, H. A., *The System of Industrial Relations in Great Britain* (Oxford, 1964).

FOX, A., *A History of the National Union of Boot and Shoe Operatives, 1874–1957* (Oxford, 1958).

FYRTH, H. J. and COLLINS, H., *The Foundry Workers* (Manchester, 1959).

GARDINER, A. G., *The Life of Sir William Harcourt*, 2 vols. (1909).

GARVIN, J. L., *The Life of Joseph Chamberlain*, I (1932).

GILLESPIE, F. E., *Labour and Politics, 1850–1867* (Durham N.C., 1927).

GILLESPIE, S. C., *A Hundred Years of Progress* (Glasgow, 1953).

GROVES, R., *Sharpen the Sickle! The History of the Farm Workers' Union* (1949).

HAMER, D. A., *John Morley: Liberal Intellectual in Politics* (Oxford, 1968).

HAMLING, W., *A Short History of the Liverpool Trades Council* (Liverpool, 1948).

HAMMOND, J. L. and B., *James Stansfield, a Victorian Champion of Sex Equality* (1932).

HANHAM, H. J., *Elections and Party Management: Politics in the Time of Disraeli and Gladstone* (1959).

HARRISON, B., *Drink and the Victorians: The Temperance Question in England, 1815–1872* (1971).

HARRISON, F., *Autobiographic Memoirs*, 2 vols. (1911).

HARRISON, J. F. C., *Learning and Living 1790–1960: A Study in the History of the English Adult Education Movement* (1961).

HARRISON, R., *Before the Socialists: Studies in Labour and Politics 1861 to 1881* (1965).

HEDGES, R. Y., and WINTERBOTTOM, A., *The Legal History of Trade Unionism* (1930).

HICKLING, M. A., *Citrine's Trade Union Law* (3rd ed. 1967).

HIGGENBOTTAM, S., *Our Society's History* (Manchester, 1939).

HINTON, R. J., *English Radical Leaders* (N.Y., 1875).

HOBSBAWM, E. J., *Labouring Men: Studies in the History of Labour* (1964).

HOBSON, J. A., *John Ruskin, Social Reformer* (1898).

HODDER, E., *Life of Samuel Morley* (1887).

HOPWOOD, E., *A History of the Lancashire Cotton Industry and the Amalgamated Weavers' Association* (Manchester, 1969).

HOWE, E. and WAITE, H. E., *The London Society of Compositors* (1948).

HOWE, E. and CHILD, J., *The Society of London Bookbinders* (1952).

HOWELL, G., *Conflicts of Capital and Labour* (2nd ed., 1890).
   Labour Legislation, Labour Movements and Labour Leaders (1902).

HUGHES, T., *James Fraser, Second Bishop of Manchester: A Memoir 1818–1885* (1888).

HUMPHREY, A. W., *A History of Labour Representation* (1912).
   Robert Applegarth: Trade Unionist, Educationist, Reformer (Manchester, 1913).

HURST, J. G., *Edmund Potter of Dinting Vale* (Manchester 1948).

HUTCHINS, B. L. and HARRISON, A., *A History of Factory Legislation* (3rd ed., 1926).

HUTCHISON, T. W., *A Review of Economic Doctrines, 1870–1929* (Oxford, 1953).

JEFFERYS, J. B., *Labour's Formative Years, 1849–1879* (1948).
   The Story of the Engineers (1945).

JENKINS, R., *Sir Charles Dilke: A Victorian Tragedy* (1958).

JEVONS, W. S., *The State in Relation to Labour* (1882).

JONES, G. S., *Outcast London: A Study in the Relationship between Classes in Victorian Society* (Oxford, 1971).

KIDD, A. T., *A History of the Tinplate Workers* (1949).

KINGSLEY, MRS (ed.), *Charles Kingsley: His Letters and Memories of His Life* (1883).

KNIGHT, F., *Bolton and District United Trades Council: Jubilee Souvenir, 1866–1916* (Bolton, 1916).

LENO, J. B., *The Aftermath, with Autobiography of the Author* (1892).

LEVENTHAL, F. M., *Respectable Radical: George Howell and Victorian Working Class Politics* (1971).

LIPSET, S. M., TROW, M. A., COLEMAN, J. S., *Union Democracy* (Glencoe, 1956).

MACCOBY, S., *English Radicalism, 1853–1886* (1938).

MACDOUGALL, I., *The Minutes of Edinburgh Trades Council, 1859–1873* (Edinburgh, 1968).

MACHIN, F., *The Yorkshire Miners: A History* (1958).

MACK, E. C. and ARMYTAGE, W. H. G., *Thomas Hughes: The Life of the Author of 'Tom Brown's Schooldays'* (1952).

MACKIE, J. B., *The Life and Work of Duncan McLaren* (1888).

MACKINVEN, H., *Edinburgh and District Trades Council: Centenary 1859–1959* (Edinburgh, 1959).

MARSHALL, A., *Principles of Economics* (8th ed, 1920).

MARTIN, A. P., *Life and Letters of the Rt. Hon. Robert Lowe, Viscount Sherbrooke GCB, DCL* (1893).

MARWICK, W. H., *Economic Developments in Victorian Scotland* (1936).
A Short History of Labour in Scotland (Edinburgh, 1967).
Life of Alexander Campbell (Glasgow, 1964).

MASTERMAN, N. C., *John Malcolm Ludlow: The Builder of Christian Socialism* (Cambridge, 1962).

MAURICE, F. (ed.), *Life of Frederick Denison Maurice, Chiefly Told in His Own Letters* (1884).

MENDELSON, J., OWEN, F., POLLARD, S., THORNES, V. M., *Sheffield Trades and Labour Council, 1858 to 1958* (Sheffield, 1958).

MILL, J. S., *Collected Works* (Toronto and London, 1965).

MORLEY, J., *Life of Gladstone* (1903).

MOSSES, W., *The History of the United Patternmakers' Association* (1922).

MUSSON, A. E., *The Congress of 1868: The Origins and Establishment of the Trades Union Congress* (1955).
The Typographical Association: Origins and History up to 1949 (Oxford, 1954).
British Trade Unions, 1800–1875 (1972).

PELLING, H., *A History of British Trade Unionism* (1963).
Popular Politics and Society in Late Victorian Britain (1968).

POLLARD, S., *A History of Labour in Sheffield* (Liverpool, 1959).

POSTGATE, R. W., *The Builders' History* (1924).

PRICE, L. L. F. R., *Industrial Peace, its Advantages, Methods and Difficulties* (1887).

QUENNELL, P., *John Ruskin: The Portrait of a Prophet* (1949).

RAVEN, C. E., *Christian Socialism, 1848–1854* (1920).

REID, T. WEMYSS, *Life of the Rt. Hon. William Edward Forster* (1970 ed.).

RICHARDS, C., *A History of Trades Councils, 1860–75* (1920).

ROBBINS, L., *The Theory of Economic Policy in English Classical Political Economy* (1961).

ROBERTS, B. C., *The Trades Union Congress, 1868–1921* (1958).

ROTHSTEIN, T., *From Chartism to Labourism* (1929).

SAMUELSON, J., *Recollections* (1907).

SAVILLE, J., *Ernest Jones: Chartist* (1952).
(ed.), *Democracy and the Labour Movement: Essays in Honour of Dona Torr* (1954).

SCHUMPETER, J. A., *Economic Doctrine and Method: An Historical Sketch* (1954).

SHARP, I. G., *Industrial Conciliation and Arbitration* (1950).

SHIPLEY, S., *Club Life and Socialism in Mid-Victorian London* (History Workshop Pamphlets, No. 5.)

SIDGWICK, H., *The Principles of Political Economy* (2nd ed., 1887).

SIGSWORTH, E. M., *Black Dyke Mills* (Liverpool, 1958).

SMITH, F. B., *The Making of the Second Reform Bill* (Cambridge, 1966).

282 TRADE UNIONS AND SOCIETY

SMITH, P., *Disraelian Conservatism and Social Reform* (1967).

SOLLY, H., *These Eighty Years* (1893).

SOUTTER, F. W., *Recollections of a Labour Pioneer* (1923).

SWIFT, H. G., *A History of Postal Agitation from Fifty Years Ago till the Present Day* (1900).

TATE, G., *The London Trades Council, 1860–1950: A History* (1950).

TAUSSIG, F. W., *Wages and Capital: An Examination of the Wages Fund Doctrine* (1890).

THOMPSON, E. P., *The Making of the English Working Class* (1965).

TRANT, W., *Trade Unions: Their Origin and Objects, Influence and Efficacy* (1884).

TREVELYAN, G. M., *Life of John Bright* (2nd ed., 1925).

TURNER, H. A., *Trade Union Growth, Structure and Policy* (1962).

VINCENT, J., *The Formation of the Liberal Party, 1857–1868* (1966).

WARD, J. T., *The Factory Movement* (1962).

WARD, T. H. (ed.), *The Reign of Queen Victoria* (1887).

WEBB, B., *My Apprenticeship* (1926).
Our Partnership (1948).

WEBB, S. and B., *The History of Trade Unionism, 1666–1920* (1920 ed.).
Industrial Democracy (1902).

WELBOURNE, E., *Miners' Unions of Northumberland and Durham* (Cambridge, 1923).

WHITTAKER, E., *A History of Economic Ideas* (1943).

WILKIE, T., *The Representation of Scotland* (Paisley, 1895).

WILLIAMS, T. G., *The Main Currents of Social and Industrial Change since 1870* (1935).

WOLF, L., *Life of the First Marquess of Ripon* (1921).

Index